Making the World Clean

Wasted Lives, Wasted Environment, and Racial Capitalism

Françoise Vergès

Goldsmiths
Press

Contents

Contents

Series Foreword

Jennifer Gabrys, Ros Gray, and Shela Sheikh

With multiple environmental crises erupting worldwide, the planetary has become a common topic. Yet while studies proliferate that speculate about the state of the planet or propose governance at a planetary scale, they often reinscribe dominant voices, knowledges, and ways of being. The Planetarities series seeks to unsettle prevailing engagements with the planetary by supporting work that grapples with the power dynamics, indeterminate relations, and poetic possibilities of eco-social transformations. Drawing on, extending, and reworking Gayatri Chakravorty Spivak's notion of "planetarity," the series takes up distinct types of "planet-thought" and "planet-feeling." For Spivak, planetarity was a concept that could undo the abstractions of globalism while expanding beyond isolated consolidations of self or identity. With "planetarities," this series further embraces the pluralistic concepts and practices that offer different connections and collectives tied to the planet.

As a series, Planetarities creates a space for work from writers and practitioners within and beyond Western and institutional contexts, with contributions from the Global South, Indigenous communities, and environmental activists working within transdisciplinary and transnational movements. This series seeks to advance theoretical and practice-based work as a plural and diverse collective project that shares a sense of urgency about planetary troubles. The texts in this series attend to planetary inhabitations and problems, from climate migration and environmental justice to multispecies world-building and the geopolitics of extraction. By considering how the planetary is at once summoned and unsettled through ecological and socio-political crises, the series poses a challenge to Anthropocene discourse by decentering the Anthropos and instead exploring how the planetary undoes and remakes humans and nonhumans as planetary subjects.

Making the World Clean: Wasted Lives, Wasted Environment, and Racial Capitalism, the second volume in the Planetarities series, delivers a powerful warning against mainstream, white environmentalism and the corporatization or techno-solutionism of cleaning. By engaging with numerous case studies from across the globe, more often than not overlooked by international media and canons of history, Vergès forcefully demonstrates that cleaning—of bodies, homes, offices, cities, the planet—is rooted in a racialized, bourgeois, gendered, and colonial binary of clean vs. dirty. Against "cleaning up"—an often industrialized form of greenwashing that erases the experiences and knowledge of those most affected—we are invited to consider what a decolonial, feminist, anti-racist, anti-patriarchal, and anti-capitalist cleaning might look like, as well as how elements of this have already long been practiced. Rather than *reform* existing practices and politics of cleaning, Vergès argues for *abolition*: "dismantling the afterlives of slavery and colonialism" and radically transforming systems of oppression.

Following Ruth Wilson Gilmore's formulation that abolition is "life in rehearsal," the book points us towards avenues for radical hope, of decolonial cleaning as "a strategy of resistance in a time of ruination." This resistance, however, is neither utopic nor pure; for those particularly affected by racial capitalism, it is often not chosen, and it entails tactics suitable to each context. Neither eventful nor spectacular, Vergès explores a notion of cleaning grounded in the *elemental*, meaning that which is banal or trivial but is necessary for sustaining and cultivating life. Where facts and figures about the wasting of lives and environments and ongoing forms of colonial violence may lead to despair (the genocide and ecocide being carried out by the State of Israel against Palestinians and their environments being a current example), and where the empirical language of reports on "waste management" provoke dreariness, Vergès instead offers the reader an impassioned and sensorial call to affirm *a politics of living*.

We are grateful to the team at Goldsmiths Press, led by Sarah Kember, for their support for this publication that has been germinating for some years and that, in our current global political context, is more urgent than ever. We extend thanks to Susan Kelly, Ellen Parnavelas, and Angela Thompson for carefully stewarding the development and production of *Making the World Clean*, and to Adriana Cloud for her sensitive copyediting and sharp-eyed attention to the extensive endnotes, which we hope will be a useful resource. Finally, we thank Françoise Vergès for her *esprit de résistance* that has infused the breadth and force of this short book.

Foreword by Ruth Wilson Gilmore

Françoise Vergès always encourages expansive and ferocious analysis. She notices patterns across and between themes, people, places, dynamics, relationships, things. Her thoughtfulness, supported by such wide and deep reading and listening, enables us to think better. She models how she thinks with such excited confidence that we readers sharpen our ability to notice more on our own. This book repeatedly shows how to bring sharp particularity to general existential questions. What has been happening to water beings on the water planet in the context of racial capitalism? The sorting and stacking institutions that shape and make sense of modernity's social reality require not only the labor but also the considered insights of cleaners to reveal contradictions from the ground up. My family were university cleaners; today, as a university professor, I am more likely to fail a student who leaves trash in the classroom than who plagiarizes. The latter's anxiety-fueled impulse invites transformative remedies; by contrast, the former assumes the reproduction of a social reality that I teach and organize to undo. As well-researched as this work is, Vergès doesn't read or listen in order to recite what she's studied. Rather, attentive to the embodied risks and beauties of modeling oppositional consciousness, she rehearses as she learns, towards dismantling racial capitalism and its imperial and colonial guarantors. She lays out motives; she suggests means. In other words, Vergès teaches us to see in order to act, and through acting to become more provisionally aware of what we might not have noticed before. This book is a gift whose value arises from being used. Abolition is emancipation in rehearsal.

Ruth Wilson Gilmore, author of *Abolition Geography*

Preface

The first thing the State of Israel did in October 2023 when it launched its attack on the Gaza Strip, where two million Palestinians live (most of them refugees or descendants of refugees of the 1948 Nakba), was to totally cut off water, then electricity, and then to stop the entry of fuel, food, and medicine. It was a perfect textbook act of settler colonialism. It justified these decisions with its "right to self-defense" after the attack on its soil by the Palestinian group Hamas on October 7, 2023, which killed 1,140 Israeli women, children, and men, while others were taken hostages in Gaza. Between October 7 and 12, the Israeli Air Force acknowledged it had dropped 6,000 bombs on Gaza,[i] which was equal to 25,000 tons of explosives or two nuclear bombs.[ii] On November 11, the toll was 11,078 Palestinian deaths, among them 4,506 children, and most of Gaza's infrastructure had been destroyed. In many cities of the world, millions marched in solidarity with Palestine, calling for an immediate ceasefire and the end of occupation and apartheid. In the West, the criminalization of the movement against the occupation exacerbated; anyone who expressed their solidary with Palestine was accused of antisemitism; artists were cancelled; activists, politicians, and journalists were threatened.

I was seeing in practice the politics of denial of vital needs on an unprecedented scale. And this was unfolding as I was finishing the revision of this book about the racial and gendered politics of wasting lands, bodies, and resources and the organized deprivation of clean water, shelter, and access to health services—in other words, about the structural denial, along racial lines, of vital needs. The word "settler" was cleansed of the charge of dispossession, extermination, and racism and was instead associated with liberal democracy, women's and gays' rights, rule of law, and freedom. Founded on the genocide of Indigenous populations, on ethnic cleansing, deportation, enslavement, mass dispossession, oppression, exploitation, and racism, the United States, Canada, and Australia have nonetheless presented themselves as the true defenders of universal and women's rights, justifying military intervention under that banner.

I considered that I might have not explored enough the link between settler colonies, modern nation-states, genocide, racial patriarchal capitalism, and the organized deprivation of vital needs. I might have made clearer the fact that the modern nation-state and its racialization of groups, its organized abandonment of the vital needs of poor women and of women of color, of Indigenous and poor people around the world, was the heir of the colonial politics of dispossession, extraction, and exploitation that capitalism has not only perfected but extended. I am not talking of a smooth continuum, but of the ways in which some foundations of colonialism survive. But I hope that this book will contribute to that conversation.

May all the dead rest in peace. We will continue to fight against occupation; against the state of permanent war; for justice, peace, dignity, and freedom; for the abolition of racial patriarchal capitalism and imperialism.

Françoise Vergès
November 2023

Acknowledgments

I never write alone but surrounded by the voices and writings of many people. To write this book, I read a lot of articles and essays, I watched many documentaries and films, I went to see many artists' exhibitions. I have an immense debt to everyone who has analyzed and written on and fought against racial patriarchal capitalism. I thank the ancestors who opened the way. May they rest in power.

I want to thank Jennifer Gabrys, Ros Gray and Shela Sheikh for inviting me to contribute to their collection by expanding on the article "Waste, Race, Gender and Capital" (*e-flux*, 2019). To my comrades in struggle, Ros Gray and Shela Sheikh, special thanks for their work on the manuscript and for their trust and patience.

Note

Throughout the book I use the terms "women" and "men," though I acknowledge the plurality of gender and the fact that some refuse to identify with any gender. As for the politically fraught term "woman," I follow the argument of the feminist transdisciplinary scholar Ariel Salleh: "if political theory is to be grounded in praxis, it has to bracket out or suspend these epistemological nuances to reach people in everyday life"; she adds that "the deformation known as womanhood should not be confused with the material potentiality of a specific embodiment."[iii]

When they say about the neighborhood we live in is dirty, why do they ask me to come and clean their house? We, the people in the slums, the same nasty women they have come to their house in the suburbs every day. If these women are so filthy, why do you want them to clean for you? They don't go and clean for us. We go and clean for them.

—Studs Terkel, *Working*[iv]

MAKING THE WORLD CLEAN

Is Cleaning a Decolonial Struggle?

The quote on the previous page is from the 1974 book by Studs Terkel, *Working: People Talk about What They Do All Day and How They Feel about What They Do*. These words are a starting point for a decolonial feminist antiracist politics of cleaning that considers as fundamental analytics the exploitation of women of color and the clean/dirty divide that racism has built.

This book looks at the social relations that have made cleaning into drudgery and into a racialized, gendered, poorly paid job that is nevertheless necessary for any society to function. If refusing the drudgery of housework assigned to women and girls all their lives has long been a feminist struggle, antiracist, Indigenous, and Black feminists have pointed to the fact that this work has been overwhelmingly done by women of color who, historically and in the present day, have been designated to that work. Cleaning will be examined here as it is structured by social-racial relations that have been shaped by colonialism and racial capitalism. Building on this understanding, I look at the racial/class and patriarchal norms of cleanliness, the waste and wasting that colonialism produces, and racial capitalism as producing goods as waste. I ask what cleaning could be, and how cleaning might be liberated from its historically racial and gendered roots. What will be a cleaning practice liberated from its racial and patriarchal bourgeois norms? In what follows, I will be calling this a "decolonial, antiracist, anti-patriarchal, anti-capitalist politics of cleaning," hereafter abbreviated as "decolonial cleaning." By this I mean the abolition of the racial industry of cleaning (whether domestic workers in bourgeois homes or public spaces); of the racial, gendered binary clean/dirty; and of the bourgeois patriarchal norms of cleanliness. "Decolonial cleaning" imagines cleaning as taking care of land, humans, plants, animals, and rivers, not seeking to discipline them or to transform living practices into dead objects. It is about cleaning for living and not for rigid conservation, that ideology that fixes or freezes a landscape, a site, a house, or a city into a display of dead objects. What will a decolonial cleaning look like? Can we (decolonial/ anticolonial antiracists) imagine this alternative form of cleaning?

Cleaning is also considered as an environmental issue: How can a world polluted, contaminated, and wasted for centuries by colonialism and racial capitalism be "cleaned" in ways that are not corporate "cleaning up" or greenwashing practices? Both of these types of practice start by agreeing that damages have been done and that cleaning must be done. But their understanding of cleaning as *cleaning up* leads to another source of profits, exploitation, and dispossession. They lead rehabilitation programs, fund grassroots initiatives and gender equality programs, and extol the benefits of an engineered conception of "nature."[1] Gender equality is now a requirement in any program of development and environment, the key word being the "empowerment" of women and girls in a world that needs—in order to remain alive—to dispossess and to exploit. Thus, the Shell Foundation has a page on its website about restoration programs that outlines its gender politics: "Women and girls—particularly those in rural areas and with lower socio-economic status whom we focus on—suffer an outsized impact from climate change and lack of access to energy products and services. They also have limited mobility as compared to men. Women entrepreneurs have less access to finance and resources to successfully setup and grow their business."[2]

The military, one of the most polluted industries, also establishes restoration programs after having wasted lands and lives. Thus, the U.S. Department of Defense (DoD), which presents itself as the "steward of nearly 25 million acres of public lands," which gives it the "responsibility to protect, maintain, and enhance the natural and cultural resources found on these lands," claims that its "environmental cleanup policy conforms to existing laws and regulations."[3] The DoD Environmental Restoration appropriations provide for "the identification, investigation, and cleanup of past contamination (prior to 1986) from hazardous substances and wastes; correction of other environmental damage; detection of unexploded ordnance; and the demolition and removal of unsafe buildings, structures, and debris."[4] Meanwhile, the U.S. Army still has to clean up the effects of, according to the U.S. National Library of Medicine, close to 75 million liters of the chemical herbicides and defoliants spilled over Vietnam between 1961 and 1971; of this, Agent Orange accounted for about 43 million liters (or 60 percent) over an area covering 10 percent of Vietnam's current territory. Clearly, the conception of protecting and conserving land and life is far from being neutral. This conception is directly inherited from colonialism, when the colonizing West gave itself the role of steward of the planet. Exposure to Agent Orange is considered today to be the cause of an "abnormally high incidence of miscarriages, skin diseases, cancers, birth defects, and congenital malformations (often extreme and grotesque) dating from the 1970s. Much of it contained a dangerous chemical contaminant called dioxin."[5] Many Vietnamese claim that this is "ecocide," defined as the "intentional, extensive and permanent destruction of an entire ecosystem by human activities," but the crime of ecocide is "not yet recognized in international law. While the destruction of the environment is already punishable in the context of armed conflict, it is only punishable if the damage is disproportionate to the concrete and direct military advantage anticipated (Article 8 (2b) (iv) of the Rome Statute)."[6] In other words, there is an expected "proportionate" damage, but who decides that threshold? The U.S. armies have left Cambodia, Afghanistan, Iraq, Laos, Vietnam, to name a few countries they have invaded, having caused disproportionate damages whose costs they have stubbornly avoided. For instance, in 2018, the U.S. withdrew from the Protocol on the Compulsory Jurisdiction to the Vienna Convention on Diplomatic Relations (VCDR), a treaty that provides the International Court of Justice (ICJ) with compulsory jurisdiction over VCDR-related disputes. That means that no U.S. citizen can be brought to that court.[7] This is organized impunity.

"Slow Violence"

This conception of damage in the eyes of international law also ignores the "slow violence" that environmental humanities scholar Rob Nixon has analyzed in his book *Slow Violence and the Environmentalism of the Poor*.[8] Quoting what Edward Said named "the normalized quiet of unseen power," Nixon encourages us to "address our inattention to calamities that are slow and long lasting, calamities that patiently dispense their devastation while remaining outside our flickering attention spans—and outside the purview of a spectacle-driven corporate media."[9] We should differentiate *cleaning up* by corporations from the *cleanup* demands of communities. The first is never neutral: it masks past and present slow violence, it recovers the damage with vibrant color, it creates a pastiche. Industrial *cleaning up* is done along class and race lines. When poor local communities demand that large corporations clean up the pollution and contamination they have caused, their demand is minimized, dismissed, and soon gets lost in the many fogs that corporations create with the support of PR, lobbying, and highly paid lawyers. Again, the fact is not that they deny damage, but that they muddle the facts, take the issue to court, where their lawyers contest the proofs communities have given, and drag out the case to exhaust the financial resources and the energy of the activists. It takes courage and fortitude to keep going.

The example of Agent Orange is one among many others. I will just add here the Niger Delta case, where Ogale communities have demanded that Royal Dutch Shell clean the large-scale, continued contamination of the water and soil that its oil and gas extraction had caused.[10] A 2011 report by the United Nations Environmental Program (UNEP) showed the concrete consequences of Shell's continuous pollution-contamination:

- Heavy contamination of land and underground water courses, sometimes more than 40 years after oil was spilled.
- Community drinking water with dangerous concentrations of benzene and other pollutants.
- Soil contamination more than five metres deep in many areas studied.
- Most of the spill sites oil firms claimed to have cleaned still highly contaminated.
- Evidence of oil firms dumping contaminated soil in unlined pits.
- Water coated with hydrocarbons more than 1,000 times the level allowed by Nigerian drinking water standards.
- Failure by Shell and others to meet minimum Nigerian or own standards.[11]

We must learn to read these data slowly, paying close attention, so that they start to take on some weight, to evoke something more than numbers. Behind the sentence "Heavy contamination of land and underground water courses, sometimes more than 40 years after oil was spilled," what we must read is the daily reality of access only to polluted water with which to wash, clean, eat, and cultivate. And that in 40 years, this has not changed. Or that Shell has not even cleaned up what it pretends to have cleaned up. In 2020, Godwin Ojo of Environmental Rights Action/Friends of the Earth Nigeria said: "After nine years of promises without proper action and decades of pollution, the people of Ogoniland are not only sick of dirty drinking water, oil-contaminated fish and toxic fumes. They are sick of waiting for justice, they are dying by the day. The Nigerian government should acknowledge this project has been a failure and reinvigorate HYPREP [the cleanup agency] with technical skills and strategic thinking, fully involving the community."[12] Faced with a government that pocketed the money allocated for cleaning, and the organized denial of Royal Dutch of the damages it had caused, the Ogale community has multiplied its actions, raising awareness, mobilizing, analyzing data, and taking Royal Dutch Shell to court.

When the UK Supreme Court ruled that Shell could be sued in English courts, Royal Dutch Shell did not dispute that pollution had been caused but argued that "it could not be held legally responsible for its Nigerian subsidiary. Shell is responsible for about 50% of the delta's oil production."[13] Corporations use all the weapons at their disposal (the media, lobbying, law, corruption, intimidation, assassinations) to avoid accountability. Around the world, what I will be calling "the politics of the elemental," of vital needs, are mobilizing people. The answers to these vital needs—for humans, access to clean and drinkable water, to clean air, to a roof over their heads, to education and health; and for nonhumans, the end of utilitarianism—will require profound changes, including the abolition of racial patriarchal capitalism. The politics of the elemental will be revolutionary because it would mean rethinking social and intimate relations.

I borrow the term "organized abandonment" from abolitionist scholar Ruth Wilson Gilmore to designate governments' relinquishing of their responsibility to guarantee these vital needs.[14] This abandonment, in order to help neoliberal corporations, was made possible by an ideological counteroffensive that harked back to the notion of "benign neglect." The latter was promoted in 1970 by Daniel Patrick Moynihan, Democrat senator and advisor to U.S. president Richard Nixon.[15] In a memo addressed to Nixon on January 16, 1970, Moynihan first listed the progress made in jobs and education for the Black communities but immediately underlined a threat: "Increasingly, the problem of Negro poverty is the problem of the female headed family."[16] "With no real evidence, I would nonetheless suggest that a great deal of the crime, the fire setting, the rampant school violence, and other such phenomenon in the black community have become quasi politicized. Hatred—revenge— against whites is now an acceptable excuse for doing what might have been done anyway."[17] He then suggested that "the time may have come when the issue of race could benefit from a period of 'benign neglect.' The subject has been too much talked about."[18] The senator claimed that the cause of high crime rates in Black neighborhoods was African-Americans' alienation from society due to their "anti-social lifestyle," such as living in female-dominated households. Moynihan pathologized poverty: "Fires are in fact a 'leading indicator' of social pathology for a neighborhood. They come first. Crime, and the rest, follows. The psychiatric interpretation of fire-setting is complex, but it relates to the types of personalities which slums produce."[19] As fires are a good indication of a crime-filled area, Moynihan affirmed, again without proof, that most fires in Black neighborhoods were found to be cases of arson, and not accidents. "Benign neglect" would mean that firefighting teams were to ignore such neighborhoods, as it was futile to fight arson. "What I was saying," Moynihan said in an interview, "was that the more we discuss the issue of race as an issue, the more people get polarized, the more crazy racists on the left and maybe crazy racists on the right shout and yell and make things seem so much worse than they are, when in fact the nineteen sixties have been a period of enormous progress."[20] The politics of "benign neglect" targeted 1960s–1970s Black militancy, the civil rights movement, as well as the Black Panthers Party, who had been transformed, he said, "into culture heroes for the white—and black—middle class."[21]

The intent was not only to justify pacification through murder and repression of Black activists and their allies but also to impose a politics of bourgeois respectability whose norms rested on the ways of life of the suburban white middle class. Benign neglect condoned the abandonment of public services in Black and poor neighborhoods by representing them as dangerous, unhealthy, and deteriorated because of inner deficiencies, female-headed households, and lack of positive male role models.[22] In a chapter of *Abolition Geography*, Gilmore comes back to that ideology by retracing the trajectory of "antistate state actors" who worked toward the naturalization of policies that went against people's vital needs. They argued "that the withdrawal of the state from certain areas of social welfare provision will enhance rather than destroy the lives of those abandoned."[23] These actors, she writes, have as their ideal "a frightening willingness to engage in human sacrifice while calling it something else."[24] Nonetheless, they "have triumphed in promoting and imposing a view that certain capacities of the state are obstacles to development, and thus should be shrunken or otherwise debilitated from playing a central role in everyday economic and social life. But their actions are contrary to their rhetoric."[25]

I propose to apply the policy of organized abandonment to the racialized, class, and gendered politics of wasting, corporate *cleaning up*, and to an urban architecture that draws a line between neighborhoods that are taken care of and those that are not, reinforcing the binary clean/dirty. "Benign neglect" or "organized abandonment" offered neoliberal ideology a terrain upon which to expand the reach of economics and markets into "noneconomic" domains of life (for instance, water and air), advocating that the dereliction of public services would be good to people who otherwise would not make the effort to uplift their lives. The poor and racialized were blamed for their situation. Under neoliberalism, everyone can claim their consumer rights on things like rivers, forests, lakes, water, air, and social needs. Neoliberalism promoted a set of calculations and consumer choices that was said to guarantee freedom against a too invasive state. The notion of freedom became key because it mobilized affective investments in privilege. Further, so the neoliberal story goes, if people's vital needs are not fulfilled, it has nothing to do with organized abandonment but everything to do with state bureaucracy, laziness, and lack of personal effort from the people themselves. Institutional responsibilities are diluted and the situation is said to be "complex" in order to muddle the basic questions of why, when, by whose hand the situation came to be like that. Social relations are masked and individualism promoted.

Collectives around the world have confronted the ways in which they are targeted by organized abandonment, and though I will come back to the consequences of organized abandonment later, let me mention two examples that have not made international headlines. One is the systemic lack of water for months in the French territories of Guadeloupe and Mayotte, a situation blamed on unexpected circumstances—drought, and the local administrative system—and without any acknowledgment of the organized abandonment by the French state of its duties. It is important to study how, when, and why the organized abandonment of vital needs happened, who its actors are, and what have been the counterstrategies communities have elaborated as benign neglect has become a governmental policy, with active ideologues, think tanks, and a range of diverse media (cinema, TV series, books). What this case shows is that the language of the politics of the elemental (land, water, air) is used to confront corporations' and governments' organized abandonment of ordinary people. The other example is from Brazil: the Movimento dos Trabalhadores Sem Teto (the Movement of Workers without a Roof)—"set up in 1997 by a group of militants from the Movimento Sem Terra [MST, the Movement of Those without Land], the rural landless workers' movement, who saw the need to go beyond the countryside and organize in the cities"[26]—who solved the problem of being relegated far from public services (schools, hospitals, public administration) and places of work by occupying empty buildings. "Fighting urban segregation means, on the one hand, fighting for housing together with public services and infrastructure, on the peripheries; and on the other, demanding the expropriation of unused property in central city districts, to create social housing in areas that already have services and infrastructure. In other words, we have to fight against the segregation of centre and periphery, which means confronting the real-estate speculators."[27]

On the other hand, rich dominant classes are assured that waste will be externalized from their surroundings, dumped in poor neighborhoods and in the Global South, and that the cleaning up of their beaches, golf courses, and neighborhoods will be swift. They support the greening of popular neighborhoods and the destruction of "slums," since for them *cleaning up* is gentrification. There is a double colonial gesture still at work in the racist and neoliberal politics of cleaning up: while they continue to extract and thus *waste* land and bodies, the dominant classes of the West demand that enclaves be created in the Global South for their own enjoyment (hunting, sunbathing, admiring birds, resting in luxury). The West pressures poorer countries to be more "sustainable," to conserve forests, to clean up their energy sources, and curb polluting industries. The planet must remain organized for its comfort.

Environmental politics scholar Helena Varkkey speaks of the "distancing of waste,"[28] of putting waste out of sight, and the people in charge of doing it. In the documentary *Urban Solutions* (2022), the invisible doormen who are ubiquitous in Brazilian rich neighborhoods know that they "hold the door and carry the groceries for a hopelessly backward elite who hate us."[29] This is an elite who "has developed a pathological hatred of the poor. It's entirely logic [*sic*], they are totally at our mercy, they don't even know how to cook."[30] The film adroitly mixes colonial paintings of slavery and nature with current images of racism and exploitation by dominant classes who cannot admit that they are dependent on domestic workers, drivers, delivery people, doormen, cooks, and nannies, showing the long history of delegating waste and dirt to people who are racialized in the process—identified as "dirty," they are assigned to "dirty" work. Their society rests on workers whose vital needs they dismiss. The externalization of pollution is being conceived in the very fabric of urbanization. Polluting industries are located in poor neighborhoods or poor countries. One historical example of that spatial division is Paris, where bourgeois neighborhoods were built in the west and poor ones in the east because winds blowing from west to the east would carry polluted air to the poor. But slow violence also exists in the world of cleaners in that the chemicals they must use enter their bodies and respiratory systems, and repeated gestures (which are part of all repetitive tasks) damage their joints. The violence of colonialism and racial capitalism has many levels, and each must be studied in every case, in the short term and the long term, how the past continues in the present.

Radical Hope

Racial capitalism is explored here in terms of how it depends on the production of waste and wasting, the tons of accumulated contaminated waste that suffocates the planet and its poor and racialized inhabitants as well as non-human lives. Rather than falling into a catastrophism and end-of-the-world discourse that can have the effect of making people feel frightened and powerless, I take the side of radical hope. I advocate the end of *this* world, and, as

Black Canadian writer and scholar Robyn Maynard wrote in a letter to Michi Saagiig Nishnaabeg scholar, writer, and artist Leanne Betasamosake Simpson, "all world-endings are not tragic" and "some versions of this world need to end."[31] I owe a debt to the way Gilmore articulates abolition when she writes that "abolition is life in rehearsal because freedom is a place."[32] What she means is that it is essential to look at how "people arrive at arranging themselves into a social force," tracing a "historical geography of the future."[33] "Abolition" here is not the European abolitionism that gave European colonial powers the good role in the abolition of colonial slavery but the radical transformation of the systems of oppression. Abolition, say Aviah Sarah Day, Black community organizer with the collectives Sisters Uncut and Hackney Cop Watch, and Shanice Octavia McBean, Black writer and activist in Sisters Uncut, "must work towards the wider goal of seizing the land, natural resources and wealth stolen from us by capitalists: abolition must work in service of proletarian revolution."[34] It is the dismantling of the afterlives of slavery and colonialism: the theft of land, racism, the organized abandonment of people of color in the areas of health, education, housing, work, life, the carceral industrial system . . .[35] Abolition work is present in all the actions against prisons, against anti-refugee politics or mega projects, against planned toxic empoisoning (locating toxic industries or toxic dumping near poor and racialized communities), against invasive and racist birth control politics, because all of these actions (and others that target projects that destroy all forms of living) demonstrate that there are other ways to live than to consume, extract, and exploit.

It bears repeating that decolonial antiracist feminist cleaning is abolitionist because it seeks the end of the racial industry of cleaning in all spaces, and the end of the racial, colonial, and gendered fabricated division between what is clean and what is dirty, of the bourgeois patriarchal norms of cleanliness. In a recent book, *A Program of Absolute Disorder*, in which I argued that the decolonization of the Western museum was impossible, I wrote that the transformation of that institution could not be only about representation, about demanding diversity on the walls, but had to also be about wondering who cleans, who cooks, who guards in that institution, how much they are paid, whether they can organize, if their work is as valued as the work of the curators, art historians, and artists, who without them would not be able to write, imagine, and realize a show.[36] I was saying that we must see cleaners, cooks, and guards as human beings with dreams, feelings, bodies, and sexualities. Already in 1969, in her *Manifesto for Maintenance Art*, the feminist artist Mierle Laderman Ukeles had asked: "The sourball of every revolution: after the revolution, who's going to pick up the garbage on Monday morning? . . . Maintenance is a drag; it takes all the fucking time. The mind bogles and chafes at the boredom. The culture confers lousy status on maintenance jobs—minimum wages, housewives—no pay."[37] But her feminist critique remained blind to race.

In the performance "The Clean-up Woman," Afro-Dutch artist Patricia Kaersenhout attended to the disappearance of the racialized body of the cleaner. Kaersenhout wanted to show the "relation between power dynamics and invisibility within white institutions. The occasional black spots in this museum represented by security, catering personal, cleaners reminded me of a passage in Ralph Ellison's book Invisible man [*sic*]."[38] Dressed up as a cleaning woman, she cleaned the museum as the public was waiting. They did not realize that the cleaning woman who went around was the artist whose performance they had come to see. By going further than Ukeles, Kaersenhout revealed how cleaning work was not only a "woman's question" but also a racial one. With the video *The Attendant* (1993), Black British artist and filmmaker Isaac Julien gave back sexual fantasies and desires to a middle-aged Black man, perceived as devoid of body and sexualities, whose work is to wander silently through an empty museum. Set in Wilberforce House in Hull, England, a museum devoted to the history of slavery, where much of the action takes place after closing time, a guard paces the galleries. As a huge 19th-century painting titled *Slaves on the West Coast of Africa* by the French artist François-Auguste Biard comes to life, the attendant lives a leather-clad sadomasochistic grouping inspired by the melodramatic scene of a white master bending over a dying Black slave. These pieces, which explore the invisibility of women and men who attend to the needs of a bourgeois society, add to the films that probe the class conflict that the intimacy of domestic work entails and they differ in form and content from films and TV series that whitewash a conflicted relation.[39] They show the multiple links (ideology, history, class, race, genders) of a social relation rooted in domination but which has succeeded in its naturalization and invisibilization.

The Elemental

To explore the questions raised above, I propose to take as an entry point the banal, the trivial, the elemental, as the terrain upon which an antiracist decolonial theory and practice of cleaning—what I have called decolonial cleaning—is imagined and developed. By *elemental*, I mean the activity necessary for the making of communal living, with the understanding that communities manage waste and cleaning differently, and that these forms of care are indispensable for good health. An example of the racist denial of the elemental is the structural neglect of women and girls of color's basic needs to have access to sanitary protection, to a private space to breastfeed, pee, poo, wash themselves—to cleaning as a necessity of caring for oneself. The *elemental* needs of women of color are considered insignificant (which is the etymological root of the word "trivial").[40] Descriptions of life in refugee camps, temporary housing, women's refuges, migrants' hostels, prisons, youth education centers, and psychiatric hospitals all paint the picture of organized neglect: dirty toilets, one shower for ten people, no warm water, dirty sheets, no soap, bad shampoo if any, cockroaches, peeling paint, bad smells, bad food. These institutions are connected by the thread of organized uncleanliness. The message is, "You'd better be thankful because you barely deserve this, and any protest will mean even less of this." Not being able to clean oneself adds to humiliation. This is class war. This is racism. Hence the importance of attending to those who are *denied the elemental*. When in the north of France the police forbid the distribution of warm food to refugees,[41] or destroy their camp every 48 hours,[42] or steal their tents in Paris,[43] these are also examples of organized attacks on vital needs.

By addressing the banal, the *trivial*, the *elemental*, I am speaking of cleaning as a necessity rather than the maintenance of a consumerist lifestyle, a condition of basic care of the body and the mind that is considered with indifference by racial capitalism, white environmentalism, and even, too often, by humanitarian organizations. It is precisely the prosaic nature of these needs that interests me. What is considered basic or mundane? How is racism maintained through these basic and mundane needs being overlooked or denied? How is neglect organized and naturalized? The revealing of what the elemental is and the demonstration of how and why the elemental is denied are central to decolonial, antiracist, anti-imperialist struggles for the Earth.

As colonialism, capitalism, climate disaster, wars around the extraction of minerals, and the production of elements indispensable to nanotechnologies and artificial intelligence increase the power of multinationals, the military, and authoritarian regimes, why look at cleaning? What changes might struggles around this mundane activity bring? I am not denying pressing issues around land, exploitation, dispossession, and extraction—far from it. I am proposing that we do not forget the trivial or the mundane because it is just this: mundane or trivial. To be clear, by speaking of the elemental, and of cleaning as a *politics of the elemental*, I am not celebrating the minutiae, the little details, the feminine touch. Neither am I advocating the *hummingbird theory*, popularized by American writer and activist Thomas Berry in his book *The Great Work: Our Way into the Future*,[44] a theory that concentrates on individual action, arguing that each of us can make a difference by taking small, positive actions to protect the environment and that individual actions can have a significant collective impact.[45] It takes as an example the burning forest and the hummingbird, which, despite its size compared to larger animals that feel the heat, carries in its beak a very small drop of water to the fire.[46] It does not look at what brought the fire or what made life possible before the burning. Of course, it will not stop the fire, but this is not what matters; what is important here is to individualize action, to weaken collective organizing and communizing. But a tiny individual action will not dismantle the organized neglect of the people of color and the Indigenous. These are not unfortunate events, the impacts of the "world as it is" that individual actions will assuage, but the inevitable consequences of centuries of fabricated vulnerability.

Cleaning, Cleanliness, Cleansing

I am aware that "cleanliness" is an ambiguous and loaded term. Cleaning, cleanliness, cleansing, clearing, purification, sterilization, purity, disinfection, scouring—all these terms belong to the same semantic field, to the racial idea that the world must be pristine and cleansed of whatever disrupts whiteness. Cleaning has been marked by racism, by colonial understandings of hygiene, and by the policies that justify the expulsion of Indigenous peoples from their lands to create parks of unpolluted nature. Throughout history, genocides have been justified by discourses of cleaning to get rid of entire populations who were seen as contaminating excess. As geographers Max Liboiron (Red River Métis/Michif and settler) and Josh Lepawsky have remarked, "at different points in history and in various places, Indigenous peoples, Jews, women, immigrants, 2SLGBTQIA + people, people with disabilities, and political prisoners are killable, not just peripheral," adding that "these details are fundamental, not incidental, to different systems and effects of waste. Genocide and sorting recycling not only are different in terms of social, economic, material, spiritual, and political systems but also they are different in terms of power, oppression, and justice."[47] Indeed, we must answer to the question "What must be discarded for this or that system to be created and carry on?" because, they argue, "to persist, systems must rid themselves of people, places and things that actually or potentially threaten the continuity of these systems."[48] Waste is then understood as what is identified as justifiably discarded by power (not only as overt domination but also as naturalizing wasting).

Cleaning, unclean, waste, wasting, wasted, discard, discarded are terms that need to be clarified because of their history. I recognize the difficulty. Cleanliness may be a term that is too loaded, too charged with a history of ethnic cleansing, genocides, and murder to be useful. But there is also the danger of idealizing cleaning or making it an all-encompassing idea. I propose looking at cleaning (work) and cleanliness (an objective or result) in relation to the production of waste, of commodities that are turned into waste by unlimited growth that it is then dumped in the Global South and near poor and racialized neighborhoods in the North. I keep as a thread the necessary work by women and men of color. Cleaning is an endless work, it is dangerous, underpaid, and undervalued, but cleaning is also a human necessity, one of the material contingencies that a posthumanism dreams of getting rid of. The desire of being freed of these material contingencies, of having to produce the very conditions of human existence—food, care, clothing, energy, housing—and to be aware of their dependency to nonhuman species, which sustained slavery, regularly comes back with the dream of robots, artificial intelligence, and so on, to alleviate the burden.

I take cleaning as an analytic and as *an elemental*, in other words constitutive of social and cultural life. Historically, cleaning has been identified by white supremacy as a dirty, racialized, and gendered job, to be exploited and industrialized, and a site of sexual violence.[49] As an analytic, cleaning brings to light the intersections of gender, class, and race, divisions marshalled by whiteness to impose its reading of cleanliness (the odorless as a sign of civilization) and to claim that dirtiness is a racial characteristic. I acknowledge the radical contribution of the Marxist feminist theorists of social reproduction, but I propose to expand this body of work to consider the current moment of exacerbated chaos. I am looking at cleaning work through the racialized lens of "environment" as a field of structuring social relations that cannot be thought apart from the "environment" as deracialized in white environmentalism. I ask how, after centuries of damage, cleaning the planet is already being imagined by Indigenous, Black, African, and Asian people, and by the collectives and communities who already construct forms of living that turn their back to the logic of waste capitalism. It is clear that the fight for better conditions of work, for the recognition of threats to health (fatigue, stress, the toxicity of chemicals, the repetition of gestures that harm joints, sexual violence, low pay) is urgent and necessary. For instance, in 2019, Black cleaning women at the Ibis Batignolles hotel in Paris protested working conditions and the low pay for cleaning 60 rooms per day instead of 12, labor that made them sick. They sang: "Scrubbing, scrubbing must be paid!" (*Frottez, frottez, il faut payer!*)[50]

Water, an Elemental

I also look at another elemental that is connected to cleaning: water. Water is an element of the Earth in continuous interexchange with humans and non-humans. Water flows through ecological, infrastructural, and bodily systems; aquifers, rivers, lakes, seas, and oceans are all connected. Colonialism privatized and diverted water to serve its benefits; it destroyed, erased, neglected, or stole the technologies of water that states or communities had created (irrigation systems, basins to collect water, canals). It enforced rigid boundaries and deprived communities of their historical access to water. Mastering water has always fascinated power: beyond ordering works to avoid floods, emperors, kings, dictators, and other leaders have asked engineers to divert and control water to demonstrate that no element will not be disciplined. Cases abound. One is the construction of the Belomorkanal (White Sea Canal) ordered by Stalin to connect the Baltic Sea with the White Sea. The digging started in 1931. In June 1933, the canal was completed; 15,000 to 30,000 *zeks* (inmates) had died during its construction from cold, accidents, or malnutrition, but the channel's depth of 3.5 meters was insufficient for most heavy vessels.[51] The canal was of no use. But by demonstrating that mega-projects can divert water work, that therefore plantations can flourish and cotton, sugar, and coffee can grow in deserts, that greening the desert is possible if the will is there, failures are forgotten or attributed to engineering faults rather than engineering being seen as hubris or at the service of power. Mega-projects around water instituted a model that became too seductive to be ignored. The Global North showed how to privatize water; it was no longer a commons. Postcolonial nation-states of the Global South followed suit. Dams, canals, and vast programs of irrigation illustrated the new states' development. Mastering water meant abundance.

But water is not only a source that proves state power. It is also necessary for daily life, for community crafts (pottery, weaving, wood, and stone carving), for raising animals, and is at the heart of religious rituals and human care. When born, a baby and their mother must be washed, the dead are washed, women and men clean themselves with water, women even more so—for decades of their lives, menstruation requires access to water every month. Water is an elemental of cleaning, of cooking, of washing clothes, for animals, for cleaning the home... Post-catastrophe images show piles of plastic bottles of water. The message is that access to drinking water is an urgent matter and is entirely justified. But what is not seen in such images is the water required for cleaning oneself. Water has become rare—more than 1.1 billion people do not have access to clean water.[52] According to a report issued by

UNESCO, the UN Educational, Scientific and Cultural Organization, "up to 3.5 billion people live under conditions of water stress at least one month a year." Furthermore, "26% of the world's population doesn't have access to safe drinking water and 46% lack access to basic sanitation."[53] Communizing water will inevitably dismantle many systems of domination, exploitation, extraction, and dispossession. This means going beyond a universal right to clean water or air.[54]

Unpacking the connections between capitalism as the production of waste and the fabricated banality of non-white women's elementary needs or of their work contributes to an antiracist and decolonial environmental politics. I oppose the *elemental* to the organized trivialization and banalization of women of color's basic needs. I approach the critique of white bourgeois environmentalism by unpacking a web of intersected relations between colonialism, state capitalism, neoliberal capitalism, and authoritarian capitalism that produce tons of waste; the cleaning work done by women of color both historically and in the present day; the organization of water scarcity; the weaponization of scarcity to impose policies of managing water that condemn non-white communities to polluted and contaminated water; the racialized notions of cleanliness/the odorless; and the consequences of warming temperatures caused by capitalist extraction, dispossession, and exploitation affecting the sources of water. In what follows, waste will thus be considered through different lenses: what colonialism considered wasted and dirty; what racism associates with dirtiness; what needs are discarded because they do not fit into bourgeois and white norms of what must be in the home; and waste as a central element of capitalist economy of consumption.

Women as a Praxis

By acknowledging the central role of Black women and women of color in the work of cleaning the world, and the facts that "pollution is colonialism"[55] and capitalism is the massive production of waste that needs to be cleaned every day while holding the thread of fabricated and weaponized scarcity, I hope to clarify what could be an antiracist struggle for cleanliness. I have written how the industry of cleanliness in the West—which includes programs of fasting, of meditation to cleanse the mind, of cleaning one's intestines, and a whole set of cleansing practices appropriated from non-Western cultures—is made possible through the exploitation of women of color.[56] In the spaces where these practices are performed, women of color work as cleaners, masseuses, and beauticians, but they do not have the financial means nor the time to participate. The extraction of their skills and life force through their racial exploitation allows white bourgeois women to adhere to a philosophy of cleanliness.[57]

Exiting Colonial Dystopia

While aligning myself on the side of radical hope, I also acknowledge that, in the words of anti-capitalist speculative fiction writer China Miéville: "It is hard to avoid the sense that these are particularly terrible days, that dystopia is bleeding vividly into the quotidian, and hence, presumably, into 'realism', if that was ever a category in which one was interested. At this point, however, comes an obligatory warning about the historical ubiquity of the questionable belief that Things Have Got Worse, and of the sheer arrogance of despair, the aggrandizement of thinking that one lives in the Worst Times."[58] The future in white environmentalism is conceived in ways that erase a past that was already a catastrophe. Racialized people have been living in dystopias for centuries; there is no pristine past to return to. In an open letter to Extinction Rebellion in 2019, the grassroots collective Wretched of the Earth clearly articulated the different notions of time in the North and the South:

The bleakness is not something of "the future." For those of us who are indigenous, working class, black, brown, queer, trans or disabled, the experience of structural violence became part of our birthright. Greta Thunberg calls world leaders to act by reminding them that "Our house is on fire". For many of us, the house has been on fire for a long time: whenever the tide of ecological violence rises, our communities, especially in the Global South are always first hit. We are the first to face poor air quality, hunger, public health crises, drought, floods and displacement.[59]

As Indigenous, Black and Brown environmental activists face criminalization and death threats, they "carefully weigh the costs that can be inflicted on us and our communities by a state that is driven to target those who are racialised ahead of those who are white."[60] As Juan Pablo Gutiérrez, delegated spokesperson for the Indigenous Yupka Nation (Colombia) writes: "The climate crisis is a COLONIAL CRISIS."[61] New perspectives must be acknowledged, in particular those that come "from the historically minimized, excluded and exterminated: THE INDIGENOUS PEOPLES who today, in spite of being 4% of the world's population have in our territories 80% of the world's remaining diversity."[62] Who speaks, who is heard and listened to, who matters, bring to light the colonial-racial making of time. The ideology of "things will get worse" and that we are living in the worst time is a surrendering to colonialism and racial capitalism. Yet, we must also recognize how destructive fossil capitalism and extractivism are and how fast they destroy. The past collides with the present and the afterlives of slavery and colonialism shape the present. The future in decolonial environmentalism is not a temporality that does not bear the traces of the past. A past whose damages are not yet repaired, a present pregnant with the past and weighed by new destructions, and a future that will be marked by the past and the present: these imbricated temporalities cannot fit into a neat "future." I return here to Ruth Wilson Gilmore's understanding of "an historical geography of the future,"[63] framed in the temporalities of struggles.

Polluting, Contaminating, Cleaning Up

By saying that capitalism is waste, and that waste, as Marxist activist writers Fred Magdoff and Chris Williams have argued, "is a sign of capitalism's success,"[64] I aim to show that cleaning is made impossible under an economy and an ideology that conceive of the Earth as a waste dump. Tons of things are produced without any socially useful purpose.[65] In 2015, advertising, packaging, and e-commerce orders alone led to the production of 35 million tons of cardboard. In 2016, the world's cities generated 2.01 billion tons of solid waste. In 2018, the World Bank estimated that 11 tons of solid waste were produced every year.[66] Region-specific data mask the fact that waste circulates (air and water do not know borders). In other words, waste generated by state productivism and Western imperialism, or produced for the comfort and consumption of privileged white people, ends up being dumped on racialized people in impoverished racialized neighborhoods or in the countries of the Global South. What I mean by waste is not only solid waste and what we know as refuse and garbage,[67] but also what is *wasted* by bombs, herbicides, chemicals, megafarms, megafires, fast fashion, toxic haze, mining, the construction industry,[68] the waste from mining minerals such as copper and lithium that are becoming more important than oil and coal, and the waste and destruction that deep-sea mining will bring.[69] Although they account for only 16 percent of the world's population, high-income countries collectively generate more than a third (34 percent) of the world's waste.[70] But these data look at waste as if waste and wasting were equally produced and distributed throughout the planet. It is not clear whether they take into account the huge amount of waste generated by imperialism, and the countries and bodies that colonial occupation (for instance, of Palestine) and imperialism have *wasted*. Armies are great polluters but most of their actions are hidden and kept secret so that the consequences are underestimated.

The little-known case of the closed-down U.S. Camp Century Base on Greenland illustrates this. In 1951, Denmark and the United States signed the Defense of Greenland Agreement, which practically gave the U.S. Army all power of decision and impunity to its personnel in a foreign country.[71] Three air bases would be built and, after extensive research of the ice sheet, a nuclear base eight meters below the ice sheet's surface would be established, and year-round accommodation for anywhere between 85 and 200 soldiers, powered by a portable nuclear generator, would be provided.[72] The Camp Century NATO base was abandoned in 1967. The North American defense took a nuclear reactor home with them, but left 9,200 tons of waste behind, low-nuclear spill water included. They assumed that ice and future snowfall would preserve the base and the various remains more or less forever. But as temperatures have risen and the ice has melted, biological, chemical, and nuclear waste may leak into the waters of the world's largest island.[73] The U.S. Army is dragging the cleaning up of a land that was a Danish colony from 1721 to 1953 and where the colonial policy of "Danization" was implemented through language, culture, and administration.[74] What this case, among many others, shows is that colonialism *lays waste* (more on this later), and that the toxic consequences of colonialism and imperialism linger for generations.

Rather than putting an end to an economy that needs to produce waste, experts and policy makers discuss whether it makes "economic sense to manage waste properly."[75] Managing waste has become a profitable market. As McKinsey Sustainability writes, "With the right approach, many waste streams can become income streams, yielding economic value with technology available today." For instance, "every metric ton of used clothing collected could generate revenue of $1,975, if garments were sold at current secondary-market prices, comfortably outweighing the cost of $680 required to collect and sort each metric ton."[76] We should be full of optimism, McKinsey tell us: "The chance to tap into new sources of value through better waste management and win the 'race against waste' is cause for optimism. There are few areas where entrepreneurial success comes with more benefits to the economy and society at large."[77] Financial institutions acknowledge now the geopolitics of racism not as inherent structural features but as aggravating elements.[78] McKinsey, the World Bank, the IMF, and private foundations such as the Gates Foundation now incorporate racial and gender discriminations in their calculus of costs-benefits.[79] The notion of management is key here: waste is approached as inert rather than as having a life of its own and being the inevitable production of capitalism. Racism runs through waste management policy, which becomes a justification for more criminalization, expropriation, dispossession, and exploitation.

Hence in 1991, Larry Summers, then chief economist of the World Bank (and then president of Harvard University), spoke of the economic argument for exporting first-world waste to developing countries: "I've always thought that under-populated countries in Africa are vastly UNDER-polluted, their air quality is probably vastly inefficiently low compared to Los Angeles or Mexico City."[80] One could not be more honest. The idea that Africa is "under-polluted" after centuries of wasting by imperialism shows how the corporate class conceives pollution: it is connected with race, and whereas a threshold exists for the West, the "rest of the world" has not yet reached this threshold. The notion of threshold, as Liboiron has argued, is in itself wrong because it masks the fact that there should be no threshold.[81] Finally, the ideology that naturalizes dumping also uses notions such as "adaptation" or "resilience" to avoid revolt. Adaptation means that we must accept things as they are and trust technological inventions that will make an uninhabitable world livable; resilience is the promise that it is possible to overcome, personally or communally, terrible cruelty without seeking justice and reparation.

The Racial Politics of Wasting and Cleaning Up

In this book, I attempt to propose a counter-politics to racist *cleaning up* by showing how the latter ends up masking the social relations of dispossession, exploitation, and devastation. However, I do not suggest that a return to pre-wasted time is desirable or possible. This could be the *terra nullius* fantasy, the colonial dream of untouched nature populated by "natives" that may be first romanticized as guardians of nature or elements of nature, before becoming a threat to a nature shaped by colonial settlers. Indigenous activists and thinkers have robustly challenged that fantasy and show that national parks were built on colonial violence worldwide. *Cleaning up* is the pursuit of the colonial dream of national parks maintained for the benefit of the health of clean white bodies.[82] The Albert National Park in the Belgian colony of Congo, established in 1925, "set the tone for decades of colonial protected parks in Africa," the violent expulsion of Indigenous communities, a few selected to add "local color."[83] Yet the colonial origins of the model persist and its methods continue to be adopted worldwide: "Scientists, politicians, and conservationists are championing the protected-areas model, developed in the U.S. and perfected in Africa. In late 2022, at the United Nations Biodiversity Conference in Montreal, nearly 200 countries signed an international pledge to protect 30 percent of the world's land and waters by 2030."[84] Despite the work of Indigenous peoples to make their voice heard, the hegemonic policy remains

one of *cleaning up* an area to offer an "untouched" nature. "European countries are not going to evict white people from their lands," said Fiore Longo,
a researcher and campaigner at Survival International. "That is for sure. This
is where you see all the racism around this. Because they know how these
targets will be applied in Africa and Asia. That's what's going on, they are
evicting the people."[85] The model is so hegemonic that it is adopted by states
around the world and by nonprofit organizations such as the World Wildlife
Fund, all helping to "fund violent campaigns against Indigenous peoples."[86]
In other words, the ideology of *cleaning up* can be found in corporate programs of crime-washing or in states or nonprofit programs of conservation
of nature. It is about building guarded enclaves whose economic objective is
to make profits, and ideological programs whose promise is a piece of regi-
mented nature, freed from any human and nonhuman presence that could
disturb the idea of nature: birds yes, but not snakes, humans yes, but in folk-
loric garb. An antiracist decolonial politics of cleaning, by contrast, seeks to
rethink cleaning within social relations of solidarity and communizing needs.

Race, Gender, Capital, and Cleaning

In recent years, I have been considering how waste, race, and gender inter-
sect and the ways in which colonial slavery, colonialism, racial capitalism,
and imperialism have constructed specific understandings of cleanliness
and, consequently, dirtiness. After looking at "Who Cleans the World" in *A
Decolonial Feminism* and at the interconnections between waste, race, gender, and capital in a 2019 article,[87] I wanted to take cleaning further as a political question and focus on the *elemental*. The racialized production of waste,
wasting, and wasted; the racialized division between clean and dirty; and the
organized denial of the elemental appeared as a good starting point to take
cleaning out of drudgery, out of the "woman's question" that could be resolved
through gender equality programs. I situate this book within the framework of
these earlier publications, whose common thread is how to abolish systems
of dispossession, exploitation, and extraction—processes of racialization and
domination. In doing so, I have addressed subjects that on first glance might
appear to have nothing to do with each other: for instance, anticolonialism,
memories, and afterlives of slavery, the work of the anticolonial figures Frantz
Fanon and Aimé Césaire, colonial psychiatry, Indian Ocean processes of cre-
olization, decolonization of the arts, the impossible decolonization of the
Western "universal" museum, anticolonial communism in Reunion Island,

and feminisms. This book is intended not so much as an academic work as a contribution to an antiracist politics that focuses on the racialization of waste and cleaning, with the objective of trying to answer the following questions: Is there an antiracist decolonial praxis of cleaning that is not only *cleaning up* the mess produced by racial capitalism? If we need to clean, why and how do we do so, and for what and by whom?

I cite here many reports from the United Nations (UN), the World Health Organization (WHO); the Climate Change Expert Group (CCXG), and other international institutions. They make for dreary reading, endlessly documenting what is wrong but never, or very rarely, addressing why things are in such a bad shape. The latter can be found in activists' articles and blogs and social networks, in decolonial scholars' books. Reports that list everything that is wrong feed either a savior syndrome among Western private foundations or civilizational feminists (those who have translated the vocabulary of the colonial civilizing mission for current colonial and imperialist endeavors)[88] or neoliberal mantras, reform and liberalization, and this despite decades of programs that have proven wrongheaded. Institutions or governments offer solutions that deliberately avoid confronting the structural causes of racism, inequities, dispossession, exploitation, and injustices. They read as wishful thinking, calling to the good sense of rich countries, to the moral consciousness of the rich, or to an abstract common humanity, and they satisfy the narcissism of the rich for whom charity demonstrates their good heart. That ideology can even reach the absurd. As Italian journalist and social theorist Marco D'Eramo writes, it shows "the gigantic practical joke being played by world leaders in their 'declaration of war' on global warming."[89] In 2023, the French government sought "to encourage the textile and footwear industries to curb their practice of planned obsolescence, by imposing warranties that would oblige them to repair defective items free of charge for several years, or requiring the use of more durable materials."[90] According to D'Eramo,

the total amount allocated for this revolutionary measure was €154 million. Assuming that this figure doesn't include the cost of employing bureaucrats to assess requests, disburse subsidies and supervise the quality of the repairs, this means a handsome €2.26 has been allocated for each of France's 68 million people. Even if one were to only consider the 29.9 million *ménages* composed of an average of 2.2 members, each household would receive a grand total of €5.13 per year. To put this in context, recall that the French state spent some €7 billion on its pointless colonial mission in Africa, Operation Barkhane, which ended in ignominy last year [in 2022]; roughly €100,000 euros per year for every solider dispatched to the Sahel.[91]

The ideology that blames poor and racialized peoples for climate chaos justifies the ravaging of the Global South, but that ideology is slowly coming to the North. For decades, austerity programs have been leading to chronic unemployment while enriching the financial class; poverty is increasing in Europe, affecting more women and members of ethnic minorities.[92] Governments in Italy, Denmark, Holland, and France have adopted laws restricting access to social allowances, targeting Muslims, migrants, and refugees, reducing the amount of social aid, and helping corporations to avoid limits on their use of toxic products. If Europe, thanks to centuries of colonial extraction and dumping, is still protected from the worst of capitalism's excess and imperialism's "shocks in return" (more on this later), the latter are starting to be felt. Given this broader context, why use this data? Because they nonetheless provide, if we resist doom and gloom, a measure of the devastation brought about by centuries of extraction and exploitation by capitalism. Rather than producing pity, they should generate rage, a rage that fuels the desire to organize and fight back and to get inspired by the people who struggle and never gave up.

The website of the World Counts, a Copenhagen-based project that collates live statistics on the state of the planet, contains the following headline: "Every year *we* dump a massive 2.12 billion tons of waste. If all this waste was put on trucks they would go around the world 24 times. This stunning amount of waste is partly because 99 percent of the stuff *we* buy is trashed within 6 months."[93] This must be immediately questioned: there is no universal "we"; it hides the identification of precise actors in the production of waste and erases those who clean, whether garbage collectors (mostly men) or garbage pickers (women, children, men), either those in the streets or those going through dumping sites to collect what they can sell or repair. There is no "we" in an economy that produces waste, there is no togetherness but a repartition of waste along class and race lines. When we read that in 2015 toxic air contamination was the single largest source of premature death in the world today with nine million people dying every year,[94] the reaction should not be lamentation but rather an urgent examination of the causes and the structures that give rise to these premature deaths and understanding where, how, and with whom to fight.

The Elemental of Cleaning

"Who is doing the cleaning?" is a question that should constantly be on our minds when we enter a museum, office, or university; when we take a train or bus; when we walk through an airport, a market, or a store. Being conscious that social, economic, political, and cultural activities are possible because women of color are cleaning the spaces where they occur, that their work holds the world, enlarges environmental studies. Cleanliness accomplished by non-white women must become a fundamental analytical element in the perception and organization of cleanliness in a world that has been shaped by colonialism, racism, and imperialism. By hindering access to water and sewage facilities, racial capitalism has enforced the division between clean and dirty and slowly naturalized it. If women of color constitute the majority of cleaners worldwide, we should not forget the role of men of color in the making of a clean world for the bourgeois class. Dalits in India, Black and Brown men in Europe, Black, Latinx, and Indigenous men and male children in North America, men from South Asia and Africa in the Gulf States are garbage collectors, cleaners in factories, slaughterhouses, mega-farms. They also occupy that space between mega-projects that requires high technicity, incredible engineering and computation, and mundane needs. The United Arab Emirates, which presents itself as a leader of green energy[95] and which hosed the 2024 COP28, illustrates very well that double need. Take a very green source of energy, the solar panel. It needs to be regularly cleaned. On the one hand, a company like Abu Hail Technical Services provides "solar panel cleaning services for a range of systems. We can create a package to match your needs, whether you need roof cleaning, ground-mounted cleaning, or a service that covers both your roof and panels. We recognize the necessity of keeping your solar panels clean, and we recognize that each system is unique and necessitates a customized cleaning schedule." And on the other hand, the company must hire men from South Asia who are prevented from organizing, are underpaid, and are separated from their families.[96] The need for a massive exploited and dispossessed workforce (only 10 percent of the population are Emirati citizens) goes alongside high technology that seeks to cut costs. Thus, the cleaning of solar panels could be accomplished by a "durable, waterless cleaning robot that 'crawls' from one solar panel to another, saving thousands of man hours and countless more litres of water." This has in fact already been invented.[97]

Liboiron and Lepawsky understand the role of waste and wasting to be "a technique of power," power referring here "not to overt domination and coercion (the ability to force people to do things) but to the way that some things seem true, natural, and good and how those meanings are reproduced in particular ways that align with particular interests."[98] Denaturalizing cleaning means narrating when and how that work was racialized and gendered to align with particular interests. Worldwide, women account for 72.2 percent of the 100 million domestic workers. In Latin America and the Caribbean, this share is 92 percent, while in Asia it is 82 percent, in Africa 73 percent, and the Middle East 64 percent. In 2011, the International Labor Organization (ILO) estimated that "women accounted for five in six (83%) domestic workers, with female domestic workers making up 3.5% of all female employment and of all female wage workers in the world—reflecting the importance of domestic work as a source of employment for women."[99] Seventy-one percent of cleaning employees are exposed to repetitive work, 61 percent to chemical risks and 52 percent to painful postures. Ninety percent are exposed to at least one physical risk, to bad smells, and risks of infection.[100] The ILO describes domestic workers as providing

direct and indirect care services, and as such are key members of the care economy. Their work may include tasks such as cleaning the house, cooking, washing and ironing clothes, taking care of children, or elderly or sick members of a family, gardening, guarding the house, driving for the family, and even taking care of household pets. A domestic worker may work on full-time or part-time basis; may be employed by a single household or through or by a service provider; may be residing in the household of the employer (live-in worker) or may be living in his or her own residence (live-out). A domestic worker may be working in a country of which she/he is not a national, thus referred to as a migrant domestic worker.[101]

Women cleaners are often long-distance migrants in Europe, North America, or the Gulf States, members of a discriminated and insulted community, targeted as racialized subjects. They are, however, not passive victims. They organize: from the enslaved women who fled the plantation and their exploitation as domestics, nannies, or field workers and went marooning to the first unions in the 19th century, women of color who clean, wash, iron, cook, and take care of children and the elderly have never stopped fighting. As labor columnist, author, and organizer Kim Kelly writes:

On June 16, 1866, laundry workers in Jackson, Miss., called for a citywide meeting. The women—for they were all women, and all were Black—were tired of being paid next to nothing to spend their days hunched over steaming tubs of other (White) people's laundry, scrubbing out stains, smoothing the wrinkles with red-hot irons, and hauling the baskets of heavy cloth through the streets. At the time, nearly all Black female workers were employed as domestics by White families, to handle the cooking, cleaning and child care, hauling water, emptying chamber pots, and performing various and sundry other tasks that the lady of the house preferred to avoid.[102]

Today, there are women cleaners' unions in Angola, Brazil, the United States, Mozambique, Malawi, India, Canada, and South Africa. It is racism that invisibilizes the work of women cleaners and their presence (they are there but not there) and justifies them being hired, fired, underpaid, called by their first name. They have to deal with a boss or with intermediaries whether it is for housework or for industrial cleaning. If everything is done to erase their presence as human beings, their work must be very visible. It is their visibility as workers that is refused by the dominant classes; the latter do not want to see that their lives need cleaning, they want their cleaning to be hidden.

Organizing means overcoming isolation, the fear of reprisal, the fear of losing an income, and the fear of being expelled, since many women are undocumented. Narratives that focus on the exploitation and the lack of visible protest mask other forms of refusal. Isolation can be broken in other ways. In the United Arab Emirates, where passports are confiscated and women are systematically mistreated and overworked, some nonetheless find ways to meet, escape the suffocating atmosphere of their workplace, and even organize the escape of those who are violated and beaten. When I was working in Sharjah in 2021, I saw in the evening or on weekends groups of Filipina women—who form the brunt of domestic workers, nannies, and beauty salon employees—along a lake in Sharjah or in parks in Dubai and Abu Dhabi sharing food and drinks, listening to music, laughing. I learned that, away from the gaze of their bosses, they organized birthdays, gatherings to do their hair and apply makeup, and karaoke sessions. I am not underestimating the organized isolation, but I want to signal different practices of refusal and of joy.

The Distribution of Time according to Class and Race

Cleaning by women of color preserves what philosopher Jacques Rancière has called the "distribution of time," a distribution between two forms of life: the form of life of those who have time and the form of life of those who do not.[103] Time is not strictly the hours that one disposes of; time—as it has been divided along class, race, and gender—is the time that one *naturally* takes as one's own, a time historically produced by social relations. The time extracted from the lives of women of color for looking for work and going to work concretely limits their own time. They have been assigned that amount of time by a racial system. The extraction of their time allows for the lifestyle of bourgeois women, those who then have time. A bourgeois woman may clean her home or do her own washing and ironing, but the fact remains that women of color are expected to clean the world, take care of children, allocate time to white bourgeois women. The racial-class division of time allows them to go to the movies, visit museums, go to work, and read women of color authors.

Women of color bear the greatest burden of social reproduction, more than white women, because they not only do that reproduction for the home but also for society, outside the home. There is nobody to take on this role for them. If it is the case that "Now there was a time / When they used to say / That behind every great man / There had to be a great woman,"[104] we could say that "behind every bourgeois white woman, there has to be a great cleaning woman of color."

In 2019, I wrote that "every day, in every urban center of the world, thousands of black and brown women, invisible, are 'opening' the city. They clean the spaces necessary for neo-patriarchy, and neoliberal and finance capitalism to function. They are doing dangerous work: they inhale toxic chemical products and push or carry heavy loads. They have usually travelled long hours in the early morning or late at night, and their work is underpaid and considered to be unskilled."[105] I added that they

are usually in their forties or fifties. A second group, which shares with the first an intersection of class, race, and gender, go to middle class homes to cook, clean, and take care of children and the elderly, so that those who employ them can go to work in the places that the former group of women have cleaned. Meanwhile, in the same early hours of the morning, in the same big metropoles of the world, we can see women and men running through the streets, rushing to the nearest gym or yoga center. They pursue the mandate of late capitalism to maintain healthy and clean bodies; they usually follow their run or workout with a shower, an avocado toast, and a detox drink before heading to their clean offices. Meanwhile, women of color try to find a seat for their exhausted bodies as they return on public transit from cleaning those gyms, banks, insurance offices, newspaper offices, investment companies, or restaurants and preparing meeting rooms for business breakfasts. They doze off as soon as they sit, their fatigue visible to those who care to see it. The working body that is made visible is the concern of an ever-growing industry dedicated to the cleanliness and healthiness of body and mind, the better to serve racial capitalism. The other working body is made invisible even though performs a necessary function for the first: to clean spaces in which the "clean" ones circulate, work, eat, sleep, have sex, and perform parenting. But the cleaners' invisibility is required and naturalized.[106]

I argued that in the age of racial Capitalocene (I explain this below), the nexus of capitalism's waste with race and gender "uncovers new borders that have been drawn between cleanliness and dirtiness in an age in which concerns are growing for clean air, clean water, clean houses, clean bodies, clean minds, and green spaces," and that it is necessary to explore the ways in which the industry of cleanliness in late racial capitalism superimposes new tropes derived from colonial and racist stereotypes.[107]

In *A Decolonial Feminism*, when I asked "Who cleans the world?," I was not looking at domestic cleaning, but at the organized industry of cleaning where a majority of women of color work, every day, in airports, schools, offices, banks, restaurants, railway stations, malls, shops, universities, museums, hospitals, factories, and so on.[108] "The maid's job is back-breaking: pushing the cleaning cart is hard on the shoulders and lumbar vertebrae; making the bed by pulling the sheets and lifting the mattresses causes numerous hand tendonitises and sore shoulders; washing mirrors and the bathroom by stretching the arms generates neck pain. Handling toxic detergents encourages the development of chronic and potentially fatal illnesses," explained the Black women cleaners who went on strike at the Ibis Batignolles hotel in Paris, on July 7, 2019.[109] I wanted to prompt a questioning of why, when we enter any public space in our everyday life, we do not wonder by whom it has been cleaned and when (usually early in the morning or late in the evening). By "we" I mean the antiracist activists, the feminists, the radical leftists. How much is she paid? Is she allowed to unionize? Is she a victim of sexual violence? Acknowledging that work that makes public events, political meetings, conferences, shopping, meeting, eating, and so on possible should become a given, not an empty gesture but an attention to the life and working conditions of millions of women of color and an active support to their struggles. Just as it is becoming common practice in settler-colonial states to acknowledge that we stand on stolen land, we should learn to acknowledge the underpaid, exploited, racialized work upon which our lives, as consumers, academics, patients, students, and so on, depend. Few conversations on decoloniality, antiracist environmental politics, or anti-capitalism start with the acknowledgment that it was not just ideas, energy, and funding that make our discussions possible, but the work of Black, Brown, and Indigenous women. We always expect the place we enter to be clean and are shocked when it is not. Cleaning work must be invisible, but not its result. Waste must be dumped out of sight by people out of sight. "We" here does not refer only to the bourgeoisie—though the latter always feels much more entitled to being served by people who must make themselves invisible—but to the whole of society.

The bourgeoisie wants to make dirt and waste invisible, so that their world, which rests on rot and decay, appears pristine and immaculate. They want it to disappear, to be put "away." But as Julia Butterfly, who spent two years in a sequoia to prevent it from being cut down, has noticed, "away" is a word that does not mean much for many peoples.[110] Indigenous communities told her that they had no words in their languages for "recycling," "reusable," or "waste disposal."[111] The borders between clean and unclean neighborhoods or those between wealthy consumer societies and countries that serve as dumping zones are strictly enforced. Growth, in capitalism and in any regime that rests on overproduction, involves the use of tons of water by its industries, which then discharge toxic wastewater in rivers, lakes, and oceans.

Why Must Cleaners Be Invisible?

White bourgeois environmentalism's notion of cleaning invisibilizes women of color's work and exploitation and favors a visual culture of the spectacular aimed at triggering outrage and action. Major environmental organizations routinely use images of ocean oil spills, pipeline disasters, beaches covered with the bodies of dead birds and fish, rivers thick with plastic, plastic in the bodies of birds and fish, open-cast mines, and vast landfill sites. It is not that these acts are blameless or that it is not important to trace responsibility and imagine action, but that the iconography of the spectacular marginalizes forms of pollution that are less visible or less potent in terms of leading to outrage. It points us to the spectacular end result, but not to the causes of the pollution, excavation, extraction, nor to the bodies that bear the greatest burden of toxicity. Thus analyzing "artist Chris Jordan's iconic photographs of albatross carcasses on Midway Atoll with plastic in their rotting guts," Liboiron warns us that such images make us miss the "wider relations, the Land relations, of albatross and plastic, and [turn] them into a resource for shock, awe, and charismatic academic *presentations*."[112] Illustrations of cleaning women of color cannot fit into the aesthetic codes of shock and awe. Their uniform has been sexualized and racialized; the white apron, the broom, or the rag are not made for producing horror but rather sexual fascination, consternation, disgust, or pity. Further, as Discard Studies scholar Grace Akese has shown, those who clean refuse to become the illustration of filth, repulsion, and disgust, and they contest degrading images of their work. Drawing on her own experience of doing fieldwork on electronic waste in Agbogbloshie in Ghana, Akese reports that refuse workers denounce the harm done "by attempting to do good research." Even though she is from Ghana, when she approached people working with scraps, they told her: "This is a place of business. You people think we are here for you, eh? You come here all the time taking pictures. Every single day, someone wants to know something. Let me tell you; we are tired." "We see you people [researchers] all the time. You come here and then write bad things about us. You bring your white people to come and see us. You take pictures of the boys there. Who permitted you to come here?"[113]

Indeed, who grants permission for images to be taken that represent degradation in the eyes of the Western viewer, the academic, the artist? Too often, these images have the effect of hiding the social relations that fabricate toxic waste dumps in the Global South and assign sorting to racialized people. They maintain in the bourgeois consciousness the racial-colonial relation between dirty and non-white people rather than showing that the racial-colonial structure is responsible for dumping and a racial division of work.

Before further examining invisibility/visibility, I want to suggest that invisibility must be amended to remark that cleaners are not "invisible" to those who hire and fire them, call them by their first name, sexually harass them, give them orders. What must be made invisible, i.e., seen with indifference and denial and hence not paid suitably, is the work they do, the amount of it, the time and effort it takes, the fatigue it causes. The construction of the invisibility of cleaners' labor and the visibility of their work's results builds a white vision of cleanliness that is regularly disturbed by cleaners or garbage collectors' strikes. The white world lives with the illusion that it does not produce waste and that the piles of filth and garbage in the Global South or poor neighborhoods are the result of inherent neglect, of a natural indifference of people of color to cleanliness. Images of dumping sites fill the Western public with horror. Warnings about hygiene and health when traveling to "these" countries add to the construction of a clean world vs. an unclean world populated by unclean peoples.[114] In "Capitalocene," I wrote that images of "mountains of garbage, of *dirty* streets, *dirty* rivers, *dirty* beaches, *dirty* neighborhoods, of plastic covering fields, of people—women, children, men—searching through garbage or pushing carts filled with refuse, of children swimming in polluted water, all this in the Global South—contribute to the creation of a naturalized division between dirty and clean."[115] The root causes remain hidden: the legacies of colonialism, of colonial urbanization and the racial restructuring of the landscape; structural adjustment programs that require governments to reduce public expenses; the externalization of polluting industries.

The feeling that cleaning "that" world is an impossible task is slowly ingrained. What becomes a pressing issue is how to keep externalized pollution from reaching "clean" areas."[116] The mystery of cleaning (of course it is clean, it is only when it is not clean that there is alarm) naturalizes the production of waste. At many conferences, we drink water from plastic bottles without thinking twice. The question of where those bottles will go afterwards does not come into consciousness. We are thankful that people care about our health and warn us about water pollution, but we also know that water is not clean because of the privatization of water and the power of corporations.

During debates around the publication of *A Decolonial Feminism*, my opening question, "Who has cleaned the place we are in?" caused some surprise, yet everyone knew the answer. It brought to light the naturalized erasure of women of color's work. Decolonizing a site that occupies an important place in the reproduction of ideology and the ways in which representation is being conceived (a museum, a university, an art school, an art center) has meant, more often than not, including a better representation of non-white authors, artists, and scholars, bringing more diversity to the books that were discussed, or changing what is hung on the walls, and has been less about examining who cleans, who guards, who serves—all of those who make the place work but who are not included in the conversation.

The Denial of Vital Needs

I want to look critically at programs of *cleaning up the planet* and examine why the access of women of color to their own cleaning needs has been impeded. In other words, I want to take waste seriously but by looking not only at how cleaning and waste have been racialized, how the "ethics of cleanup" are "based on separation" while "those of purity" are "based on annihilation,"[117] how waste and cleaning are regimes of power, but also the gendered and racialized work of cleaning waste. I am asking: What will we do with the tons of waste being dumped in the Global South and near the poor and racialized neighborhoods in the North? How can we clean the contaminated land, rivers, and forests left behind by the mining and chemical industry, the polluted land left behind by imperialist armies, the huge dumping sites where the fashion industry sends its overproduction, the cesspools yielded by the car, maritime, and oil industries, the toxic waste generated by agribusiness and the weapons industry? Rather than restore what existed previously, what can we learn from Indigenous philosophies, antiracist scientists, Black, Brown, and Indigenous feminists, and decolonial activists and thinkers to rethink the notions of dirtiness and cleanliness necessary for a society to function? What would make the world clean while rejecting the white patriarchal bourgeois norms of cleanliness, with its colonial, gendered, and racial genealogy? If cleaning is also a practice of care that makes social relationships livable, then what kind of cleanliness we are talking about? If it is not the whitening of space, its organization into clean vs. dirty places, then what is it?

If today in Western Europe women from the peripheral countries of the EU who are hired in the service and care industry are exploited, underpaid, and considered expendable, they are hierarchically above women of color. What militant Marxist and Black feminist political activist Angela Davis wrote in 1981—"more Black women have always worked outside their homes than have their white sisters"[118]—is still in place. Alongside many feminists, she noted that "housework, after all, is virtually invisible: 'No one notices it until it isn't done—we notice the unmade bed, not the scrubbed and polished floor.' Invisible, repetitive, exhausting, unproductive, uncreative—these are the adjectives which most perfectly capture the nature of housework."[119] Davis concluded that "neither women nor men should waste precious hours of their lives on work that is neither stimulating nor productive."[120] Should we then put our efforts into inventing robots to abolish all drudgery? Davis is convinced that nothing good can be found in cleaning and encouraging women to get out of their home can only do them good—they will be free of isolation, find comrades, understand exploitation, learn to organize. She is right. By listening to women who do tedious, tiresome work, we learn that they do not want to be deprived of the camaraderie they have found, of their sisters, as they often describe those who share their situation and with whom they also organize. Women cleaners do not like when their work is criticized or mocked by supervisors or bosses, whom they see as lazy, unable to do what they do and to see that they do it well. And they can also say how much they want to escape that work. Taking pride in one's work does not mean that one is not aware of exploitation and racism; it is a reaction against the contempt with which of one's work is considered.

Strikes by cleaners are always remarkable and powerful because they bring into the field of the visual the amount of rubbish societies living under colonialism and capitalism throw away every day, as well as how much waste people living in rich countries produce (a quick reminder: a white American in the USA produces 1,361 pounds of rubbish per year, 4.9 pounds per day).[121] Rubbish collectors' strikes and strikes in hotels, hospitals, or universities bring to light what must remain behind the scenes, the piles of trash in the streets produced by what is thrown away in the spaces of domestic intimacy every day. The media, however, tends to reproduce images of cleaners strikes in ways that induce hostile reactions; seeing the waste piling up in the streets is an irritating reminder of what the city's inhabitants discard. Opinions about threats to public health, about rats invading the streets, and the rotten smell that drives away tourists reinforce not only the idea that trash must not be seen but that it is the strikers who are responsible for the threat to public health rather than capitalism.

Studying the role of images of a 2021 cleaners' strike in Lyon, France, director and researcher Jordane Burnot and Lina Cardenas remark that "far from being neutral, the photos accompanying the articles highlight the negative consequences of the strike for local residents. These representations shift the focus from the strike to its consequences, whatever the content of the article. Journalists use images to displace the problem, making overflowing garbage cans the main subject. The work of the garbage collectors, the consequences of the job on their bodies, the reasons for the mobilization, the demands or the picket lines are practically absent from the illustrations."[122] They then analyze how the production of images by a friendly filmmaker and by the strikers themselves offered a counternarrative that builds a "controlled representation of the struggle that challenges the hegemonic image of the mainstream media . . . . Beyond this symbolic use of conflict, these supports also played an important role in the legalization of the struggle."[123] The cleaners' strikes highlight the ways in which their work is perceived, insisting on the fact that when they work, they are "confronted with the invisibility and structural indifference that assigns them the status of non-person in the public space ('You don't exist for people,' 'You're part of the scenery')."[124] These daily situations maintain and reinforce an already existing feeling of devaluation linked to the performance of a "dirty job" ("We pick up other people's shit," "We're shit to people").[125] Cleaners say that people voluntarily throw their waste in front of them, that racist and sexist remarks are constant, that adults loudly warn their children that if they do not work at school, they will end up as a cleaner.[126]

During the 22 months the Ibis Batignolles strikers picketed in front of the hotel, banging pots and pans, dancing and singing to keep their spirits up, in the summer heat and winter snow, hotel guests showed their displeasure by pelting the strikers with garbage from their rooms. "Guests were throwing cans, apples, coffees, newspapers at us because we were making too much noise," striker Rachel Keke recounted.[127] Guests who expected to find a clean room did not want to see and hear the Black women who did the work. They did not want to be reminded that Black women saw their waste, saw the disgusting state in which some of them left their rooms, broke the quietude the guests expected when checking into a hotel. "Their" space was disturbed as they had to go through the picket line of Black middle-aged women dressed in vibrant African fabrics chanting and dancing. This was not the Paris they had paid for. They made their displeasure known to the hotel management who took recourse in an injunction from the administrative court requiring the picket line to be relocated to a certain distance from the entrance and chants not to exceed a certain noise threshold. A bailiff was sent every day to measure the distance and sound level, and if the women did not respect these thresholds, they were fined. The customers' discontent was symptomatic: it reflected the ideology of consumers' rights according to the market, for whom the conditions of production must be masked in order not to disturb the consumers' pleasure. This is how the racial-colonial mode of life has been constructed historically—enjoy what the market sells you and don't ask how it was produced and brought to you.

In Paris, during the 2023 strikes against the governmental pension reform, the uncollected waste—10,000 tons on the twelfth day of the strike, March 17, 2023[128]—brought into the field of the visual the work garbage collectors accomplish and the waste we produce. When such strikes make the daily production of waste visible in the cities of rich countries, the bourgeoisie, suddenly realizing that daily cleaning is indispensable for its comfort, demands not only that the state intervene to end the strike but also army and police involvement, greater privatization of cleaning to prevent future strikes, and even making striking illegal. Cleaners' struggles challenge the fabricated invisibility (of work) versus the visibility of results. The decay of social life under racial capitalism, usually masked behind the beauty of Western cities, is rendered visible. An antiracist decolonial feminism insists on the fact that "without them [cleaners], we'd be living in filth. They're exhausted, really tired, scrubbing, scrubbing, hurts your back, hurts your feet, hurts your kidneys. Scrubbing, scrubbing, you've got to pay for it."[129] By occupying the space outside the work space—the streets in front of the hotel, a space where people who are not workers must go through, as in a railway station—they challenge the racial division between clean and dirty: they show that things do not get clean by miracle but by people who have voices and bodies.

Cleaners fighting for their rights turn to storytelling and refusal, making the broom and the mop into symbols of intersected oppressions.[130] They restore dignity to the job of cleaning, asking for safer working conditions, better pay, and respect. They reject the shame associated with cleaning and fight to make cleaning recognized as being based on forms of exploitation that are gendered and racialized, but also as *elemental* to social and planetary functioning and wellbeing. Against the politics that require a victimized body whose conditions of victimization must remain hidden and an accumulation of images of "wasted bodies and lands" that provoke horror and pity, what is needed is a visual activism that contributes to decolonial politics. Fully conscious of this, cleaners but also artists and writers have turned to narratives to bring to light not only the full content of the exploitation and the value of the work, but also why it cannot be considered trivial.[131]

How to Name the Age of Waste and Wasting

To discuss waste is to discuss the naming of our current predicament. Anthropocene? Wasteocene? Plantationcene? Racial Capitalocene? Chthulucene? Anthropo-obscene?[132] "Anthropocene," which describes the "human dominance of biological, chemical and geological processes on Earth," was first introduced in 2000 in an article jointly written by Paul Crutzen and Eugene Stoermer. They dated its emergence to the latter part of the 18th century, admitting that "alternative proposals can be made (some may even want to include the entire Holocene). However, we choose this date because, during the past two centuries, the global effects of human activities have become clearly noticeable. This is the period when data retrieved from glacial ice cores show the beginning of a growth in the atmospheric concentrations of several 'greenhouse gases,' in particular CO_2 and CH_4. Such a starting date also coincides with James Watt's invention of the steam engine in 1784."[133] Geologists, paleontologist, geographers, historians, and stratigraphers started to work on "climate change," and in 2016, the Anthropocene Working group (AWG), created by paleontologists and stratigraphers of the University of Leicester, declared the "Anthropocene" to be stratigraphically real and recommended formalization at epoch/series rank based on a mid-20th-century boundary.[134] Criticism of a term that encompassed all humans emerged quickly. "This 'anthropo-' blocks attention to patchy landscapes, multiple temporalities, and shifting assemblages of human and nonhumans: the very stuff of collaborative survival," anthropologist Anna Lowenhaupt Tsing remarked.[135] In 2017, environmental historian and historical geographer Jason Moore argued that the term "Capitalocene" was better suited to describe the epoch, writing that "the Anthropocene is a comforting story with uncomfortable facts. It fits easily within a conventional description—and analytical logic—that separates humanity from the web of life. This makes for a familiar story, one of Humanity doing many terrible things to Nature."[136] Making the Industrial Revolution the birthdate of a geological turning point erased capitalism's early origins and "its extraordinary reshaping of global natures long before the steam engine, is therefore significant in our work to develop an effective radical politics around global warming . . . and far more than global warming alone!"[137]

Choosing the Industrial Revolution was far from neutral. It erased the colonization of the Americas and the Caribbean, which "marked a turning point in the history of humanity's relation with the rest of nature. It was greater than any watershed since the rise of agriculture and the first cities."[138] To Moore, the era of primitive accumulation gave rise to a "new world-praxis: Cheap

Nature."[139] Moore dated the beginning of the Capitalocene to the 16th century, which also witnessed the "discovery of the New World, people brought through the force of 'blood and fire,' the slave trade, the division of colonies among European powers, as well as the organization on a global scale of a mobile, racialized, gendered, and bonded workforce. Hence the term Capitalocene, a "world-ecology of power, capital, and nature" that situates the "rise of capitalism, historically accumulation of capital, and geographically, within the web of life. This is capitalism not as economic system but as a situated and multispecies world-ecology of capital, power and re/production."[140] Even if he wrote that "nature, women and colonies, in this perspective, are not only plundered but actively created through symbolic praxis, political power, and capital accumulation,"[141] Moore did not assign a central role to social reproduction or to race.

Scholar of inhuman geography Kathryn Yusoff situated her critique of the Anthropocene firmly in the struggle against anti-Blackness: "As the Anthropocene proclaims the language of species life—anthropos—through a universalist geologic commons, it neatly erases histories of racism that were incubated through the regulatory structure of geologic relations."[142] Yusoff sees a continuum between "indigenous dispossession of land and sovereignty in the invasion of the Americas through to the ongoing petropolitics of settler colonialism; of slavery, 'breaking rocks on the chain gang' (as Nina Simone sings it), to the current incarnations of antiblackness in mining black gold; and of the racialized impacts of climate change. To redress how geology makes property relations and properties a relation of subjugation is to challenge the incompleteness of address in the Anthropocene."[143] "The mine and the afterlives of its geomorphic acts constitute the materiality of the Anthropocene and its natal moment, from the transformation of mineralogy of the earth in the extraction of gold, silver, salt, and copper to the massive transformation of ecologies in the movement of people, plants, and animals across territories, coupled with the intensive implantation of monocultures of indigo, sugar, tobacco, cotton, and other 'alien' ecologies in the New World."[144] Yusoff insisted: "The histories of the Anthropocene unfold a brutal experience for much of the world's racialized poor and without due attention to the historicity of those events (and their eventfulness); the Anthropocene simply consolidates power via this innocence in the present to effect decisions that are made about the future and its modes of survival."[145] To human geographer Andreas Malm, Moore was abolishing "even the opposition between the classes—in language."[146] "Capitalism makes nature. Nature makes capitalism"—none of these propositions is true, Malm wrote. Malm saw Moore as being closer to French philosopher and anthropologist Bruno

Latour and his hybridity theory than Moore thought: "Capitalism emphatically does not make nature; nature most definitely does not make capitalism."[147] Malm rejected constructionism, which was transforming global warming into a discourse: "a storm is not a speech act"[148] and "oceans are not polluting themselves; humans are doing it" (or rather colonialism-capitalism).[149] Latour, who had declared that his aim was to blur "the distinction between nature and society durably, so that we shall never have to go back to distinct sets,"[150] depoliticized climate disaster. As scientists protesting political inaction claimed in 2016: "Ice does not have a program. It simply melts."[151]

In 2015, feminist scholar Donna Haraway, thinking that "a big new name, actually more than one name" was warranted, named the moment "Chthulucene—past, present, and to come,"[152] "after the diverse earth-wide tentacular powers and forces and collected things with names like Naga, Gaia, Tangaroa (burst from water-full Papa), Terra, Haniyasu-hime, Spider Woman, Pachamama, Oya, Gorgo, Raven, A'akuluujjusi, and many many more."[153] "'My' Chthulucene, even burdened with its problematic Greek-ish tendrils, entangles myriad temporalities and spatialities and myriad intra-active entities-in-assemblages—including the more-than-human, other-than-human, inhuman, and human-as-humus," she wrote.[154] All distinctions were blurred. Hence her call for "'Make Kin Not Babies!'" Making kin is perhaps the hardest and most urgent part. Feminists of our time have been leaders in unraveling the supposed natural necessity of ties between sex and gender, race and sex, race and nation, class and race, gender and morphology, sex and reproduction, and reproduction and composing persons."[155] This is "dissolutionism," Malm argues,[156] and the "hybridist dissolutionism" that Haraway and Latour defend leads to a lack of rigorous analysis. As they "wage war on distinctions," they "not infrequently end up with a prose evacuated of meaning."[157]

This is what I want to avoid: transforming exhaustion, premature death, suffocation, and lack of water into narratives or discourse. Hence the notion of "racial Capitalocene" that I proposed in 2017 in a text that took leave from the work of Cedric J. Robinson, of the Black radical tradition, on racial capitalism.[158] The term took into account slavery and colonialism, bringing to light the fact that the full ecological consequences of slavery and colonialism can appear centuries after colonies became independent, as historian Joachim Randkau has shown.[159] "There is also a different kind of violence, not rapid but slow motion, not instantaneous but incremental, not body-to-body but playing out over vast stretches of times through the medium of ecosystems,"[160] as Malm has argued, after Nixon. "Blindness to our ancestors' crimes, and to the ways we 'whites' continue to live from these crimes, keeps the suffering of those already exposed to the devastation of climate crisis impossible for us to see or feel," philosopher Donna M. Orange has written.[161] But as we saw with the Wretched of the Earth collective, it cannot be a question only of seeing and feeling—it has to be a question of doing. What transforms seeing into action? And "feeling," as I sought to show in an earlier analysis of 19th-century French abolitionism, can stop at paternalistic abolitionism.[162] I spoke of a politics of feelings, of a dangerous pity (*une pitié dangereuse*), and looked at all the declarations of love toward the freed enslaved and toward the colonized as the exact counterpoint of the cruelty and brutality that was actually occurring in the age of post-slavery colonization and imperialism.[163] Remaining within the frame of seeing and feeling often leads to sentimental politics that feed the savior syndrome. This is not what Orange is arguing, but we must attend to the long history of the fields of visibility and feeling in a Western humanitarianism that does not confront power.

Robinson's theory of racial capitalism offered a corrective to Moore's and Malm's notion of Capitalocene (even though they differ). The colonial continuum that Robinson theorized added to the debate. Robin D. G. Kelley explains racial capitalism thus:

Capitalism and racism did not break from the old order but rather evolved from it to produce a modern world system of "racial capitalism" dependent on slavery, violence, imperialism, and genocide. Capitalism was "racial" not because of some conspiracy to divide workers or justify slavery and dispossession, but because racialism had already permeated Western feudal society. The first European proletarians were racial subjects (Irish, Jews, Roma or Gypsies, Slavs, etc.) and they were victims of dispossession (enclosure), colonialism, and slavery within Europe. Indeed, Robinson suggested that racialization within Europe was very much a colonial process involving invasion, settlement, expropriation, and racial hierarchy.[164]

In other words, racialism "permeates the social structures emergent from capitalism."[165] In her *Rethinking Racial Capitalism: Questions of Reproduction and Survival*, sociologist Gargi Bhattacharyya clearly summarizes the different elements of racial capitalism. Her ten theses are useful: racial capitalism, she says, is 1) "not a way of understanding capitalism as a racist conspiracy or racism as a capitalist conspiracy"; 2) "feminist debates can help us understand the role played by 'non work' as part of an expanded conceptualization of social reproduction"; 3) "racism had a history that precedes capitalism"; 4) racial capitalism combines the "exercise of coercive power and the mobilization of desire"; 5) "new and unpredictable modes of oppression must be understood"; 6) "we must grasp how people are divided from each other in the name of economic survival or in the name of economic well-being"; 7) racial capitalism "describes a set of techniques and a formation, and in both registers the disciplining and ordering of bodies through gender and sexuality and dis/ability and age flow"; 8) racial capitalism is "intimately intertwined with the processes precipitating ecological crisis"; 9) "dehumanization seems to be an unavoidable outcome of the processes of capitalist development"; and 10) racial capitalism is a "way of understanding why we seem so divided and yet so intimately intertwined with each other."[166]

But sociologist and cultural studies scholar Paul Gilroy has also urged us to be "paying careful attention to the specific dynamics both of race as a matter of political ontology, and of racism as a variety of political speech. Race and nation are now primary sources of groupness and absolute ethnicity. They are supposedly endowed with a special power to restore certainty and find stability amidst the flux of precarious life in increasingly dangerous conditions."[167] Commenting on the daily drowning of sub-Saharan Africans in the Mediterranean or the English Channel, he says: "Clear, moral and juridical choices are involved in salvaging people from the water, as they are in the tasks of naming the drowned and promoting dignity by burying their bodies. In many circumstances, we are referred to the forms of care and sociality conditioned by disaster and what might be called the banality of good. They operate on smaller scales than the revolutionary opportunities we associate with disaster capitalism. These responses are closer to the ordinary virtue that can be glimpsed in disaster altruism and disaster solidarity."[168]

It was during the conference "Confronting Racial Capitalism: The Black Radical Tradition and Cultures of Liberation" in 2014 at the Center for Place, Culture and Politics at City University of New York that I first talked of "racial Capitalocene." In the 2019 written piece, I insisted on earlier struggles and cited the organization of farmworkers led by Cesar Chavez and Dolores Huerta in California in the early 1960s for workplace rights, including protection from toxic pesticides, and the African American students in 1967 who opposed a city dump and in 1979 a landfill in Houston. Work on environmental racism had come from grassroots movements. The publication in 1987 of *Toxic Waste and Race in the United States*, a report by the Commission for Racial Justice, showed that race was the single most important factor in determining where toxic waste facilities were in the United States and that the siting of these facilities in communities of color was the intentional result of local, state, and federal land-use policies.[169] In the 1980s, in fact, the Reagan administration's practice of cutting the budgets of federal environmental agencies had aggravated racist decisions. I also pointed to the October 1991 "Principles of Environmental Justice" that the delegates to the First National People of Color

Environmental Leadership Summit drafted, and which became a defining document for the growing grassroots movement for environmental justice. I quoted the preamble:

WE, THE PEOPLE OF COLOR, gathered together at this multinational People of Color Environmental Leadership Summit, to begin to build a national and international movement of all peoples of color to fight the destruction and taking of our lands and communities, do hereby re-establish our spiritual interdependence to the sacredness of our Mother Earth; to respect and celebrate each of our cultures, languages and beliefs about the natural world and our roles in healing ourselves; to ensure environmental justice; to promote economic alternatives which would contribute to the development of environmentally safe livelihoods; and, to secure our political, economic and cultural liberation that has been denied for over 500 years of colonization and oppression, resulting in the poisoning of our communities and land and the genocide of our peoples.[170]

The preamble contained everything that would inform future anticolonial, antiracist environmental movements. It was a way of saying that no discussion on global warming could afford to ignore race. "Global warming and its consequences for the peoples of the South is a political question and must be understood outside of the limits of 'climate change' and in the context of the inequalities produced by racial capital,"[171] I wrote. By joining race and capital, I was still siding colonialism, which I am now emphasizing.

To Martinican scholar Malcom Ferdinand, the afterlives of slavery and colonialism cannot be separated from the struggle for environmental justice. "The ecological crisis began before these [before the Industrial Revolution]. It comes from a certain way of inhabiting the earth, from some believing themselves entitled to appropriate the earth for the benefit of a few."[172] The model of that organization is the "colonial habitation," which was "a violent way of inhabiting the earth, subjugating lands, humans, and non-humans to the desires of the colonizer."[173] The colonial habitation is a "violent and misogynistic process, an awful way to inhabit the earth promoted by a colonizer for whom other human beings were dehumanized and for whom colonized lands and the non-humans that inhabited them mattered less than his desires."[174] To Ferdinand, if we exclude racism from political environmentalism, we will continue "to see slogans devoid of social thought. This allows others to co-opt the environmental imperative and advocate a technocratic response, such as combatting pollution and resource scarcity through geo-engineering or carbon markets."[175] Ferdinand adopts the term "Plantationocene" generated by the participants of a conversation recorded for Ethnos (Aarhus University, October 2014).[176] Plantationocene is the devastating transformation of human farms, pastures, and forests into extractive and closed plantations, based on slave labor and other forms of exploited, alienated workforce.

Tsing has looked at the "scalability" that colonialism created. Although scalability is "not an ordinary feature of nature," "progress itself has often been defined by its ability to make projects expand without changing assumptions."[177] She argues that "scalability requires that project elements be oblivious to the indeterminacies of encounter," which "banishes meaningful diversity, that is, diversity that might change things."[178] Tsing cites the example of Brazil: "In their sixteenth- and seventeenth-century sugarcane plantations in Brazil, for example, Portuguese planters stumbled on a formula for smooth expansion. They crafted self-contained, interchangeable project elements, as follows: exterminate local people and plants; prepare now-empty, unclaimed land; and bring in exotic and isolated labor and crops for production. This landscape model of scalability became an inspiration for later industrialization and modernization."[179] Historians have shown how sugarcane plantations were the model for factories during industrialization.[180] And I argue that agribusiness is the heir of the plantation system.

"Wasteocene" is what environmental historian Marco Armiero proposes to describe the "planetary mark of our new epoch."[181] He writes that it is "not solely because of its ubiquitous presence—after all, even CO2 emissions are basically atmospheric waste—rather I argue that what makes the Wasteocene are the wasting relationships, those really planetary in their scope, which produce wasted people and places."[182] "Wasteocene" is the narrative linking waste, justice, and the making of our present world," "waste being the planetary mark of our new epoch."[183] To Armiero, "wasting, as socio-ecological relations creating wasted people and wasted places," is "a social process through which class, race, and gender injustices become embedded into the socio-ecological metabolism producing both gardens and dumps, healthy and sick bodies, pure and contaminated places."[184] Armiero describes the historically fabricated frontier between bodies and land that can be wasted versus those that are protected from being wasted. But wasting is also the process of invizibilization that "erases even the traces of what/who has been wasted, the domestication of memory is perhaps a more sophisticated strategy to continue reproducing wasting relationships."[185] Domesticating memories is, Armiero writes, the process that hides the "systemic intersection of racism/colonialism, heteropatriarchy, class inequality and human supremacy."[186] The "Wasteocene logic," he suggests, "unites humans and nonhumans in its production of wasted lives and places. An entire ecosystem was subjugated to the mining industry under the usual extractivist regime which produces the ultimate other, disposable places and people to be exploited up to their exhaustion."[187] The wasteocene is "about cleanliness and aseptic environments as much as it is about griminess and contamination,"[188] a view that Liboiron and Lepawsky share in their book, *Discard Studies: Wasting, Systems, and Power*, in which they remark that the ways in which cleanliness and griminess have been constructed and distributed are two sides of the same coin. "The main theories, concepts, and techniques we know from discard studies are able to describe and help interpret instances of value and devaluation, the wasting of some lives and not others (necropolitics), dominant structures and how they are maintained or threatened, and how hierarchical categories are formed and do their work."[189] Liboiron and Lepawasky examine this by looking at "wider system of waste and wasting" (rather than at "material waste and trash") and why "wasting is a technique of power," referring "to the way that things seem to be true, natural, and good and how these meanings are reproduced in particular ways that align with particular interests."[190] Waste here is thus not about how different cultures consider what is waste and how they organize cleaning, but about the fact that wasting is inseparable from colonial and capitalist regimes, which have given value to objects obtained through wasting (gold, silver, sugar, tobacco, cobalt) upon dispossession and exploitation.[191]

Although it did not seek to impose a name, ecofeminism, which emerged in the 1970s, offered and explanation to the environmental crisis that has since provided important literature in recent years proliferating blogs and social networks, inspiring influencers and movements. The term "ecofeminism" was first introduced by French feminist scholar Françoise d'Eaubonne in her book *Le féminisme* (1972).[192] Ecofeminism appeared in a moment of intense debate in 1970s France around nature, society, and ecology that culminated with the candidacy of the agronomist René Dumont at the 1974 presidential elections. His *L'Utopie ou la mort!* (Utopia or death!) of 1973[193] signaled a tone, either change or death, that was echoed in d'Eaubonne's 1974 *Le féminisme ou la mort* (Feminism or death).[194] In his book, Dumont predicted that "the total and inevitable collapse of human civilization will occur over the next century if population growth and industrial production continue at high levels."[195] His theory echoed 1950 U.S. Malthusianism,[196] although he added a great concern for what was then called the Third World.[197] D'Eaubonne was greatly influenced by social psychologist Serge Moscovici and feminist philosopher Simone de Beauvoir. Moscovici's *La société contre nature* (Society against nature), published in 1972, argued that "society is not outside nature and against nature, it is in and by nature."[198] To him, "society is radically unnatural: the human species is the absolute end of nature and its crowning achievement, the highest form of all present, past and future existence in the universe."[199] His idea was that "nature does not exist in itself, but is a social construction. It exists neither outside society nor beyond the action that human beings have over it."[200] This matched Beauvoir's theory that women's "nature" had been invented to dominate them. She saw an antinomy between society (where women can be free) and nature (which relegates women to assigned roles) and was convinced that only by leaving the home and being financially independent would women acquire freedom.[201] From these arguments, d'Eaubonne concluded that women and nature are both victims of male domination.[202] To Gandon, d'Eaubonne argued that "the relationship between man and nature was more than ever that between man and woman. The destruction of nature was not the fault of mankind as a whole, but of men, who have built a sexist, scientistic civilization and, more broadly, a society of domination."[203] Opposing masculine and feminine values, she warned: "Yes, the bill is going to be heavy, in a sexist world where man has reduced himself and identified with the destructive Masculine, leaving the conservative Feminine to woman. He had thought he was investing his forces of aggression and destruction in the creation of techniques. . . . The values of the feminine, so long scorned because they are attributed to the inferior sex, remain the last chance for survival for man himself. But we need to move fast; even more than revolution, we need mutation."[204] D'Eaubonne was not for revolution; rather, since "the two ecological consequences of the social on women and nature are agricultural overproduction and the over-reproduction of the human species," only feminism "by liberating women liberates humanity as a whole, in other words, wrests the world from today's man today, to pass it on to tomorrow's humanity."[205] Ecofeminism is a humanism, she insisted, and the "sole aim is to destroy the very notion of power: then, and only then, will the proletariat be able to define itself as proletariat, and women be able to assume themselves as proletariat, and women to assume universality: the human race."[206] Ecofeminism will even transform the content of development (which was much discussed then either around the development of the Global South or through the modernization of Europe), because it invents "a mode of development that is other than Western and patriarchal, and a sustainable development that takes into account a differentiated gender analysis in all activities, whatever the field, so that it is not reduced to environmental concerns alone."[207] The term ecofeminism was embraced around the world by feminist writers on the environment such as Carolyn Merchant, Val Plumwood, Vandana Shiva, Maria Mies, Selma James, Ariel Salleh, and Karren Warren, among others.[208]

There is renewed interest in ecofeminism. In 2021, feminist writer and activist Selma James argued that the struggle she has led for decades (Wages for Housework, the history of which I will outline below) needed to be linked to the struggle for the care of the planet. "The kind of caring work that in every area of our lives is done by women who are enabling, who are protecting, who are preventing, who are making it possible for all of us not only to survive but to find some happiness—that work is hidden. It's hidden because we live in a capitalist society where the reproduction of the human race is not the priority."[209] Such work is not unlike the care for the planet. She argued that "skilled work, which requires judgement and, above all, self-discipline and selflessness" needed to be paid because "all the injustices that the women's movement has targeted, which shape our lives and relationships—rape and domestic violence, pay inequality, exclusion from land ownership, sexual repression, lack of power in the family and in society generally—can be traced to women's lack of financial power."[210] A "CARE Income" would bring together wages for housework and care of the planet. It would speak

to the movement to end government subsidized factories in the field, which torture animals, poison the soil, and undermine local food production. It can increase the power of Indigenous communities and small farmers, the carers for the soil, providing land, water, and seeds that ensure food and economic independence, and methods of organic agriculture which can regenerate the health of people, wildlife, and the soil. As women in the Southern Peasant Federation of Thailand who are supporting a Care Income have said: "We care for the land in the same way we care for our families, trying always to do what is best for the life and wellbeing of all."[211]

To Jones, women have always been prominent in "environmental struggles," which "are far from new," by "protecting or reclaiming ancestral land from mining, dams, military bases, pipelines, cash crops, factory farms, and a variety of multinational takeovers that have led to poisoned land and water, disease, disability, death, displacement and destruction of communities, and mass migration to the city or to other countries."[212] Her slogan was "Invest in caring, not killing."[213]

The connection between women's practice and caring for the planet is being reconsidered by a new generation of feminists worldwide, and one must also add to this debate the literature around the intelligence of trees, plants, insects, and birds that challenges anthropocentrism and calls into question the idea that "man" has power over nature.[214] Ecofeminism has its "schools," Marxist[215] or hybridist.[216] The philosopher and yoga teacher Jeanne Burgart Goutal comes back to the remark that "the exploitation of nature and male domination have deep roots in common, and implement similar mechanisms (objectification, devaluation, violence)."[217] Ecofeminism thus "seeks to make visible that which is invisible, yet indispensable to our lives and our economy, such as domestic work (preparing meals, taking care of the house and children . . .), the overexploited work done on the other side of the world to manufacture the objects of our daily lives, or the work of self-regeneration of ecosystems."[218] The task ahead is to "evaluate these vital tasks both morally and financially, and undoubtedly share them more equitably, or even move towards a different division of labor."[219]

These calls to mutation, this trust in the power of visibility, forget that it comes back to power relationships. Patriarchal racial capitalism will never be convinced by moral injunctions. It will never pay cleaners as well as engineers and bankers, and if they are women and men of color, it is even unthinkable. Women cleaners obtain better salaries and working conditions because they fight back, they defy power. The ecofeminists who acknowledge colonialism, racism, and the North/South divide seem nonetheless to trust change as mutation. But again, why would capitalists renounce a power that guarantees increasing profits? Being counted as a social group is not only about making that group visible. Any oppressed group must force the entry, even in a feminist assembly. This is what Argentinian feminist theorist and activist Veronica Gago recounts when she narrates the struggle of domestic workers in the gated communities of the Nordelta district in Argentina. The latter were identified by their bosses through smell and noise: "They were told that they smelled bad, that they talked too much. They were forbidden from traveling with their bosses or property owners, who did not want to share seats with them in the vans to and from gated communities, the only way that these women had to getting to their workplaces. Yet they do want those workers to clean for miserable wages and to silently suffer abuses."[220] In a feminist assembly that was discussing the women's strike of 2020, they insisted that "their situation be taken into account in the strike call and organization."[221] In other words, in their discussion of domestic work and women's strike, feminists must listen to the voices of those engaged in industrial or informal cleaning work. What the words of workers engaged in industrial or informal cleaning show is that the lived experience in its thick materiality (body exhaustion, pride in work, knowledge accumulated with years of work, mixing of collective and individual life) is not just a narrative, a testimony or an illustration, but what determines the way in which any kind of resistance, of struggle (strike, march, occupation, going underground) will be organized, led, and sustained. It is not just about privileging the "first concerned" but about finding how radically different experiences (of the workers, the feminist academic activists, the activists, the women who work at home, the workers, the artists, the intellectuals) build a common platform of struggle. It is about embracing contradictions and differences, living in them.

Racism and Waste

A great majority of peoples live among nonbiodegradable materials: plastic (which takes 100 to 1,000 years to degrade); glass; metals; cardboard; paper; old clothes; thermocol sheets; cans; man-made polymer; biomedical waste; chemical waste; batteries (which take 500 to 1,000 years to degrade); electronic waste such as discarded mobiles, laptops, and batteries; steel waste from steel utensils; glass derived from households; metal waste; mineral waste; syringes, medicines, and other equipment from hospitals; and agribusiness waste. Colonialism and capitalism's economy of extraction, dispossession, exploitation, and extinction leaves in its paths land exhausted by monocultures; forests lost forever; extinct species; cultures erased; cities obliterated; seas disrupted by mining; mountains hollowed; islands disappearing; expunged memories; lives that do not matter; children of color condemned to premature death; Indigenous, Brown, and Black women murdered every day; migrants and refugees drowning, maimed, and killed. The thinking of Western modernity seeks to domesticate memories, to transform wasting into sublime images of ruins, to recreate "nature," or to advocate for excessive hygiene. All this aims at control and power rather than at ending devastation. It naturalizes the consequences of racial capitalism; catastrophes become acts of God, about which there is nothing to be done. It wants us to learn to be resilient and to adapt, to be fascinated by images of ruination, to accept that recreating nature is "better than nothing," or to abide by excessive norms of cleanliness.

The cartography of bordered social and racial segregation explains why catastrophes are more murderous among poor communities of color. In "The Case for Letting Malibu Burn," American political activist and historian Mike Davis, after having explained how racial and social segregation in Los Angeles was built, shows that similar conflagrations (in this case, the 1995 fire) were "inverse mirror images of each other."[222] On one side, Westlake, a neighborhood populated by migrants, and Black and Latinx working-class residents; on the other, Malibu, one of the wealthiest neighborhoods in the USA. While, as Davis tells us, the wealthy inhabitants of Malibu were protected from the consequences of wildfire by "the largest army of firefighters in California history" and "benefitted from an extraordinary range of insurance, land use, and disaster relief subsidies as well as obsessive media coverage,"[223] in Westlake, there were 100 fatalities. Davis details the intersected history of wealth, fire, water, protection, poverty, and cuts in public services like firefighting to demonstrate the differentiated vulnerability to death in catastrophes and the reasons why fires are so destructive in the area—the lifestyle of the rich hinders protection in that they oppose "prescriptive burning" because blackened landscapes negatively affect the value of their property and they favor technological solutions. These technological solutions have always gone against Indigenous peoples', farmers', and gardeners' knowledge that is now in some parts recognized again. In Australia, for instance, long before it was invaded and colonized by Europeans, fire management techniques—known as "cultural burns"—were practiced by Indigenous peoples who understood the role of prescriptive burning in controlling fires.

Shannon Foster, knowledge keeper for the D'harawal people and an Aboriginal knowledge lecturer at the University of Technology Sydney, remarks that the ways colonial settlers have controlled fires has led to barren, wasted land: "We can't eat, drink or breathe assets. Without country, we have nothing."[224] On the contrary, "Indigenous cultural burns work within the rhythms of the environment, attracting marsupials and mammals which Aboriginal people could hunt."[225] Foster explains that "cool burning replenishes the earth and enhances biodiversity—the ash fertilises and the potassium encourages flowering. It's a complex cycle based on cultural, spiritual and scientific knowledge."[226] The same indifference toward local knowledges can be found in Asia, Africa, the Americas, or the Pacific, where colonialism imposed the engineer over the farmer, the craftsperson, the worker. The power of the engineer rests on their capacity to treat the multiple lives in the world (forests, rivers, plains) as objects. In California, "the double standard of fire disaster was rubbed in the face of the poor,"[227] Davis says before examining the ways in which they are criminalized, made responsible for the rate of deaths and for the destruction of property. The fact that "safety" for "luxury enclaves and gated hilltop suburbs" has become a major social expenditure is almost never debated, Davis concludes.[228] The lifestyle of the rich rests on the exhaustion—on the depletion of the energy and life—of the poor and of their environment.

The Racial Stain of Cleanliness

As slavery and colonialism drew a rigid line between clean and dirty, white cleaning translated into an excessive and obsessive attention to be protected from the "stain" of Blackness. The racial genealogy of excessive industrial cleaning justifies programs of *cleaning up* that aim at erasing the conditions of wasting, keeping the illusion of pristine and immaculate nature, and does not acknowledge the way "nature" works in the first place, with germs and viruses. This is why it can be useful to develop an ethics of cleanliness that is not afraid of waste and germs, that rejects wasting and does not dream of an untainted planet, that recognizes the colonial-racial brutality and indifference to the multiplicity of forms of living, and that takes into account the myriad of initiatives that are repairing wasted lands, bodies (including of water) and minds, in connection with nonhuman species. Against the fantasy of escaping Earth and colonizing Mars that demonstrates white bourgeois and male hubris and the incapacity to imagine the abolition of colonization, queer, feminist, Indigenous, and decolonial speculative fiction offers ways to confront what cannot be brought back through mourning, collective intelligence, and creativity. Authors of antiracist, decolonial speculative creative work, from Octavia Butler to M. E. O'Brien and Eman Abdelhadi,[229] have imagined collective alternatives after the collapse of capitalism. These are not some kind of reverie, Hollywood scenarios of women and men surviving in a postapocalyptic world where one must show one's ability to kill fast and without second thought, but scenes of living with differences as well as understanding the difficulties of collective living and finding ways to resolve conflicts outside the logic of carceral and punitive solutions.

The white escape for Mars is exactly what artist Thirza Jean Cuthand imagines in her film *Reclamation* (2018).[230] "White people," Cuthand writes, "have left Earth for Mars after the climate wars and have left the Indigenous people behind, who are working to restore their lands and communities. A lesbian couple and a gay man all discuss the work they are doing and how they are cleaning up after the colonisation, pollution and destruction of their lands."[231] What matters, she says, is a "possibility of hope and restoration in the hands of the rightful caretakers: Indigenous people."[232] Escaping Earth is not the ground upon which abolitionism is envisioned because, as Cuthand says, "feeling tied to your land as an Indigenous person makes leaving this planet behind incomprehensible."[233] Cuthand thinks that envisioning decolonization is "easier once the colonizers have gone and once the people left behind realize that not only is their planet healing but also their minds and hearts."[234] Capitalism and engineers never leave aside an opportunity to make profit. Waste management, as I've already said, has become big business not only in terms of getting rid of garbage but also by offering a way of life that is "sustainable"; in other words, there is no need to revolt, just recycle.

The premise that "recycling is environmentally friendly" does not hold because, as sustainability scholar and urban waste governance professional Samantha MacBride has shown, recycling "does not necessarily conserve resources or preserve nature" but "produces pollution."[235] Regarding the recycling of paper that is supposed to preserve forests, MacBride remarks that "to save trees in a way that matters ecologically and socially means something more. It means that forests, including forest ecosystems and surrounding live-lihoods in all of their complexity, are actually protected in today's world."[236] And she warns that "both the economy of metals and as well as the material properties of metals make them relatively easy to be recycled over and over again and be reintroduced back into production, especially in comparison the heterogeneous range of synthetic polymers we call plastics. Yet we see growing rates of metals extraction taking place *alongside* growing recycling rates, worldwide."[237] In other words, recycling does not stop extraction and the production of waste, nor its cleaning.

Recycling provides a market for an experience that connects the customer to emotion, authenticity, and the feeling that they are doing something for the planet while enjoying exclusivity. The notion of exclusivity is key as it signals both being singular in a mass and joining the people who understand the risk the planet is facing while being able to consume. The excess of waste under capitalism is repackaged by owners and founders of sustainable brands who contend that "there is an opportunity to process materials that are Earth-friendly and reusable. Piñatex, Bloom Foam and Orange Fiber are just some examples [of brands doing this well]. So let's clean up; not only the waste that we have produced thus far, but [let's] also look at each of our production processes to find out how to [be] less wasteful and more resourceful."[238] Asked what a world without waste meant, the owners of Rusticae, which offers exclusive boutique hotels and rural retreats in Spain and Portugal, answer: "The take, make and throw away model has to give way to movements such as the circular economy to achieve zero waste. We cannot keep filling our shopping cart in the supermarkets with plastics and more plastics that will end up filling our containers the next day. In our sector, we want to reduce the volume of waste by suggesting hotels offer solid or bulk cosmetics instead of infinite toiletries."[239] Hannah Coffins, founder of the company Needle & Thread, claims that "responsible sourcing is a core value at Needle & Thread, and our aim is to create timeless, beautiful pieces. Every fabric and component is carefully selected to stand the test of time and, as part of a company-wide commitment, the majority of our collection now includes organic cotton, recycled sequins and recycled polyester." Coffins declares: "To me, a world without waste means a much cleaner and brighter future. My aim has always been to operate a responsible business and in order to do this, I believe it is important to consistently review the impact of our actions. Needle & Thread's timeless pieces are designed to have longevity to reduce landfill waste."[240] Brands have learned the vocabulary of sustainability, recycling, and well-being to make consumption guilt free.

Recycling addresses waste by transforming it into "naturalized commodities,"[241] and by masking the links between waste, wasting, and racial capitalism. To unpack these links requires going beyond waste management. Let us look at fast fashion, which produces over 92 million tons of waste a year, whose workers are mostly women of color, and which dresses women for a low cost, notably in the West.[242] Let's start with the Rana Plaza, an eight-story building in the Dhaka suburb of Savar in Bangladesh, a country which has 4 million garment workers, more than 58 percent of whom are women. Workers of Rana Plaza "produced garments for the transnational commodity chain that stretches from the cotton fields of South Asia, through Bangladesh's machines and workers, and on to retail houses in the Western world. Garments for famous brands such as Benetton, Bonmarché, Prada, Gucci, Versace, and Zara are stitched here, as are the cheaper clothes that hang on Walmart racks."[243] On April 24, 2013, the building collapsed in the span of two minutes, killing at least 1,132 people (the majority of them women) and injuring over 2,500 more. One thread is to ask where most workers of these workers come from. Vijay Prashad, Indian historian and Marxist intellectual, tells us that they "bring with them the desolation of the countryside, its overworked soil and poisoned water ravaged by industrial agriculture as well as by the law of value that makes the small farmer redundant before the might of capitalist farms."[244] In garment factories that can be found in Haiti, Sri Lanka, Cambodia, or Mexico, violence is viewed as necessary. Prashad quotes one of the factory owners as saying:

Factory owners want to maximise profits, so they will cut corners on safety issues, on ventilation, on sanitation. They will not pay overtime or offer assistance in the case of injuries. They push workers hard because they don't want to miss deadlines . . . Workers have no unions, so they can't dictate their rights . . . Some of this can also be blamed on the branded retailers who place bulk orders and say, "Scale up production lines because it is a big order and improve your margins". Even 2–3 cents can make the difference, but these companies don't want to factor [labour rights and safety] compliance into costing.[245]

A first thread is the loss of land, a legacy of colonialism and a consequence of neoliberal policies imposed by the IMF and the World Bank and accepted by governments. Organized poverty is another, as well as systemic violence and racism. In her study of rural Bangladesh in the late 1990s and early 2000s, anthropologist Lamia Karim traced the trajectory from rural farms to factories. Women in Dhaka told her about "the horrific conditions inside these factories," and that "on the job they have no recourse against irregularity in payment of wages, verbal and physical abuse and sexual harassment."[246]

Out of the two options that they have, to be factory workers or domestic servants, "most women prefer the garment sector."[247] They are not passive, they have fought many times but they face many enemies, not just local actors but also powerful international institutions—for example, an agreement by the World Trade Organization that "removed tariffs from clothes manufactured in Bangladesh and reinvented Bangladesh into a manufacturing site for cheap clothes."[248] The Rana Plaza collapse triggered a lot of soul searching and calls for boycotting fast fashion. To "evade criminal liability, global brands more readily entertained the demand for compensation. In less than three weeks after the collapse, long before the Rana Plaza Arrangement and the Rana Plaza Donors Trust Fund was established, PRIMARK injected money to steer the situation in their favour."[249] Six years after the disaster, one in five survivors' health had deteriorated.[250] Ten years later, "more than half (54.5%) of the survivors are still unemployed. The key reason is health conditions such as breathing difficulties, vision impairment and physical challenges, including not being able to stand or walk properly."[251] Mushrefa Mishu, president of the Garment Workers Unity Forum (founded in 1995), asserted that "buyers and the international community should ask garment factory owners about workers' wages, freedom of expression, registration of government opponents' unions, clean washrooms, safe food, and clean drinking water in the factories. They should ask the garment factory owners about forced overtime until midnight, torture and harassment, illegal dismissals, and a lack of compensation."[252]

Things got worse with the COVID-19 pandemic when fashion orders "were abruptly cancelled, which left millions of workers unemployed without severance pay."[253] Recycling clothes in the West produced in these factories does not address the systemic and structural violence that justifies their creation. What the women workers demand is practical solidarity: not being forced to be landless, getting higher pay, the right to unionize, schools for their children, clean washrooms, safe food and clean drinking water in the factories, the end of sexual violence. Boycotting fast fashion or recycling the tons and tons of clothes do not provide an answer to the organized abandonment of racial capitalism. Corporations and their subsidiaries will not answer the demands of garment workers unless a power relation is instituted. Why can simple things as clean washrooms, safe food, and clean drinking water not be found in factories? It is not ill will or conspiracy. A decolonial antiracist *politics of the elemental* is not humanitarian, but targets the reasons why "simple" things like vital needs are to be considered. Looking back at the Rana Plaza disaster, Prashad quotes Karl Marx: "But in its blind unrestrainable passion, its werewolf hunger for surplus labour, capital oversteps not only the moral, but even the merely physical maximum bounds of the body. It steals the time required for the consumption of fresh air and sunlight. . . . All that concerns it is simply and solely the maximum of labour power that can be rendered fluent in a working day. It attains this end by shortening the extent of the labourer's life, as a greedy farmer snatches increased produce from the soil by robbing it of its fertility."[254] The merely physical maximum bounds of the body indeed.

The Politics of the Elemental

Reading reports on the aftermath of the terrifying earthquake that hit eastern Turkey on February 6, 2023, I learned about the causes of the earthquake's strength, why so many buildings fell apart so fast even when they were new, why survivors had to dig through the ruins with their own hands, why there was so much delay of state aid, and the different treatment of Turkish citizens and Syrian refugees. Buried among these facts, I read that in Turkey, women, girls, and trans people suffered the most from the lack of access to water, but also that "female survivors of earthquakes find it very difficult to ask for sanitary pads. There is an assumption that within the broader picture of devastation and destruction, such matters are a trivial concern."[255]

In Pakistan, following the 2022 floods, more than 400,000 pregnant women found no medical support for themselves and their newborns, no food, no security, and no basic medical care, and miscarriages rose drastically. Girls with their periods had no menstrual care, and an estimated 70 percent of women in flood-affected areas suffered urinary tract infections (UTIs) from lack of access to bathrooms and from using dirty fabric in the place of clean pads.[256] Generally, UTIs are not attended to even though they pose a serious threat to health. Indeed, if they are not treated (and they can disappear in two days with antibiotics), the infection can spread to the kidneys and other parts of the body, and if the infection gets in the bloodstream, it is lifethreatening. Since water is the best cleanser of a woman's urinary tract, and washing must be done daily, we can guess why a lack of water and privacy cannot be considered a trivial matter. Furthermore, if in all these situations, LGBTQ+ communities meet sexual harassment and violence, "women and girls often suffer the most during humanitarian emergencies," wrote Racha Nasreddine, regional director of ActionAid Arab Region, in February 2023. "Violence against them increases and they are more at risk of being exploited. There's very limited access to services like hospitals and so pregnant women are at risk of complications if they can't receive the medical care they need.

Those who are menstruating will also need to manage their periods without the right products and with very little privacy."[257]

Six months after the floods, researchers from Islamic Relief talking to people in affected areas in Pakistan found that "40% of the children they surveyed had stunted growth and 25% were underweight as families struggle to access food and healthcare . . . Women and girls reported being particularly affected, with pregnant women still struggling to access health services and girls most likely to be underweight. Many of the women displaced by the flooding do not have the privacy to breastfeed, meaning poorer health for their babies."[258] A study of women's health in the Rajanpur district of Punjab revealed that "women had been suffering from abdominal pain, gastric diseases and kidney issues because of contaminated water, inadequate nutrition, and insanitary conditions in camps."[259] After catastrophes, women and girls, pregnant or not, menstruating or not, systematically find themselves with a lack of toilets, cleaning facilities, and access to medical resources, in greater number than men, which creates a "major source of distress."[260] "Distress" does not seem the correct word to express the consequence of what should be termed a structural denial of the elemental. It does not adequately describe the depth of anxiety, even panic and dread, that women, girls, and trans people experience when they need to pee, to poop, to wash themselves, and thus involuntarily expose intimate parts of their bodies, and what these feelings do to their bodies and minds.

The representation of the lack of privacy, the unbearable irritation of intimate parts of a woman's body, the shame of talking about these needs, and the threats that the lack of access to clean water, intimacy, sanitary pads, pills pose to women's health do not make for shocking images. The visual culture of catastrophes must not only hide the conditions of production of lack of water, but the fact that women and girls will be the first to be deprived of access to cleaning. A sanitary pad does not make good visual culture of catastrophe. The triviality of women of color's basic needs, which demonstrates how structurally racist politics deeply affect women's health and bodies, is connected to cleaning as something *trivial*. Trivializing women of color's needs for privacy and cleaning associates them with being dirty according to patriarchal norms and structural racism, while making cleaning one of the jobs they can easily access because it is associated with being a woman and with race. Structurally racist built environments that have made Black, Brown, and Indigenous women, and trans and queer people more susceptible to premature death and climate disaster (not "climate change") are exacerbating preexisting inequalities. Yet the narrative that presents women of color's displacement as new and unique is wrong; it erases the forced deportation of

African women during the slave trade, or the migration (forced or autonomous) of women from South and East Asia as indentured workers in the 19th century.

What matters is an approach that acknowledges inequities, autonomy, systemic violence, and class among women who move. Currently, as Disha Shetty, a science journalist based in Pune, India, has argued, the data that has become standard among international institutions—that women make up 80 percent of global refugee and displaced populations—is not solid. It is important to distinguish why and when women flee. Studies show that "refugees fleeing from armed conflict are especially likely to be women and children, with men often staying behind as combatants," but "by contrast, women made up the vast majority of people who remained in New Orleans in the wake of Hurricane Katrina, mainly because they didn't have the means to flee."[261] Shetty warns about the objective to shock by using the 80 percent figure: it "distracts from the needs of women who haven't been displaced but are impacted by climate change nonetheless," and treats them as passive victims whose needs are then missing from media coverage or programs on gender vulnerability.[262] Michelle Bachelet, UN high commissioner for human rights, said in 2022 regarding the women who do move: "While they sleep, wash, bathe or dress in emergency shelters, tents or camps, the risk of sexual violence is a tragic reality of their lives as migrants or refugees," adding: "Compounding this is the increased danger of human trafficking, and child, early and forced marriage which women and girls on the move endure."[263] These remarks are not wrong in themselves. In their testimonies, women speak of the systemic violence they encounter, but by insisting on victimization, such claims do not include women's practices of resistance, nor do they clearly point to structural causes. Women and girls become an indistinct mass that must be protected by international agencies or private foundations. Their own forms of organization are ignored.

In *Les damnées de la mer* (The wretched of the sea), geographer Camille Schmoll, after reminding us that the reasons of displacement can also be personal (escaping family, husbands, companions), describes the "sexual humanitarianism" that "articulates sexuality and gender to construct, hierarchize and organize vulnerabilities," and hinders women's autonomy and right to privacy. Privacy in humanitarian and state refuges "is a privilege," she concludes, underlining that daily life in these spaces is monitored in ways that are experienced as paternalistic.[264] What is needed, it must be repeated, is not victimization but an end to political and racist organized denial.

Studying the effects of climate disaster on Black women, sociomedical sciences scholar Naomi Michelson writes that "the notion that Black women are dying at higher rates to benefit private corporations is not a new one; it is just being reiterated by the climate crisis. Just like imperialism, anthropogenic climate change is inextricably linked to a history of theft, power, and greed."[265] She cites the facts that "greenhouse gases emitted within racially segregated neighborhoods are likely to increase the incidence of infectious diseases within the Black community" and that "Black infant and maternal mortality are being exacerbated by climate change, the mental health effects of climate change."[266] According to Michelson, women of color worldwide "are projected to face a unique set of health outcomes under climate change."[267]

A 2019 study showed that "2.1 billion people lacked safely managed drinking water and 4.5 billion worldwide lacked a safely managed sanitation service in 2015."[268] Behind the bureaucratic language, what can be deduced is that the privatization of water by big corporations, together with state indifference and racism, deprives the majority of humanity of water. Children of color are particularly affected: in war zones, "more girls and boys die from diseases linked to unsafe water and sanitation and lack of hygiene than from direct violence," a United Nations report said.[269] Not only are women and girls usually excluded from decision-making processes, but the water knowledge of Indigenous peoples has so far been ignored. However, we must pay attention to the ways in which the inclusion of women and girls is enacted by foundations such as the Gates Foundation and to the cultural appropriation of water knowledge. This is because the notion of "gender equality" chooses to ignore the social relations that racial-colonial capitalism has created. Indeed, though the number of studies focused on menstruation, sanitation, and hygiene has increased in recent years,[270] many remain within the field of "gender equality" and "empowerment," which does not account for the systemic racial organization of the deprivation of water. As historian J. R. McNeill has shown, during the twentieth century, rich countries of the North "customized their share of the hydrosphere much more thoroughly than poor ones," adding that, at century's end, the West "directly consumed 18% of the total available freshwater runoff of the globe and appropriated 54% of it one way or another."[271] The "West" here refers to the colonial/racial world, the rich countries of the North, whose administrators, engineers, and scientists devised the distribution of freshwater in order to serve its industries regardless of the needs of people who ended up deprived of water or unable to pay the fees that the privatization of water distribution imposed.

But is it possible to build an argument from these two case studies: the organized denial of women's needs in Turkey and Pakistan? Is it possible to generalize? Is this denial of the elemental systemic? Is it the same everywhere? What can be inferred from different cases is that menstruations remain a problem in patriarchal-racial capitalism, which requires neutral bodies. Ignored, seen as an obstacle to work, a source of shame and pollution, menstruations become a source of punishment. In India, reports show that "many female sugarcane cutters—primarily from Maharashtra's Beed district—have had their wombs surgically removed. The everyday lives of these female labourers are extremely challenging. Long workdays along with inadequate housing and limited access to healthcare facilities have a negative impact on both their physical and mental wellbeing. Women in this profession also frequently develop multiple infections and serious reproductive issues as a result of unhygienic sanitation practices."[272] Women are encouraged to have a hysterectomy by doctors and sugar mill owners who do not "provide basic facilities such as running water, adequate bathroom facilities and suitable living accommodations for all of their employed laborers."[273]

Mahadev Chunche, associate professor at the Kumbhalkar College of Social Work in Wardha, Maharashtra, who spoke to more than 400 women in Maharashtra for his PhD on India's sugar laborers, said that "almost 80% of them told him they faced sexual harassment, were molested or raped by male sugar labourers, drivers and middlemen."[274] The women constantly "complain of stomach aches because of bad nutrition, inability to have access to hygienic care during their periods, heavy loads to carry and insufficient postpartum care. To get a hysterectomy done, many of them take a loan of about INR 50,000 from the contractor who then starts to deduct the amount through the six months of labor. Surgeries, often performed by quacks, also means that may lead to serious health hazards, abdomen pains, vaginal infections, cervical problems and also cancers at a young age."[275] As medical studies have shown the link between a hysterectomy and osteoarthritis, this surgery leads to incapacitating health problems.

In a 2015 study in Odisha, India, women demonstrated their understanding of the consequences of the denial of their viral needs. They "ranked seven sanitation activities (defecation, urination, menstruation, bathing, post-defecation cleaning, carrying water, and changing clothes) based on stress (high to low) and level of freedom (associated with greatest freedom to having the most restrictions)."[276] Menstruation was "most likely to be ranked as the most stressful behavior," "followed by defecation and urination,"[277] though sources of stress vary from one site to another (rural vs. urban, differences from one community to another), and water appeared as an "essential component of sanitation related behaviors in this setting and was used in post-defecation cleaning, bathing and for menstrual hygiene management."[278] Water's deprivation is a major source of "emotional distress" and "fear, worry, anger, and bother."[279] "Women are disproportionately burdened by the persistent lack of access to safe sanitation. Women's experiences and/or fear of physical and sexual violence associated with having to walk to and use sanitation facilities, particularly in more violent neighborhoods (e.g., informal settlements), have forced many to revert to forms of sanitation that increase their risk of direct contact with untreated waste (e.g., plastic bags or bucket toilets)."[280]

These facts have not been ignored. There is a literature about the lack of access to space for cleaning oneself and to water, about the stress that menstruation bring to girls and women during decades of their lives, the danger that peeing represents to billions of women. Data and analyses can be found in public health and medical journals; in the media; in WHO, UN, UNESCO, and NGO reports; and in feminist journals of the Global South. Articles speak about the shame of what I have been referring to here as *the elemental*, the negative effects on mental health, the threat of rape and murder when girls and women go to release themselves at night, or the lack of adequate toilets in refugee camps, in cities, and in the countryside. Nothing is new. But there is much more money invested in technological progress for mining, identifying sources of rare metals, for surveillance and policing, for exploring the universe than for imagining an antiracist decolonial politics of the elemental. If programs of gender equality may bring some relief, and that should not be dismissed, they do not put an end to a structural denial, they do not radically abolish the structures of racism, colonialism, and patriarchy that perpetuate indifference and denial.

As I have been arguing, these structures are rooted in racialized and colonial ideologies of clean/dirty, in the whitening of cleanliness, in the assignation of cleaning to women (and to men) of color, in the organized denial of vital needs, and in considering cleaning a job without great importance. Of course, I could be told that as soon as technology sees an opportunity to make money, huge progress will be made (there already are intelligent vacuum cleaners, refrigerators available to some that regulate by themselves the level of cold for different food, better cleaning chemicals, more "bio" or "green" cleaning products). But what I am arguing for, which will become clearer as we proceed, is a decolonial antiracist feminist cleaning, i.e., a cleaning that does not adopt white bourgeois norms of cleanliness.

Framing women, self-care, and water exclusively in terms of availability is limited because it is "implicitly suggesting that if facilities are accessible, they will be used. A more nuanced view that takes into account not only the existence of facilities but also the factors influencing their use is needed to understand the dynamics of women's sanitation use in the region."[281] This is what I have tried to clarify: there is a need, there is a solution for that need, and there is the way in which that solution is implemented. This process is too often left to engineers or administrators, who will calculate the time a woman needs to pee and the space she needs, neat calculations that will be entered in a computer and spat out. The women's "sanitation" (toilets, privacy, access to water) question has become an important human rights issue that appears in all international institutions reports. Solutions go from UNESCO training women and girls as masons, as in Jharkhand, India, where "girls who have dropped out of school because of the lack of facilities for dealing with their periods are becoming *rani mistri*, toilet-builders, in their communities,"[282] to corporate philanthropy. Gender equality programs will not answer the denial of vital needs because, as I have attempted to show, it is a structural denial, an organized abandonment.

In 2011, in a keynote address at the 2011 AfricaSan Conference in Kigali, Sylvia Mathews Burwell, president of the Gates Foundation's Global Development Program, called "on donors, governments, the private sector, and NGOs to address the urgent challenge, which affects nearly 40 percent of the world's population" and announced "$42 million in new sanitation grants that aim to spur innovations in the capture and storage of waste, as well as its processing into reusable energy, fertilizer, and fresh water. In addition, the foundation will support work with local communities to end open defecation and increase access to affordable, long-term sanitation solutions that people will want to use."[283] The foundation was "reinventing toilets" since they were "working to develop new tools and technologies that address every aspect of sanitation—from the development of waterless, hygienic toilets that do not rely on sewer connections to pit emptying to waste processing and recycling. Many of the solutions being developed involve cutting-edge technology that could turn human waste into fuel to power local communities, fertilizer to improve crops, or even safe drinking water."[284] Before being amazed by the claim of reinventing toilets, let us remember that "philanthropy is the private allocation of stolen wages," as Ruth Wilson Gilmore has said.[285] What she calls the "non-profit industrial complex" works thusly:

The first line of defense is the market, which solves most problems efficiently, and because the market is unfettered, fairness results from universal access to the same ("perfect") information individuals, households, and firms use to make self-interested decisions. And where the market fails, the voluntary, non-profit sector can pick up any stray pieces because the extent to which extra economic values (such as kindness or generosity or decency) come into play is the extent to which abandonment produces its own socially strengthening rewards. That's their ideal: a frightening willingness to engage in human sacrifice while calling it something else.[286]

Girls and women's sanitation in the Global South has become a concern for private foundations and international organizations while the economy rests on the structural ignorance of women of color's vital needs. Corporate philanthropy leads to depoliticization and dependency and satisfies the white savior syndrome and the still-alive colonial civilizing mission. As Gilmore tells us, "the grassroots groups that have formally joined the third sector are in the shadow of the shadow state. They are not direct service providers but often work with the clients of such organizations as well as with the providers themselves."[287]

Refusing dependency and white saviors, South African activist Sibusiso (S'bu) Innocent Zikode, a cofounder in 2005 of the South African shack dwellers' movement and of the University of the Poor, reflected in a 2009 interview how, upon his experience as a young activist trained into killing, he moved to a conception of a politics of "humanizing the world" and "living communism" and understood that

a living politics is not a politics that requires a formal education—a living politics is a politics that is easily understood because it arises from our daily lives and the daily challenges we face. It is a politics that every ordinary person can understand. It is a politics that knows that we have no water but that in fact we all deserve water. It is a politics that everyone must have electricity because it is required by our lives. That understanding—that there are no toilets but that in fact there should be toilets—is a living politics. It is not complicated; it does not require big books to find the information. It doesn't have a hidden agenda—it is a politics of living that is just founded only on the nature of living. Every person can understand these kinds of demands and every person has to recognize that these demands are legitimate.[288]

"Real politics" is not about the exercise of power and the capacity to impose consent, "not about how many people you are willing to arrest, threaten or kill; . . . a real politics is not a fight to be able to abuse state power but . . . a real politics is in fact about how many people you are willing to listen to and to serve—and to listen to them and to serve them as it pleases them, not yourself."[289] Zikode defends a "living communism" which is "a living idea and a living practice of ordinary people. The idea is the full and real equality of everyone without exception. The practice, well, a community must collectively own or forcefully take collective ownership of natural resources— especially the water supply, land and food. Every community is rightfully entitled to these resources."[290] "What is needed for your life, for your safety, for your dignity" should always be the starting point of living communism.[291]

I find Zikode's remarks powerful and persuasive because they set the tone for establishing a praxis grounded in the elemental and whose objective is the abolition of all structures that hinder access to the elemental. S'bu Zikode's living communism is what I saw in the making in Reunion Island, to which I will return, in the 1960s to 1970s: a fight for land and dignity, for equality and solidarity, which has forged my thinking, when the *trivial* is the basis of politics. A living politics is a politics of the elemental, because understanding that there are no sanitary pads but that in fact there should be is a politics of living care and cleaning. I add to this Gilmore's "abolition ecology" with its "political ecological imperatives of access to fresh air, clean water, sufficient land, amelioration of toxic chemicals and beyond."[292] "By centering attention to those most vulnerable to the fatal couplings of power and difference signified by racism, we will develop richer analyses of how it is that radical activism might most productively exploit crises for liberation ends," Gilmore argues.[293] Abolition as a "theory of change," "a theory of social life," echoes S'bu Zikode's "humanizing the world" and "living communism." This is what activist Fannie Lou Hamer articulated when she said the following in 2018 about food production in the South of the United States: "Down where we are, food is used as a political weapon."[294]

Since then, studies of food in the Global South and poor, Black, and Brown communities in the North have shown how it is indeed a political weapon against mental and physical health. Analyzing environmental racism means thus looking at the past and the present that capitalism, colonialism, and imperialism have produced and the future they prepare, paying attention to local cosmologies, their understanding of waste and cleaning, their practice of life in rehearsal. Decolonial environmentalism is abolitionist because it looks at the multiple racial institutions that make the world irrespirable and uninhabitable for the many.

Among the sites of irrespirability and uninhabitability (mining, plantations, factories, youth education centers), prisons stand as "daily environmental injustice."[295] In her work in the U.S., Gilmore has shown how the state unevenly distributes risk, fatality, and access to resources across different social groups over time; why prisons deserve to be studied; and why abolitionism targets the political and economic forces that choose to invest in mass incarceration rather than in education and health. Such forces encourage a huge increase in prison construction, a vast expansion of domestic police forces, and the "common sense" that treats these violent institutions as catch-all solutions to social problems.[296] Furthermore, prisons pollute. In the USA, most are built on landfills or near former coal mining sites, exposing prisoners to high levels of toxic chemicals in the ground and waste,[297] and "zip codes with prisons had higher toxic contamination than zip codes without prisons."[298] French prisons are overcrowded, four to five persons are forced to cohabit in 12m² cells full of cockroaches and rats, eat their meals "close to the toilet" and wash in showers that "show traces of mold and do not guarantee privacy."[299] In the French overseas departments, the prison situation is worse—a legacy of slavery, colonialism, and structural racism. No health measures were taken during the COVID-19 pandemic, which brutally hit their populations. In Brazil, a policy of mass incarceration has resulted in "severe overcrowding. Cases of ill-treatment are widespread in prisons across the country," "torture and other cruel, inhuman and degrading treatment or punishment" take place daily.[300] This is repeated worldwide. Decolonial antiracist feminist theory cannot ignore prisons. Inspired by the work of Gilmore, Study and Struggle's curriculum for October 2021 (under the title "Green") reads:

As you study the environmentalisms that sustain prisons and imagine an environmentalism without them, consider the physical space necessary for mass incarceration. On whose stolen land do America's prisons and jails sit? What types of violence were necessary to establish and then to maintain a system of private property? What sorts of historic and current value extraction from the earth can you think of? Who decides whether to use land to build a prison or to grow food? How does the nation-state's promise of exclusivity and security to property owners perpetuate militarism at home and abroad? Why must we be in solidarity with nonhuman relatives with whom we share the land?[301]

Chronic sore throats, thyroid disorders, cancer, shortness of breath, headaches, sores, cysts, tumors, and vision problems are the symptoms of the destruction of human and nonhuman lives. The struggle for food, adequate and affordable housing, clean water, quality education, healthcare, and employment defines the political terrain of the *trivial* and the *elemental*, which are actively opposed by colonialism, racial capitalism, and imperialism.

The Marxist Feminist Theory of Social Reproduction

There cannot be a discussion of cleaning without referring to the Marxist feminists' theory of social reproduction. Maria Dalla Costa, Selma James, Maria Mies, Tithi Bhattacharya, Silvia Federici, Angela Davis, and many others, have argued that, as Federici puts it, "unpaid labour is not extracted by the capitalist class only from the waged workday, but . . . it is also extracted from the workday of millions of unwaged house-workers as well as many other unpaid and un-free labourers."[302] To Marxists, hetero-patriarchy and capitalism organized the division between unpaid (housework) and "real" (paid) work. Black feminist historians and theorists showed early on that the Black women's position in the labor force was linked to the historical legacies of sexism and racism, dating back to the division of care work in slavery and domestic service. It was not just a question of hetero-patriarchy and capitalism. The racialization of cleaning emerged with colonial slavery and colonization, preceding the Industrial Revolution.

In her classic *Women, Race, Class* (1989), Angela Davis wrote that during slavery, cleaning and caring became associated with Black women who "worked as cooks, nursemaids, chambermaids and all-purpose domestics" and that "white women in the South unanimously rejected this line of work."[303] Later on, white women who worked as domestics "were generally European immigrants who, like their ex-slave sisters, were compelled to take whatever employment they could find." Yet, white women could more easily escape the drudgery of cleaning for others and "proportionately, more Black women have always worked outside their homes than have their white sisters."[304] Cleaning work, rift with sexual violence, was soon "considered degrading because it has been disproportionately performed by Black women, who in turn are viewed as 'inept' and 'promiscuous.' "[305] Reflecting on the white feminist demand that housework be equally shared between women and men, Davis remarked that "neither women nor men should waste precious hours of their lives on work that is neither stimulating, creative nor productive" and observed that "the structural separation of the public economy of capitalism and the private economy of the home has been continually reinforced by the obstinate primitiveness of household labor. Despite the proliferation of gadgets for the home, domestic work has remained qualitatively unaffected by the technological advances brought on by industrial capitalism. Housework still consumes thousands of hours of the average housewife's year." To Davis, since housework should not be "considered necessarily and unalterably private in character," "a substantial portion of the housewife's domestic tasks can actually be incorporated into the industrial economy . . . Teams of trained and well-paid workers, moving from dwelling to dwelling, engineering technologically advanced cleaning machinery, could swiftly and efficiently accomplish what the present-day housewife does so arduously and primitively."[306]

Davis's conclusion was consistent with that of Western Marxist feminists who, in the 1970s, borrowed from Karl Marx's observation that every system of production involves not only the production of necessities but also the reproduction of the tools and labor power required for production. They showed that women have been responsible for the social reproduction necessary for the industrial economy to function, maintaining homes, raising children, and sustaining community ties.

Selma James, an anticolonial and anti-imperialist activist, who supported Palestinians' rights for a land and against Israeli occupation, was a forceful voice in the struggle for the recognition of what she called "unwaged work." James popularized the demand that the state recognize the need for a salary for unpaid work in the home and in the community.[307] At the 1985 UN Women's Conference in Nairobi, James explained why "Time Off" should become a worldwide slogan: "It's time now, today, that we begin to acknowledge that we are every woman, each of us, carrying the burdens of the world, two-thirds of the world's work, and that in the course of acknowledging that burden and making governments acknowledging that burden, we are in the process of lifting that burden, finally, once and for all, off our shoulders."[308] "Time off" was inspired by the "Women's Day Off" that took place in Iceland on October 24, 1975, the first day of the UN Decade for Women. The Icelandic Redstocking movement was the leading force behind the idea of a one-day women's strike, advocating the idea that there are indissoluble links between class struggle and women's liberation. Its activists agitated for the women's strike idea at a conference they held together with the largest women's labor unions in January 1975.[309] On October 24, some 90 percent of women all over Iceland stopped working to protest the wage gap and their status compared to men. James, who had initiated the International Wages for Housework Campaign, suggested adopting their slogan: "When women stop, everything stops."

In her 2018 book, *Wages for Housework*, feminist political scientist Louise Toupin reminds her readers that the objective of the movement was "to bring together people assigned to perform domestic work and housework—as it happened, women—in order to change their situation of dependency, reverse the relations of power, and redistribute the wealth that they produced. The vast majority of women who had waged jobs returned to being houseworkers once they got home, having worked during the day in specialised sectors associated with housework. It turned out that waged and unwaged women were, in reality, the same people. This was a potentially unifying force, and the strength of the Wages for Housework demand."[310] The approach was revolutionary for it meant "analyzing housework and reproductive work through the prism of work and using union strategies disrupted the entire value system on which the age-old role of the houseworker was based. Demanding a wage was, first of all, to discover oneself as a worker."[311]

Wages for Housework's political thought deeply transformed the way to look at the socioeconomic system of capitalism and understand how it was reproduced on a global level and "the central role that the vast majority of women and wageless people played in it."[312] Workers might be wageless, but they could nonetheless strike. The Global Women's Strike was launched in 1999 at the United Nations headquarters in New York with this demand: "Payment for all caring work—in wages, pensions, land, and other resources. What was more valuable than raising children and caring for others, we asked"; and "invest in life and welfare, not military budgets and prisons."[313] Critical of bourgeois feminism, which "largely chose the market" to escape the drudgery of cleaning, James declared that its refusal to fight for wages for housework had enabled "governments to demean rather than recognize caring."[314] But the opportunity to build a strong feminist movement that would have connected race, class, and gender was lost, James observed. "The women's movement faced a choice. It could embrace the market: careers for some and low-paid jobs for most. Or it could find another way to live: demanding that the work of reproducing the human race was recognized as central to all priorities. Getting wages from the State for this work, carers would help reshape all social relationships: reorganizing work to incorporate men into caring and women into—everything."[315] Imposing a salary for housework was fundamental because "pay is social power; it determines how we live, with whom, and on what terms,"[316] and because "in a capitalist society, money is power, and if you don't have money, you don't have power, and that's how it is."[317]

Worldwide, women recognized themselves in James's remarks that "women's capacity to populate the world and to breastfeed the newborn, fundamental to any society, should have been a source of power for us. Instead, we were robbed of the financial recognition and support that this unique contribution should entitle us to. Instead, we have had to be dependent on the wages of other workers, that is men. When we earned our own wages, they were lower than men's, and we were financially punished every time we went on maternity leave or had to meet other caring obligations."[318] Marxist feminists warned about the "profound crisis of social reproduction that entire populations across the world are experiencing because of the impoverishment capitalist development is producing, due to the defunding of social programs, the politics of extractivism and the now permanent state of warfare."[319] By insisting that "all women were workers who kept the cogs of capitalism turning, and that all households were workplaces," they claimed that the demand for a wage was not the only objective. The ultimate objective was to refuse housework: "what mattered was that women's grueling and thankless work was recognized, such that its conditions could be fought against—and, indeed, ultimately refused."[320] To feminist Marxist thinker and activist Silvia Federici, remuneration for unpaid work was a revolutionary strategy because it made invisible work more visible, demystified and disrupted the structural reliance of capitalism on the unpaid work of (mostly) women, and subverted the supposedly natural social role of "housewife" that capital had invented for women.[321]

Social reproduction feminists might have shown that reproductive labor involves both emotional and manual work for *all* women, but Black feminist Dorothy Roberts argued that there has been a racialized distinction within the housework itself.[322] Historically, she said, housework was divided into "spiritual" and "menial," a dichotomy "inextricably connected to a racial division between domestic laborers, a division that has survived dramatic changes in women's relationship to the market."[323] "It is true that housework has always been women's work, but polishing floors, scrubbing clothes, and tending to children for pay has been seen as Black and other minority women's work."[324] To white women of privilege, "paying someone else to perform menial housework freed time for these women to engage in housework's spiritual aspects, supervising their servants and educating their children."[325]

According to health policy and care work scholars Janette Dill and Mignon Duffy, the spiritual side, "dominated by White women of privilege, was work that was considered to require moral character and relational skills: serving as hostess, supervisor of the daily work, or a role model for children. In contrast, the most strenuous and unpleasant tasks (scrubbing floors and washing laundry, caring for the bodily needs of household members, and preparing and cleaning up after meals) were thought to require little or no skill. This menial labor was relegated to slaves and domestic servants and was ideologically associated with women who were Black, Indigenous, and people of color."[326]

The paid labor force and the increased commodification of household chores did not affect these divisions, and "the shift to a service economy had a different impact on white and Black women: while many white women 'moved up' to jobs formerly occupied exclusively by men, most Black women only 'moved over' to the less prestigious jobs traditionally reserved for white women."[327]

That Black women are overwhelmingly represented in low-wage jobs in the cleaning and caring industry is therefore not surprising.[328] "Racial-ethnic women are employed to do the heavy, dirty, 'back-room' chores of cooking and serving food in restaurants and cafeterias, cleaning rooms in hotels and office buildings, and caring for the elderly and ill in hospitals and nursing homes, including cleaning rooms, making beds, changing bed pans, and preparing food."[329] "In these same settings white women are disproportionately employed as lower-level professionals (e.g., nurses and social workers), technicians, and administrative support workers to carry out the more skilled and supervisory tasks."[330] The Black Women for Wages for Housework, founded in 1976 as an international network campaigning for people, the environment, and ending poverty and racism, declared in 1977: "We have never been paid enough for all the work we have already done." To this, they added: "We don't need more work. We need *money* to work less,"[331] connecting reparations for centuries of low pay and the need to earn more to work less. Care was not sentimentalized. It was work, and women of color had never been paid enough for it. Their understanding of motherhood, care, work, and cleaning was deeply shaped by their living experience as racialized human beings. Already in the 1950s and 1960s, poor Black women, making up "the bulk of the Welfare Rights Movement wanted to prioritize motherhood instead, arguing that economic justice was about more than job opportunities. To them, it meant a guaranteed standard of living, regardless of whether or not you worked outside the home."[332] The "single mothers of the Welfare Rights Movement developed bold welfare policy proposals that prioritized their dignity and agency. In a country that *still* defines poverty as an issue of individual poor choices, the insistence that their economic condition wasn't a personal failing was a significant intervention in 1960s America—especially as poor, mostly Black women advocating for themselves."[333]

Women cleaners want to decide for themselves what will ameliorate their lives, and protection as it is conceived by the International Labour Organization (ILO) and Left governments does not always fulfill their needs. For instance, in Brazil, which counts the greatest number of domestic workers, 7.2 million—out of which 93 percent are women—the ratification on February 1, 2018, of ILO Convention 189, covering decent work for those carrying out domestic tasks in the home, was not always felt as progress. As well as social protection rights, ILO Convention 189 reinforced a law from 2015 that had introduced an eight-hour limit to the working day, a ban on child labor, fines in cases of unfair dismissal, and the right to paid holiday and a thirteen-month salary. Researcher Lilian Steiner has shown that to women cleaners, although progress has been real in many instances, the law's provisions do not always help. Rosa Alves, a cleaner Steiner interviewed, said that "she prefers to keep working through her 30 days' paid holiday, so she has a bit more money at the end of the year. Although her employers pay her above the minimum wage, the mother of three, who has been working since she was 12, still has difficulty making ends meet in raising her children. 'I pay taxes now, but the state school and health system are still just as bad,' she laments."[334] In 2020, Luiza Batista Ferreira, president of the National Federation of Domestic Workers, was worried about the "introduction of a new 'intermittent employment' contract that allows hourly payment for domestic tasks, with no guarantee of minimum wage or number of hours. 'It makes it easy for employers: they can reduce the hours of work and pay less,' says Ferreira."[335]

Cleaning under racial-colonial capitalism has never been anything else than a backbreaking job that deals with smelly, contaminated, polluted waste and that remains viewed with contempt and assigned to people of color, in particular women of color, because it is about waste and, as we have seen, waste has been constructed as unrelated to whiteness.

The Whitening of Cleanliness

As I have begun to argue, unpacking the connections between colonialism and capitalism as the production of waste, the whitening of cleaning, and the fabricated triviality of non-white women's elementary needs or of their work means looking at how colonialism and racism historically constructed a division between the clean/civilized/odorless world and the unclean/uncivilized/smelly worlds while making cleaning a racialized and gendered job. Hygiene and smells became connected with the calculation of the level of civilization that had been reached.

Colonial narratives insisted on the smells of food, homes, and bodies in the colonies that naturally irritated a European nose, even though the two capitals of the most important colonial empires (post-slavery) in the 19th century, London and Paris, were known for their horrific smells, pollution, and lack of hygiene, and the Thames and the Seine were so thick with waste of all kinds that disgusting bubbles were bursting on their surfaces.[336] Historically, in the Arab and Asian worlds (as well as imperial Greece and Rome), washing one's body was esteemed highly, and a close attention to perfuming bodies and to intimate hygiene was a sign of culture and self-esteem. Europe remained insensitive to daily bathing, thinking even that it was bad for the health. Indeed, historical records have informed the racial-colonial description of a dirty non-European planet. In ancient Babylon (2800 BCE), soap or soap-like products were known, found in clay cylinders. The Egyptian Ebers Papyrus, a medical document from about 1500 BCE, described combining animal and vegetable oils with alkaline salts to form a soap-like material used for treating skin diseases, as well as for washing. Medieval authors have mentioned the presence of *hammam*s (public baths) in Muslim societies, in accordance with Islamic recommendations for skin care and hygiene practices, whereas King James VI of Scotland wore the same clothes for months on end, even sleeping in them on occasion. Hilal al-Sabi' (969–1056) estimated that Baghdad at its height had 60,000 bathhouses.[337] Arab chronicler Ahmed ibn Fadlan, born in the late 9th century, described the Vikings he encountered (he called them "Rus") during his journey along the Volga River as the "filthiest of God's creatures."[338] In 1580, Ambroise Paré, one of the most revered scientists of Europe, wrote: "Baths must be forbidden because the pestiferous vapour can enter a man's body quickly and make him die suddenly."[339]

In 17th-century Europe, doctors continued to advise against drinking water, which, "given its nature, brought too much cold and humidity to the stomach. This could cause a dangerous drop in body temperature, which was thought necessary for digestion." In his 1668 *Anatomical History of the Genitals of Man and Woman*, the physician Reinier de Graaf stated that it was enough for a virgin to bathe in water in which men had previously ejaculated in order to become immediately pregnant.[340] The aristocrats barely bathed, and palaces such as the Louvre or Versailles were known to stink and be filthy. It wasn't until the end of the 18th century that the bourgeoisie started to bathe, but it soon became a class and race distinction. Bourgeois literature described the lower classes as smelly, dirty, and living in horrific hovels; women of the lower classes, sex workers, and Jewish or Roma women were constructed as even more smelly and dirty than aristocrats and bourgeois white women. Processes of racialization based on foul odor happened in Europe, affecting populations that colonial imperialist Europe (France, England, and Germany) perceived as inferior: Italians, Spaniards, Greeks, and Polish. Everywhere, the poor and racialized inevitably stank.

Colonialism pitted a clean Europe against an unclean "rest" of the world. The colonial obsession with smells and hygiene barely masked the putrid and decayed smell of colonization, of bodies decomposing, of contaminated rivers, of open mines. In Europe, the bourgeoisie depicted the peasantry and the working class as smelly and unhygienic and associated cleanliness with bourgeois whiteness and its naturally higher level of civilization. Colonial narratives insisted on the smells of food, homes, and bodies in the colonies that naturally irritated a European nose, even though, for long, Europe remained insensitive to daily bathing, even thinking, as we have seen, that it was bad for the health.

Captured African women, children, and men, who had bathed in the rivers and lakes of their countries, were forced into the filth and stench of the barracks, then of the slave ship. To be sold, they were washed and oiled and presented naked. On the plantation, the slave owner's house had to be cleaned and shined daily, which still barely covered the stench of slavery. Plantations, ships, mines, and then the factories of the Industrial Revolution contributed to the race, class, and gender regimes of cleanliness.

Though they had been declared dirty and unclean by the dominant classes, in Europe, women of the lower classes did the cleaning until the 1960s, when they were replaced by Black and Brown women. In the Caribbean, the Americas, and Indian Ocean European colonies, Black women continued to clean homes and wash white people's bodies and clothes. That apparent paradox, asking "unclean" people to clean the white bourgeois homes and bodies, was in fact a direct implementation of structural racism: cleaning had to be done by people stigmatized as unclean to keep the whitened division between clean and unclean alive. Europe's own processes of racialization were globalized, and the colonial and racial construction of uncleanliness and smell against Black and non-European peoples further whitened cleanliness.

Olfactory Racism

Smell plays a role in the production of historically situated racial otherness. French historian Alain Corbin has described how, from the 1750s onward, a stigmatization of groups associated with strong smells was part of a "perceptual revolution" that encouraged a growing intolerance of odors that increased in the 19th century among the bourgeoisie, which associated them with the crowd and the people, and it was how bourgeois hygienists began the enterprise of deodorization.[341] The poor stank like death, like sin, the bourgeois said. To stop the sources of foul smells, roads were paved, swamps drained, and garbage dumps located away from bourgeois neighborhoods, leading progressively, according to Corbin, to "olfactory silence," but only in certain parts of the city. Corbin left aside the racial ideology of smell. The racial making of an odorless world and its connection to conceptions of washing and cleaning described how in Europe, Jews, Roma, Irish, workers, and peasants were said to have distinctive smells that situated them outside of a civilized group. Food and hygiene became markers along a racial hierarchy of smells, which consolidated as colonialism expanded. "At the beginning of the eighteenth-century [sic] Native Americans were described as sweet but by the end of the period, they were said to project 'outward stench.' By the early eighteenth century the cause of the racial perceived stink of the Jews, the 'foetor judaicus,' was now seen as the product of distinctive hygiene and diet rather than a curse from god."[342]

White supremacy drew a very detailed nomenclature connecting non-whites and foul odor and, by the 18th century, it made an association between the African's dark skin and stench. Non-whites were situated along a scale of putridity and foul odor. Slavery and colonization were the matrix of the racist discourse linking non-whiteness, foul odor, and uncleanliness. Beauty was connected to an odorless white body that could then be perfumed, whereas non-whites were said to have an odor that could never be overcome, even with repeated baths. An example of this are the letters and writings of Lady

Anne Lindsay Barnard, a Scottish travel writer, artist, and socialite, from when she lived in Africa with her husband, the colonial secretary of Cape Town, South Africa, for five years.[343] In a 1799 letter to Melville, then secretary for war and the colonies in England, she complained that "one of the worse points of [female] slaves . . . is the dreadful smell which they leave behind them—a 'fox is a rose to it'" and subsequently complains that she would rather slaves were not able to attend a ball since she did not "'much like the smell' of their oil."[344] Distinctions, based on pure fantasies, were made among Africans according to their smells. In his natural history, the French naturalist Buffon argued that "those of Guinea are extremely ugly, and have an insufferable stench" whilst "those of Sofala and Mosambique are handsome, and have no bad smell."[345] As historian Andrew Kettler has shown, "the African subject was defined as a scented object, appropriated as filthy to create levels of ownership through discourse that marked African peoples as unable to access spaces of Western modernity. Embodied cultural knowledge was potent enough to alter the biological function of the five senses to create a European olfactory consciousness made to sense the African other as foul."[346] The European nose became the arbiter of nice smells, imposing its perception of foul/smelly not only on non-white women and men but also on non-European fruits, spices, or ways of cooking. The gaze was not the only sense convoked to racialize; olfactory racism, as Kettler calls it, was as important in the formulation of racial ideas.

All throughout the 18th century, white supremacy perfected its discourse of race and odor, which had concrete consequences. By the 19th century, whites used dogs to track runaway slaves because they could supposedly detect "racial odor," foreseeing the use of dogs by the Nazis to detect the "odor of dissent."[347] Ideas about odorous women, the lack of sensitivity to foul smells among the poor, and the peculiar odor of inferior races mutually reinforced racism. The racist trope of smell constructed a false history where whites and European have always been odorless and clean. Yet, as Italian journalist and social theorist Marco d'Eramo (whom we encountered earlier) reminds us,

domestic running water—for toilets, cooking, personal hygiene, washing clothes and dishes—is a very recent and ephemeral phenomenon, dating back less than a century. In 1940, 45% of households in the US lacked complete plumbing; in 1950, only 44% of homes in Italy had either indoor or outdoor plumbing. In 1954, only 58% of houses in France had running water and only 26% had a toilet. In 1967, 25% of homes in England and Wales still lacked a bath or shower, an indoor toilet, a sink and hot- and cold-water taps. In Romania, 36% of the population lacked a flushing toilet solely for their household in 2012 (down to 22% in 2021).[348]

In France, the modernization of bathrooms came with the end of the colonial war in Algeria, as scholar of urban and revolutionary history Kristin Ross has shown in *Fast Cars, Clean Bodies: Decolonization and the Reordering of French Culture* (1996).[349] Ross draws a connection between torture and shampoo, between water in the bathtub and colonial war, between the new modernized hygienic France and the *sale guerre* across the sea. She describes a cartoon showing a "French paratrooper in camouflage bending over a sudsy bathtub, his hands submerged; a box of Pax laundry soap ('extraordinaire pour la lessive!') standing next to the tub—but a man's feet stick out of the water; the bubbles aren't suds, but rather the tortured man exhaling."[350] The year the Algerian revolution started, in 1954, only 17 percent of Parisians had a shower or bath in their dwellings, Ross reminds us.[351] The racist tropes around smelly Arabs and dirtiness were used to justify torture and murder. The war in Algeria and its presence in France was a cleansing operation: the French army burned forests, bombed with napalm, and forcibly relocated the Algerians into camps. As architect Samia Henni has shown, "the French civil and military authorities profoundly reorganized Algeria's urban and rural territory, drastically transformed its built environments, rapidly implanted new infrastructure, and strategically built new settlements in order to keep Algeria under French colonial rule and protect France's interests in Algeria."[352] As Henni explains:

The construction of militarily controlled camps dubbed *centres de regroupement* (regrouping centers) in Algeria's rural areas resulted from the creation of the forbidden zones—free fire zones—and engendered massive forced relocations of the Algerian population. Special military units called the Sections administratives spécialisées (Specialized Administrative Sections) supervised the evacuation of the forbidden zones, the regrouping of the Algerian population, the construction of temporary and permanent camps, the conversion of a number of permanent camps to villages, and monitored the daily life of Algerian civilians.[353]

Fanon had explained why the divide between the white and non-white town had to be clear and visible.[354] The settlers' town "is a brightly lit town; the streets are covered with asphalt, and the garbage cans swallow all the leavings, unseen, unknown and hardly thought about . . . His feet are protected by strong shoes although the streets of his town are clean and even, with no holes or stones," while the town belonging to the colonized people is "a world without spaciousness; men live there on top of each other, and their huts are built one on top of the other."[355] The settler's town must be clean because it must project his own image, the one that is built on racism and white supremacy. His city is clean because non-white people have cleaned it, and garbage has been dumped in their neighborhood because of supposed natural white superiority. In the aftermath of French colonial wars against movements of national independence and as the French state was reorganizing itself along capitalist modernization ideology, the colonial discourse on the threat by natives to cleanliness and hygiene was imported into France.

If we look at Paris, the bourgeoisie has historically made every effort to delimit the white/clean city from the non-white/unclean neighborhoods. Transformations of the city, already undertaken at the beginning of the 19th century, accelerated a growing concern for cleanliness following the revolutions of 1830 and 1848. "Paris is an immense site of putrefaction, where misery, pestilence and disease work in concert, and where air and sunlight hardly penetrate. Paris is a bad place, where plants wither and perish, where six out of every seven children die in a year."[356] In the 1840s, French statesman Adolphe Thiers ordered the construction of city fortifications transforming Paris into a fortress, and Georges Eugène Haussmann, the official who made Paris the city it is still today, started to redraw the city in 1852. The Paris Commune was a turning point, and a terrified bourgeoisie was intent on pushing away an international working class, which had the temerity to challenge its power and invent new ways to live. Later, the destruction of the fortifications was decided and completed in 1929 and replaced at the beginning of the 1930s by social housing. It was called the "zone," inhabited by *zonards* (a deprecating term for someone from a deprived area) in their "insalubrious housing." In 1956, the government decided to construct a *périphérique* that would separate Paris proper from the *banlieues* (outskirts). The zone was cleared, its inhabitants evicted, and the *périphérique* was inaugurated in 1973.

Olfactory racism remained alive in the postcolonial West. In an infamous 1991 speech, Jacques Chirac, then mayor of Paris and later French president, declared:

How do you expect the French worker who lives in the Goutte-d'or,[357] where I was walking with Alain Juppé three or four days ago, who works with his wife and who, together, earn about 15,000 francs, to see a family with a father, three or four wives, and about twenty kids, on the landing next to his HLM, crammed together, earning 50,000 francs in social benefits, without of course working! [loud applause]. If you add to that the noise and the smell [loud laughter], well, the French worker on the landing, he goes crazy. He goes crazy. That's the way it is. And you have to understand, if you were there, you would have the same reaction.[358]

The group Zebda, based in Toulouse and created by sons of migrants from North Africa and French youth, answered in 1995 with a rap song reminding the French that those who "smell" had built their society:

Who built this road?
Who built this city?
And who doesn't live here?
To those who complain about the noise
To those who condemn the smell
I introduce myself
My name is Larbi, Mamadou Juan and make way
Guido, Henri, Chino Ali I am not ice
A voice told me "Marathon" seeks the light
From the abyss I drew a fight "the good deal."[359]

Olfaction, which is "possibly our most primitive sense," has been very useful in many jobs: medicine, cooking, gardening, taking care of animals, babies, the elderly, but racial capitalism has imposed a perfumed and deodorized world where some smells are found offensive.[360] The distinction between the open market with its smells of fish, fruit, meat, and piles of rotten vegetables and the odorless supermarket with its packaged fruits, vegetables, and meat, where even fresh fish has no smell, is made everywhere. In the Global South, tourists are warned that if the local market makes for great pictures, beware of the smell of the durian fruit or any other smell that assaults the Western nose, of fresh and dry fish, of raw meat, and certainly do not buy fruit there. Rather, go to the supermarket, whose brands (U.S., French, British) are familiar. On the other hand, smells have been a source for marketing perfumes, deodorants, creams, and home or office ambiance smells. Olfactive branding is a new field based on neuroscience research on the link between smell and emotions, which has expanded the field of fabricated smells in a search for authenticity in fashion (the "authentic" smell of cotton or wool, for instance). Dawn Goldworm, cofounder and nose, or scent, director of the olfactive branding company 12.29, "uses the 'visceral language of scent to transform brand-building' in the actual buildings where clients reside (mostly through ventilation systems or standalone units)."[361] Goldworm designed Nike's signature scent, which she explains in a video "was inspired by, among other things, the smell of a rubber basketball sneaker as it scrapes across the court and a soccer cleat in grass and dirt." She says her goal is to create "immediate and memorable connections between brands and consumers."[362] What this shows goes beyond perfumes and the ways people in different cultures like or dislike certain smells; it points to a manufactured world of scent.

The distinction between smells (odorless/foul) has had concrete consequences on the *elemental* by hindering access to water, by justifying massacres and murder, by denying public health, by segregated housing, and by considering the needs of women of color to be *trivial*. The notion of cleanliness of white bourgeois bodies and the cleanliness of their cities and of the planet they wish to inhabit must be analyzed along the axis of Global North and Global South, but also by looking at the ideology that ascribed cleaning that which is dirty to certain groups of people.[363]

Wasting and Protecting under Racial Capitalism

Waste has become the measure of the potency of racial capitalism. The effort to "green" waste or hide the fact that it is colonizing the planet is essential to its regime. This strategy of dissimulation harks back to colonial time and its division between clean bodies and societies (white) and unclean ones (Black and Brown) to the reduction of bodies to a vital force that must be extracted as fast as possible and then discarded. Since racial capitalism has become hegemonic and concern about climate disaster entered the public conversation, cleaning has become *cleaning up* the excess of waste that neoliberalism overproduces. "Green capitalism" was then presented as a solution to disaster capitalism, and research centers, corporations, and universities opened programs on "sustainable disaster," preparedness, response and mitigation, and sustainable recovery.[364] The latter concerns environmental catastrophe and its management, and there is a growing body of academic, governmental, and corporate literature that discusses what to do with waste, advocating a "green" cleaning up industry as well as international institutions, foundations, and governments with their own experts, engineers, and technicians. In the words of World Bank urban development specialists Sameh Wahba and Silpa Kaza, a good management of waste will be "leaving no one behind," because "when properly supported and organized, informal recycling can create employment, improve local industrial competitiveness, reduce poverty and reduce municipal spending."[365]

International organizations and private foundations of billionaires find in environmentalism as dispossession a reason to claim the greening of a region. For example, in 2011, in Uganda, 22,000 farmers were evicted for the UK-based New Forests Company (NFC) plans.[366] The company had planted and harvested timber on tree plantations in Uganda, Tanzania, Rwanda, and Mozambique, claiming that the timber produced satisfied all the population's needs and would prevent logging in natural forests. But the reason that pine is "favored by carbon farmers is that it grows quickly," meaning that the "native trees which held up well during the cyclone, live for longer therefore sequestering carbon for longer, and encourage biodiversity" are deprioritized.[367] Further, studies have shown that "pine trees are one of the biggest contributors to air pollution. They give off gases that react with airborne chemicals—many of which are produced by human activity—creating tiny, invisible particles that muddy the air."[368] In other words, they contribute to what I will be calling *unbreathing*: the organized pollution of air because capitalists know they contaminate the air people breath.

In Brazil, the Guaraquecaba Climate Action Project, bankrolled by Chevron, General Motors, and American Electric Power, restricts and discriminates the communities' traditional ways of life, locking the Guarani people away from their own forest. To do so, and to intimidate local communities into submission, it employs armed guards, the environmental police of the state of Paraná, known as the Força Verde (the Green Force).[369] Força Verde officers have forcibly entered and searched private homes without due authorization. A local community member reports:

They wanted us to collaborate with them, and we agreed to collaborate . . . but then they started sending the guards in. Around three days went by and they started to send the guards to my house. They came in saying that I had hidden things there, it was completely wrong, if the door was closed they would come in anyway. They would bang on the door and say they had a court order, they didn't care about anything, they would just come right in. . . . The Força Verde came into our house numerous times, not once or twice, many times. . . . If there was any kind of weapon in the house, they would grab it and take it with them. . . . You couldn't even have a knife, they would take it away, they wanted everything. . . . They never showed us anything, they just turned up and came right into the house.[370]

This is environmentalism as dispossession, what the Indigenous Environmental Network calls "carbon colonialism." Arms trading, dictatorships, and murder are environmental politics.[371] But as we already saw in the discussion on industrial cleaning-up, corporations not only know how to avoid responsibility, but even turn environmentalism against environmental activists or victimized communities.

Take the Bhopal example. On December 3, 1984, more than 40 tons of methyl isocyanate gas leaked from a pesticide plant in Bhopal, India, owned by an Indian subsidiary of the U.S.-based Union Carbide Corporation (now Dow

Chemical), immediately killing at least 3,800 people and causing significant morbidity and premature death for many thousands more. It was the worst industrial accident in history. Union Carbide immediately tried to dissociate itself from legal responsibility and finally accepted to pay "$470 million in compensation, a relatively small amount based on significant underestimations of the long-term health consequences of exposure and the number of people exposed."[372] Tens of thousands more people have died since. Thirty-nine years later, a 2023 study has found "that the impacts of that horrific accident span generations. Researchers show that the disaster has burdened people who were born in the year after the accident with cancer, disabilities and poverty."[373] Again, this is a slow violence that is also systemic, racial, structural. In 2003, William Stavropoulos, CEO of Dow—who has, recall, "no responsibility to the chemically maimed of Bhopal—said in a press release, 'Being environmentally responsible makes good business sense.' "[374]

The geopolitics of clean/dirty draws a line between areas of dirtiness—characterized by disease, "unsustainable" birth rates, violence against women, crime, and gangs—and areas of cleanliness, which are heavily policed and where children can safely play, women can walk freely at night, and streets are occasionally closed to traffic to allow shopping, dining, and other leisure activities. The clean/dirty division is connected to the militarization and gentrification of cities, with poor people of color blamed for their innate dirtiness and driven out of their neighborhoods in order to make the city "clean." The economy and geography of dumping-recycling of waste is clearly racial, from Western countries to the Global South. The most important global recycling market has settled in Asia.[375] Most of the sites are in Africa, Asia, and South America/the Caribbean, with two in the margins of Europe (the biggest one is in Belgrade, Serbia).

In data on waste dumpsites from the mid-2010s, featured in the top 50 were the Jam Chakro in Pakistan (extending over 202 hectares, it is one of the largest dumpsites in the world), three in the Gaza strip alone, and six in Nigeria, with Agbogbloshie in Accra receiving 192,000 tons of e-waste annually.[376] It is easy to observe that all are in poor neighborhoods in the Global South or in a territory occupied by a colonial state. By dumping trash on poor, colonized, and non-white people and in countries of the Global South, racial capitalism continues to trace the border between clean and unclean that slavery and colonialism produced. If it were not for the dumping of e-waste and fast fashion waste in the Global South or for shipbreaking in Bangladesh where more than 100 out of 700 ships are scrapped each year,[377] or for the dumping of tons of waste by the State of Israel in in the occupied territories of Palestine, the postcards of clean beaches, romantic streets, or glamorous neighborhoods in which to enjoy a stroll or a nice dinner would not be possible. Trash does not disappear, it is "managed" or "dumped" somewhere far from bourgeois living spaces. Racial capitalism suffocates the planet with its waste, which can never be totally discarded, despite the industry of waste management and the work of millions of people involved in the informal waste recycling and cleaning, 80 percent of whom are waste pickers.[378] These workers, who tend to be seen with contempt or pity, demand better pay and working conditions. One percent of the urban population in developing countries makes their primary household income through informal sector waste management activities, and in Latin America alone, 4–5 million waste pickers earn their livelihood by being a part of the global recyclables supply chain.[379]

Recycling rates in Argentina are at 11 percent of the total waste stream, with 95 percent of this material recovered by the informal sector. The latter are specialists of waste, and if their work is dangerous for their health, neither pity nor disgust is helpful. They demand dignity and respect and fight against the privatization of working in dumping sites. Indeed, private companies, suddenly aware of the potential benefits they can gain from transforming recycling into a business, are using the arguments of protection and amelioration of the living conditions of pickers to appropriate cleaning and recycling.

The effort of greening waste or hiding the fact that it is colonizing the planet is essential to its the regime of racial capitalism. This strategy of dissimulation harks back to colonial time, and its division between clean bodies and societies (white) and unclean ones (Black and Brown) to the reduction of bodies to a vital force that must be extracted as fast as possible and then discarded.

In *Is Racism an Environment Threat?*, anthropologist Ghassan Hage makes the link between racism, particularly Islamophobia, and Western anxiety about the environment.[380] His argument that "the racial crisis manifested by Islamophobia and the ecological crisis not only happen to have an effect on each other; they are in effect one and the same crisis, a crisis in the dominant mode of inhabiting the world that both racial and ecological domination reproduces" expands the literature on environmental racism.[381] Speaking about waste management, he addresses the way in which the vocabulary used to speak about refugees is comparable to the one used to speak about nonrecyclable waste. "Rubbish and waste," he writes, are "an inevitable leftover of the process of colonization that one has to live with and manage but that one can do without. In a way, the racialization of the Arabs as 'waste' prefigures the current forms of neoliberal racialization where the uselessness of the racialized to the racist displaces the earlier racism where the figure of the useful laborer or slave dominated."[382] By imagining Arabs into "ungovernable waste," he writes, "Islamophobia points us most clearly to the ecological cri-sis as it is experienced today. For what is the ecological crisis if not a crisis of ungovernable waste, whether in the form of plastic in the oceans, toxic chem-icals in the rivers and the soil, or greenhouse gases in the atmosphere?"[383]

To Hage, by inventing waste as ungovernable, thus threatening and deadly, "the civilized space of legality and democracy is dependent on the racist colonial space of unregulated accumulation for its existence, suste-nance, and regeneration."[384] Hage argues that "the colonial and the ecological crises generate similar affective tendencies associated with a sense of loss of control and sovereignty, point to them sharing more than just an objectivist 'logic of capitalist exploitation.' "[385] The sense of loss of control that the climate crisis induces, what psychologists have called "eco-anxiety," thus creates sim-ilar affective tendencies that capitalist exploitation alone cannot explain.

The Pleasure of Water

"The people's history of bathing is one of shared space. Histories and prac-tices of the bath belong to histories and practices of the commons. Bathing routines are cultural rituals, architectural forms, and natural environments combined to make arts of living out of everyday necessity. The aquatic land-scapes that make us want to jump into and splash about in—rivers, pools, waterfalls, springs, and sea—are where we have always washed and where we might like to immerse ourselves each day if we could," architect and urban interventionist Christie Pearson writes.[386] We live with and in water. The Earth is a watery place (about 71 percent of the Earth's surface is water covered, and the oceans hold about 96.5 percent of all Earth's water).[387] Water is indispen-sable to live and wash and breathe. It washes the newborn and the dead, is offered to goddesses and gods, and is present in cooking and cultivating, for enjoyment and pleasure. Babies have a high percentage of water in their bod-ies, which decreases with age, and up to 60 percent of the human adult body is water.[388]

Water was a central element of beauty in the gardens of Mexico, Granada, or Baghdad. The sound and the sight of water were said to soothe and facili-tate reverie; peoples invented architecture on water, organized a maritime nomad life, learned to fish, navigate, and play in water. Baths in Arab, Roman, and Asian cultures were sites of social life. European travelers and historians, arriving with set racial ideas about cleaning in non-European countries, have described their astonishment when they saw the sophisticated architecture around water, the care taken in cleaning the body and the environment, and bathing in steam or in water. As bathing in steam was "a common practice throughout the Mediterranean world, Scandinavia, and Eastern Europe," it was seen as an element of European culture, whereas, for instance, it "was also the principal form of bath for the people of Mexico before and after conquest, all the way up to the nineteenth century. This Mesoamerican steambath—the *temazcal*—was called a *baño* or 'bath' throughout the colonial and national periods, and the bathhouses, or *baños*, of Mexico would usually include tubs for immersion as well as a *temazcal*."[389] In 1449, "Nezahualcóyotl, the ruler of Texcoco who was allied with Moctezuma Ilhuicamina, the ruler of Tenochtitlán, designed and built an enormous earthen levee across the entire lake, protecting the city as well as the rich agricultural lands and the fresh waters of the western shore from the salty waters that surged into the eastern end of the lake."[390]

Water was used in rituals and in spiritual practices among Indigenous and enslaved Black communities. Bathing in water has been seen as an act of purification from humiliation and violence. Iya Osundara Ogunsina, a priestess, explains how Blacks practice spiritual bathing: "People are into cleansing their homes, smoking out their homes with sage, palo santo, and incense."[391] Baptism, not only in Christian rituals, is done in water. The classical African American spiritual "Wade in Water" is "enmeshed with multiple subtle references to water as a cleansing and liberating space, not just biblically, but as a cue for slaves to communicate with each other as they sought an escape to freedom."[392] Water in the Black tradition "expresses spiritual decontamination, salvation, self-care, and survival. It is the ultimate life force that compels consistent acknowledgment and consumption, both internally and externally. Hygiene has been intertwined with Black traditions even in the direst of circumstances, and that anchored reverence is a genetic imprint that no pop culture trend can divorce us from."[393] Among Indigenous peoples, relations to water and cleaning vary according to context, but they are also founded on a spiritual relation to cleaning in water.

The Enclosure of Water

The hydrologic cycle that has brought water to Earth is threatened by the warming of temperatures, a consequence of climate catastrophe. The lack of water—no water at all, not enough water, or contaminated polluted water—is structural. Water is a colonial tool to discipline and punish, it is capitalized, it serves in diplomatic or economic bargains. Making cleanliness into a tool of racial and gendered domination is linked to the organization of lack of water or of polluted water. The production and existence of water, which did not need humans' intervention to exist, have been affected by racial capitalism and imperialist armies.

About the latter, it is worth knowing that imperialist armies devised a politics of water to serve their needs as early as 1920. Charles H. Lee, a captain in the 26th Engineers Water Supply in the U.S. Army, remarked on "the important relation water supply bears to the successful execution of military operations,"[394] which need several million gallons of water per day. He was just following in the military tradition of appropriating water. After carefully examining the sources of water available to satisfy the needs of the U.S. armies in France during World War I, Lee concluded that hydrology played a central role in the success of military operations. And indeed, it does. The privatization and weaponization of water are as old as war: protecting sources of water, carrying water, depriving populations of water, poisoning or contaminating wells and sources of water to subdue the enemies or the civil populations. In the USA, from 2001 to 2020, market opportunities engineered by the occupation of Afghanistan and federal contracts for weapons grew by $119 billion. "Military hegemony also aids in securing profitable markets through the installation of compliant political regimes. Capitalist Elon Musk alluded to this fact in July 2020 when he proclaimed on Twitter, 'We will coup whoever we want! Deal with it.' "[395] Could we then look at the military strategy of scorched earth that is intent to leave nothing behind but the deliberate and widespread destruction of resources, as what imperialist wars do?[396]

"War is a racist enterprise," activist and political analyst Danny Haiphong has written.[397] He adds that "as the market for private military contractors has grown, so too have profits for Wall Street investors. Fossil fuel corporations supply one of the largest polluters in the world, the U.S. military, with the crude energy necessary to facilitate its endless expansion. Oil shares frequently rise with each prospect for war."[398] Haiphong notes that "the truth is that the U.S.'s wars at home and its wars abroad cannot be viewed as separate entities. Military contractors are cashing in on weapons transfers to local police departments based upon a litany of racist justifications for the mass incarceration state to terrorize Black Americans. They also benefit from the erection of a deportation machine that labels undocumented people 'illegal' for the sake of 'border control.' "[399]

The enclosure of water has led to death. A 2006 United Nations Human Development Report stated that "on average, a child dies from a water-related disease every 15 seconds in the Global South. Unsafe drinking water and poor sanitation are leading causes of death in the Global South for children under age 5."[400] Close to half of all people living in the Global South suffer from a health problem related to water and sanitation deficits. Trachoma—which threatens 400 million individuals with blindness and is prevalent in children—is a direct result of living in dry, dusty, water-scarce environments where sanitation is lacking, according to the WHO.[401] According to a 2010 UNEP/Pacific Institute report, "every year, more people die from the consequences of unsafe water than from all forms of violence, including war. And, every year, water contamination of natural ecosystems affects humans directly by destroying fisheries or causing other impacts on biodiversity that affect food production"; we can assume that things have gotten worse since.[402] Two-thirds of the world's population may face water shortages in 2025, and we know that this two-thirds will primarily be in the Global South or among poor and racialized communities in the North.[403] Already some 1.1 billion people worldwide lack access to water, and a total of 2.7 billion find water scarce for at least one month of the year. Inadequate sanitation is also a problem for 2.4 billion people, who are then exposed to diseases, such as cholera and typhoid fever, and other water-borne illnesses.[404] Two million people, mostly children in the Global South, die each year from diarrheal diseases alone, which can be easily avoided with access to clean freshwater. According to the WHO, "unsafe or inadequate water, sanitation, and hygiene cause approximately 3.1 percent of all deaths—over 1.7 million deaths annually—and 3.7 percent of DALYs (disability adjusted life years) worldwide."[405] Scientists even showed in 2023 that "gravitational surveys have measured the depletion of underground reservoirs, which is caused in large part by irrigation, especially in northwestern India and western North America. These surveys show that groundwater pumping shifted enough mass into the oceans to cause 6.24 millimetres of global sea-level rise between 1993 and 2010," which led to a "substantial impact on the Earth's rotation axis."[406] It was not caused, as many articles said,[407] by "humans" but by the insatiable thirst for water by agribusiness growing water-dependent crops despite near-desert conditions[408]—in occupied Palestine, northwestern India, or in the western United States (for instance, with Saudi alfalfa farms expanding into the Arizona Sonoran Desert).[409]

The vocabulary of these reports carefully masks the responsibility of ideologies and of political choices by using "human activities" to denounce the facts that "metals, such as arsenic, zinc, copper, and selenium, are naturally found in many different waters. Some human activities like mining, industry, and agriculture can lead to an increase in the mobilization of these trace metals out of soils or waste products into fresh waters. Even at extremely low concentrations, such additional materials can be toxic to aquatic organisms or can impair reproductive and other functions."[410] These "activities" are not "human," they are dictated by colonialism, imperialism, and capitalism. Crops such as corn, rice, cotton, or sugarcane; the garments and textile industry; meat production; the beverage industry; automotive manufacturing;[411] and militaries the world over all need a lot of water. The privatization of water, leading to higher cost of water, and the monopoly over sources of water by a dozen corporations in the world[412] belie the principle of universal access to water. The accumulation of such data may have a numbing effect. What can be done against so many assaults on the bodies and minds, on the mental and physical health of billions of racialized people? Where to start?

Water has been made scarce by structural racism, and that scarcity is manipulated to restrict even more access to water. It is expropriated to wash the streets of wealthy neighborhoods; make their trees, lawns, and flowers grow and flourish; fill up their swimming pools; allow for showers three times a day; answer to the avidity of the agribusiness, fashion, chemical, building industries. The racial distribution of water impacts peoples living under the regime of fabricated scarcity. Water scarcity takes a greater toll on women and children because they are often the ones responsible for collecting it. When water is farther away, it requires more time to collect, which often means less time at school.

In *Caliban and the Witch: Women, the Body and Primitive Accumulation*, Federici mapped the connections between the forms of enclosure that occurred with the birth of capitalism and the destruction of the commons. She looked at the multiple attacks launched by capitalism on the vulnerable, the poor, on women exercising healing practices, on midwives curing people with herbs or charms, on mutual aid and on popular powers.[413] More recently, looking at the "new enclosures" at the heart of the present phase of global capitalist accumulation from a feminist perspective, Federici centered on women and "reproductive work as crucial to both our economic survival and the construction of a world free from the hierarchies and divisions capital has planted in the body of the world proletariat."[414] The commons, she said, should not be understood as happy islands in a sea of exploitative relations but rather as autonomous spaces from which to challenge the existing capitalist organization of life and labor. The commons (light, air) were neither public nor private land or goods, they could not be "owned by particular groups or individual and were enjoyed by all."[415] As politician and politics scholar Derek Wall has written, prior to the period of European colonialism, "commons were the rule rather than the exception across much of our planet." Wall notes that although "commons were never pure," the "global assault on the commons did real damage to formerly communal peoples, and such attacks on indigenous people and commons continue in the twenty-first century."[416]

Weaponizing Water

Capitalism needs water to run its economy, and the military, an institution vital to its protection, consumes a lot of water and will do anything to keep its privileged access to that resource. There is a long history of water management to serve the interests of the colonial extraction economy, racial capitalism, and neoliberal economies. From the canals built to bring water to the sugar plantations' mills, to white enclaves, to the Industrial Revolution came the pollution of rivers and the diverting of water. Armies have been known to poison water or bomb dams. In the 20th century, diverting rivers and building dams to bring water to large irrigation projects for different industries and agribusiness, and increased use of pesticides, became a requirement.

Let me refer to some of the numerous criminal projects around water. Colonial states, empires, and armies have threatened to flood a city or a valley, to poison wells and rivers, to hinder access to water. The Water Conflict Chronology dates the oldest example in 2500 BCE, when Urlama, King of Lagash (from 2450 to 2400 BCE), in Mesopotamia, diverted water from this region to boundary canals, drying up boundary ditches to deprive Umma of water. But weaponizing water does not belong only to old empires or to Biblical times. Western colonial civilizing missions did not hesitate to poison wells or deprive populations of water. In 1904, as German colonial troops brutally suppressed a rebellion by the Herero people of German South West Africa (modern-day Namibia), General Lothar von Trotha pledged to exterminate the Herero people. Germans drove the populations into the Namib Desert, which led to massive death from dehydration and starvation; they also reportedly poisoned desert water wells. Seventy percent of the Herero population was killed in what became known as the Herero and Namaqua Genocide. In the 1960s, the U.S. Army bombed irrigation water supply systems in North Vietnam. An estimated 661 sections of dikes were damaged or destroyed; and between 1967 and 1972, its "Operation Popeye" used silver iodide for cloud seeding over Vietnam, hoping to provoke floods. In Mozambique in 1976, the apartheid Rhodesian government dropped bacteriological agents in groundwater. And, as I will come to in more detail, the State of Israel systematically deprives Palestinians of water or pollutes their sources of water.[417]

Under colonialism, the appropriation of water went hand in hand with land theft. In India, for instance, where an irrigation network was well developed, the British interest in water resources in the Indus Basin "was closely related with plans for large-scale agriculture production in the sub-continent which subsequently would boost the British Empire," and "preference was given to the reclamation of large barren and unoccupied wastelands and transforming them into productive land. There were well-developed canal command areas or colonies, which cultivated a variety of crops, such as cotton, rice, wheat, barley, sugarcane among others."[418] It is important to notice the long afterlife of this colonial policy when the British Raj turned "representative chiefs into unrepresentative aristocrats, granting them magisterial powers, a paramilitary apparatus and immense landed estates (*jagirs*) on newly irrigated land," siphoning "off rents, land revenues, and export cash cops like indigo, opium and cotton, all at the expense of previously pastoral tribesmen now forced to settle and toil as local farmers."[419] Large estates, monoculture, and exploitation no longer protected the land from the worst of floods or droughts.

Contaminating water does not occur only in the Global South; the Love Canal case in the 1950s United States shows how inhabitants of the same polluted water site were treated differently along racial lines. Looking at the role of racism offered a "wider perspective, emphasizing how gender, race, and class shaped the environmental movement.[420] The Love Canal was originally planned as a community settlement powered by a canal connecting the Niagara River with Niagara Falls.[421] Only one mile of the canal had been dug when the project came to a halt due to lack of funding. The site was sold to Hooker Chemical Company, which, from 1942 to 1953, with government sanction, used the partially dug canal as a chemical waste dump. Public awareness of the disaster unfolded in the late 1970s when investigative newspaper coverage and grassroots door-to-door health surveys began to reveal a series of inexplicable illnesses—epilepsy, asthma, migraines, and nephrosis—and abnormally high rates of birth defects and miscarriages in the Love Canal neighborhood. Wet winters in the late 1970s raised the water table and caused the chemicals to leach into the basements and yards of neighborhood residents, as well as into the playground of the elementary school built directly over the canal.[422]

Race played a role in how the damages were assessed. Those living in the "projects"—the racialized poor neighborhoods called Griffin Manor— were ignored in the allocation of damages. As a 63-year-old Black grandmother said in response to the lack of attention that low-income renters had received: "Mostly black people live in these projects, what do they care? Kill them all (laugh)."[423] White workers created the Homeowners' Association, with membership based on home ownership because many were owners of their homes, while many Black residents living in Griffin Manor were renters. Finally, white owners receive compensation or moved away; Black people stayed and did not receive the same amount of compensation. When the scandal erupted, Hooker Chemical and Plastics Corporation sold the territory to the municipality of Niagara Falls, arguing that their contract absolved them of all responsibility. The canal was backfilled with earth, and a new Niagara Falls neighborhood was built on it. If the Love Canal scandal brought awareness to contamination, structural racism maintained the division between the uncontaminated and the polluted, as we saw in 2016 with the lead seepage into the drinking water of Black communities in Flint, Michigan.[424]

In the Global South, the Green Revolution—the 20th-century agricultural project initiated by the USA that utilized plant genetics, modern irrigation systems, and chemical fertilizers and pesticides in the name of increasing food production and reducing poverty and hunger—began in Mexico, then reached India, Pakistan, China, the Philippines, and farther.[425] It led to increased water consumption, soil degradation, and chemical runoff that did significant environmental damage; simultaneously, fertilizers and pesticides polluted air and water. The Green Revolution had harmful consequences on agriculture and human health. In India, for instance, the increase in the use of pesticides led to a "large amount of water pollution and damage to the soil. Another major issue is the pest attack, which arises due to an imbalance in the pests." It added to the problems brought by the canal systems and by the "irrigation pumps that sucked out water from the groundwater table to supply the water-intensive crops, such as sugarcane and rice."[426] Since it was led by scientists and engineers trained in the West, or applied by foundations or NGOs linked to the West, the Green Revolution dismissed Indigenous knowledge and crops.[427] In the 1990s, "under the patronage of the international financial institutions and certain governments of the North, the big multinational groups of the sector managed to gain control of the water services in many cities of the world, particularly in the Global South."[428] This was when a major global offensive in favor of the privatization of water services and sanitation, which ended up benefiting large multinational corporations, was orchestrated by international financial institutions such as the World Bank and International Monetary Fund. But, as journalist Olivier Petitjean has remarked, "it was also supported with great enthusiasm by the governments of the countries where these multinational groups originated (first and foremost by France) as well as by the European Union."[429] The promises of corporations proved to be misleading, leading to increased costs of access to freshwater, corruption, and mismanagement in the cities of the Global South and the Global North.[430] Large and modern irrigation projects obstruct access to water for people of color and Indigenous people. One example is the Majes Project, a large-scale irrigation system in Peru that "aimed in its first stage to turn 22,000 ha of arid lands of the Majes desert into a highly modern and profitable agriculture oriented towards growing commercial export crops."[431] Juana

Vera Delgado and Margreet Zwarteveen, in their detailed study of Indigenous resistance to the project, show how what was considered "a key element of the modernization of the Arequipa region in Peru," which "included the resettlement of people, development of roads, generation of electricity and reform of land tenure systems," was "carried out by centrally financed bureaucratic institutions, highly dependent on international funds."[432] The colonial ideology that had seen Indigenous water systems as "'anomalous', 'abnormal' and even 'unnatural'" persisted among "those who propagate modern 'universal' models of water management."[433] Globally, existing ways of managing and using water have not been "seen and judged on their own merits and terms but are evaluated against the universal and ideal model."[434]

Management of water under racial capitalism is like neoliberal *cleaning up*: it does not listen to communities' needs; it looks at numbers, computer tables, and profits. In *A Vital Frontier: Water Insurgencies in Europe*, anthropologist Andrea Muehlebach retraces the history of a "Global Water" structure[435] whose objective was to facilitate the creation of water markets where investors could insert "the logic of private property and profit 'into the heart of a public infrastructure.'"[436] The "number of people globally served by privatized water companies" thus grew "from 335 million in 2000 to 1.1 billion in 2015."[437] The water insurgencies in Italy or France, she then described, oppose the "possessive individualism so central to capitalist modernity."[438] We might look to Bernard Barraqué's genealogy of "water management."[439] His three-step approach on the development of the water industry goes like this: (1) in the 19th century, a quantitative water management based on civil engineering; (2) from the end of the 19th to the beginning of the 20th century, a qualitative management based on sanitary engineering and local institutions; and (3) since the end of the 20th century, a heritage management with an environmentally engineered approach.[440] This approach includes neither colonial or imperialist policies, nor Indigenous programs of water in the non-West (in India, Cambodia, or China, for instance), nor movements in the Global North that oppose the privatization of water commons.

A decolonial antiracist feminist and abolitionist critique studies how access to water, as *elemental*, is privatized, racialized, and gendered. By doing this, it anchors environmental politics in the experience of Black, Indigenous, and Brown peoples. If their needs for water were fulfilled, then it would mean that clean water has been communized. Water scarcity limits access to safe water for drinking and for practicing basic hygiene at home, in schools, and in healthcare facilities. When water is scarce, sewage systems can fail, and the threat of contracting diseases such as cholera surges. Scarce water also becomes more expensive. Water is at the core of national and global policies but as long as we do not attack racial capitalism, racial and gender inequities will continue.

Discourses and policies that rest on data and call for a universal right to water use the vocabulary of "humanity" and "humans" as a single category. As Jamaican novelist and philosopher Sylvia Wynter has warned us, the "human" was reconceptualized in relation to concepts of Blackness and modernity. She explains that "the word 'native' really means the European is 'generically human' and its 'natives,' 'others.' "[441] And she adds: "If we are the bearers of 'human otherness,' it means that the world of the human remains subordinated to the world of 'Man.' We are going to have to struggle for an entirely new definition of what it is to be human. The West has 'unified' the world, but it has 'unified' the world increasingly under one, what I call the 'ethno-class' or Western bourgeois conception of what it is to be good man and woman of one's kind."[442] Or, to say it more bluntly: "Do you realize what is happening? YOU HAVE '*PEOPLE*,' WHO ARE THE 'REAL' HUMANS!"[443] Historically, the distribution of water has been geared toward the satisfaction of "real humans." Reports on "humans" and humanity" continue to maintain the division Wynter analyzed.

Around the world, communities have adopted the dual strategy of resistance practices that Delgado and Zwarteveen have observed among Andean Indigenous communities "to obtain legitimacy as citizens and water-right holders." On the one hand, they affirm their "own culture, language and traditions to demonstrate their own 'otherness' "; on the other, they "pragmatically and strategically appropriate and borrow elements of these same hegemonic discourses and insert those into their own modes of thinking and doing to construct a dynamic alternative to modernity and development."[444]

In 2023, the population of Guadeloupe, whose native name is Kerujéra, "the island of beautiful waters," had lived for thirty years with water cutbacks. An obsolete network, its poor maintenance, and a poor water quality have demonstrated the persisting colonial domination on water. Furthermore, domestic tap water has been unfit for consumption due to chlordecone contamination. Under ministerial dispensation, chlordecone, a pesticide that was banned in France in 1990, continued to be authorized until 1993 for use in the banana plantations in Martinique and Guadeloupe owned by descendants of slave plantation owners. It has caused significant and long-lasting pollution on both islands. Over 90 percent of the adult population is contaminated by chlordecone, according to Santé publique France, and the population has one of the highest rates of prostate cancer in the world.[445] The French state made exceptions to the law forbidding the use of chlordecone to "satisfy the voracity and financial appetites of the descendants of slavers, who unfortunately found accomplices in the political class in Martinique," Garcin Malsa said.[446] Malsa, the former mayor of the town of Sainte-Anne in Martinique and the former president of a local ecological association, Assaupamar (Association pour la sauvegarde du patrimoine martiniquais), founded the first Martinican ecologist party, Modemas.[447] To Caribbean scholar Malcom Ferdinand, not only "As [*sic*] no viable decontamination method has yet been found, this molecule is likely to remain in the soil for many generations to come," but also "extending to all the ecosystems of these islands, this pollution is widespread. All of Martinique's water sources and 80% of Guadeloupe's are located in contaminated areas."[448] As early as 2006, the associations SOS environnement Guadeloupe, Union régionale des consommateurs, Agriculture-santé-société-environnement, and Union des producteurs agricoles de la Guadeloupe filed a complaint against X (X in French law is when the author of the damage or crime cannot be identified), so that those responsible for the chlordecone pollution affecting Guadeloupe's soils and food chain might be "identified and punished."[449]

After sixteen years of investigation, on January 2, 2023, a French tribunal dismissed the chlordecone scandal and ruled out any criminal liability of the state and plantation owners, while young activists who had protested against the chlordecone scandal were quickly indicted and tried.[450] To Ferdinand, the chlordecone poisoning was a case of ecocide, the crime characterized as " 'an extensive damage or destruction which would have for consequence a severe alteration of the global commons or the Earth's ecological system'—upon which rely all living beings in general and humankind in particular—and in compliance with the known planetary boundaries."[451] The "economy of the French West Indies is largely agricultural. But this agriculture is still structured by a colonial logic. From the outset, these colonies were conceived as 'gardens' to be exploited by Western players, with no regard for the land or its inhabitants, to supply their own markets with exotic food products, bananas in particular. This is what I call colonial living [*l'habiter colonial*]," Malcom Ferdinand said.[452] A month after the criminal case of chlordecone contamination had been dismissed, five Guadeloupeans took legal action in the Pointe-à-Pitre court against the private and public players responsible for water distribution in Guadeloupe. The plaintiffs claimed that the restricted access to water and sanitation on the island, as well as the contamination of water by chlordecone, penalize and endanger the population. The contamination of water and the fabricated water scarcity also mean that water corporations are making a lot of profit, as Guadeloupeans must buy over fifty million plastic bottles a year.[453] Finally, after decades of fighting by the peoples of Martinique and Guadeloupe, in March 2024, the French National Assembly unanimously voted a proposition for a law that establishes the responsibility of the French state in the Chlordecone pollution and establishes compensation for its victims.[454]

The French colonial mode of living can be found in all French "overseas territories" (*outre-mer*), the territories of the former colonial empire (slavery and post-slavery) that are not independent and remain under French law.[455] Let's look at Mayotte, an island of the Comoros archipelago in the Indian Ocean with a Black and Muslim population. The French state, with the complicity of a local pro-France elite (the leader of the far-right party National Rally, Marine Le Pen, is always received with flowers and grandeur), separated it from the Republic of the Comoros in 1974, making it a French department.[456] The French State has economic and geopolitical interests; there is a Foreign Legion that has had a base there since the 1970s; gas has been found, so French companies are interested in Mayotte as a site of extraction;[457] the island is in the Mozambique Canal, where oil tankers pass through; and it serves as a military base for French interventions in the region. As protests against the pension reform mobilized people in France in May and June of 2023, the French state was preparing a vast campaign of expulsion of "illegal" tenants and the destruction of houses in a context of a months-long lack of water. Freshwater is now flown by planes from Reunion and Mauritius, but it's sold at a price few people can afford. On June 12, 2023, the authorities decided to cut off the water supply four times a week, from 5 p.m. to 7 a.m., and declared that this frequency could rise to five, then six, weekly cuts.[458] Local elected representatives blamed the water crisis upon a lack of maintenance of the water system and on migrants;[459] the government blames it on an exceptional drought. But rather than an exceptional drought, the pollution of rivers, accelerated deforestation (Mayotte is the most deforested French department), neocolonialism, and racism explain the situation of dispossession and racial politics on the island.

On September 2, 2023, the French minister of the *outre-mer* announced proudly that every "vulnerable" person (he cited pregnant women and babies) would receive two bottles of water per day, while others would have access to water every third day.[460] The declaration was flabbergasting and cynical. How will two bottles of water satisfy the daily needs of a pregnant woman to wash herself and the children she may have, to prepare her food, wash her clothes? Who calculated the amount? Upon what facts did the expert who declared that two bottles were enough base their decision? What about women and girls who are menstruating? What about the toilets? Toilets in schools are already closed, which means that children cannot relieve themselves all day long; by the end of September 2023, many schools had to close because they could not deliver water to the children, and analyses revealed noncompliant water quality, deemed unfit for consumption.[461] It is certain that none of the whites who make these decisions have ever experienced what it is to have only two bottles of water in the heat. Furthermore, to attribute the crisis to exceptional weather and to practice magical thinking by affirming that rains will come and save the situation reveals the chosen heedlessness of French state administrators. Not a word about the structure that has led to a lack of water—the power cuts that made the pumps unable to operate, the "suspected pollution of a raw water catchment," the consequences, according to Mayotte elected officials, of "the State forcing us to transfer, in 2017, millions of euros to a private operator [SMAE] that has shown itself incapable, in five years, of meeting its commitments to increase water production by desalination."[462] And all the reports that draw a link between colonialism and the worsening of the consequences of climate disaster were ignored. The water situation in Mayotte is exemplary of the ways in which the *elemental* needs of people of color, especially women (in this case Black, Muslim women), are not only ignored but treated with contempt.

Indeed, armies, either legal or extralegal, work closely with the police to protect the privatization of water, extraction, border control, colonial occupation . . . Economist Claude Serfati has studied how France has become what he has called "l'État radicalisé" (the radicalized state) by making "arms sales and nuclear power the last levers of its industrial policy, to the detriment of sectors otherwise useful to the population. By arrogating national defense issues to themselves, successive presidents have accentuated the authoritarian features of the Fifth Republic, a regime shaped by military coups de force. Today, the French army is present in the streets, on Health Defense Councils, and wherever Total, Bolloré and consorts take their interests around the globe. Freedom-destroying laws follow one another, giving more power to the administration and the police, beyond any democratic control."[463] These remarks can be applied to most states defending neoliberal extraction, racial capitalism, and occupation, since armies and the police are two major protectors of environmental racism's interests and colonization.

Palestine under Colonial Water Politics

Expropriation, dispossession, and restriction of water under colonial occupation and the role of the army in these strategies are well illustrated in Palestine. In June 1967, after Israel occupied the West Bank, including East Jerusalem, and the Gaza Strip, the Israeli military authorities instituted complete power over all water resources and water-related infrastructure in the Occupied Palestinian Territories, introducing sweeping bans and restrictions. In November 1967, Military Order 158 stated that "Palestinians could not construct any new water installation without first obtaining a permit from the Israeli army." Palestinians were forbidden to "drill new water wells, install pumps or deepen existing wells, in addition to being denied access to the Jordan River and fresh water springs. Israel even controls the collection of rain water throughout most of the West Bank, and rainwater harvesting cisterns owned by Palestinian communities are often destroyed by the Israeli army."[464] The Israeli state declared parts of the West Bank "'closed military areas,' which Palestinians may not enter, because they are close to Israeli settlements, close to roads used by Israeli settlers, used for Israeli military training or protected nature reserves."[465] Palestinians were forced to use the new access gained to water sources, especially in the Jordan Valley. Israel "connected all the settlements built in the West Bank, with the exception of the Jordan Valley, to the Israeli water grid."[466] The Water Agreement entrenched Israel's monopoly over water sources and cemented its status as regulator and sole authority for strategic decisions concerning water. "Israelis have access to water on demand, while Palestinians receive water according to predetermined allocations."[467] In 2023, a report stated that "since 2021, Israeli authorities have demolished nearly 160 Palestinian reservoirs, sewage networks and wells across the occupied West Bank and East Jerusalem—claiming they were unauthorised—according to the United Nations humanitarian agency, OCHA."[468] During the first half of 2023, authorities knocked down almost the same number of Palestinian water installations as they did during all of 2022. Defending the demolitions, the Coordination of Government Activities in the Territories (COGAT) said that "the allocation of water for agriculture is performed in accordance with the law."[469] "According to Amnesty International, Palestinians in the occupied West Bank each consume, on average, 73 liters of water a day. Israeli citizens, meanwhile, consume approximately 240 liters of water a day. And, even worse, illegal Israeli settlers consume more than 300 liters per day. The Palestinians' share of the water is not only far below the average consumed by Israelis, but is even below the recommended daily minimum of 100 liters as designated by the World Health Organization."[470] According to another report, "Palestinians say they can barely get enough water to bathe their children and wash their clothes—let alone sustain livestock and grow fruit trees," while "in sharp contrast, neighboring Jewish settlements look like an oasis. Wildflowers burst through the soil. Farmed fish swim in neat rows of ponds. Children splash in community pools."[471]

The Israeli army "has confiscated approximately 1000km^2 of land to create closed military zones, which amounts to more than 20% of the West Bank territory. Excluding the areas that fall between the green line and the segregation barrier, Palestinians are barred entry to all of the military zones which are mainly on the eastern slopes of the Bethlehem and Hebron Governates in the Jordan Valley."[472] The army not only confiscates land for its own purpose and protects the privatization of water and its racialized distribution, but it also contaminates sources of water. Hence, Doctor Mahmoud Sa'ada, former head of the Middle East Division at International Physicians for the Prevention of Nuclear War, gives the example of nuclear facilities in Israel in the contamination of water: "the radiation from the facilities and its waste burial sites is causing increased rates of cancer and birth deformalities [*sic*] in the Palestinian communities of the West Bank." He also notes the "incidence of radiation leakages into the subterranean water systems in both Wadi Araba and the aquifers of the Naqab Desert."[473]

When in March 2023 Itamar Ben Gvir, Israel's national security minister, whose portfolio includes overseeing prisons within the Green Line, ordered "an end to what he calls 'the summer-camp conditions of murderous terrorists,'"[474] nobody was surprised that it meant, among unprecedented measures against all Palestinian prisoners, the limitation of showers to four minutes per person. Furthermore, each prison wing would be curbed to one hour of running water each day (less than one minute per person).[475] Ben Gvir clearly showed how, under colonialism, cleanliness is reserved for the occupiers. His decision is one among many taken in the Israelis' water war against Palestinians.[476] By violating a basic human need, to wash oneself, Ben Gvir was weaponizing the necessity of washing and cleaning oneself. His decisions were simply the borrowing of colonial racial politics that had declared that the colonized were smelly and unclean, in order to legitimize torture and denial of rights. They are also connected to racial colonial representations that seek to confirm the line between clean/civilized: here the green lawns of Israeli streets, the clean beaches of Tel Aviv, a people who "literally made the desert bloom; and over there, deliberately polluted sites.[477]

For years, millions of liters of sewage were discharged into the coast of Gaza every day.[478] Dr. Abdallah al-Kishawi told the Associated Press that in Gaza alone, there has been a 13–14 percent increase every year in the number of patients admitted with kidney problems to Gaza City's Shifa Hospital.[479] Not only is the State of Israel organizing the lack of water, it is forcing the Palestinian Authority to "purchase water from the national Israeli water company, Mekorot, at several times the cost. In total, Palestinians in the West Bank consumed 239 million cubic meters (mcm) of water in 2020, 77.1 of them purchased from Israel and then distributed unequally throughout the West Bank."[480] The State of Israel has "established at least 15 waste treatment facilities in the West Bank to recycle waste largely produced inside Israel," processing "hazardous waste and dangerous substances such as medical waste, solvent waste, oil waste, metals, electronics and batteries, as well as sludge."[481] At the same time, it has "prohibited Palestinian communities from developing essential infrastructure, including waste treatment facilities."[482] The waste dumped in Palestine also arrives "from the illegal Israeli settlements," exacerbating the "already dire situation of these overburdened landfills. Currently, there are over 200 Israeli settlements in the West Bank housing a settler population of more than 620,000."[483]

To Mohammad Shehadeh, Euro-Med Monitor regional manager in Europe, Gaza is a place where "a civilian population caged in a toxic slum from birth to death are forced to witness the slow poisoning of their children and loved ones by the water they drink and likely the soil in which they harvest, endlessly, with no change in sight."[484] The Israelis' war on water against Palestinians (and neighboring countries) knows no limits, and is made even worse by the climate crisis. The European Union has remained passive when confronted with the fact that Israel "has caused destruction worth more than $2 million to EU aid projects in the occupied West Bank over the past five years . . . Israel has 'demolished or seized' almost 560 'structures' within aid projects since 2015. The projects were financed by the EU collectively and by its governments individually. More than 70 of those structures were destroyed or confiscated between January and October [2023], according to the note."[485] Cases abound of organized spoiling of soil and water scarcity caused by colonialism, the army, and the state. The state can thus turn off water or drastically limit its use by prisoners, patients in mental hospitals, or the elderly in hospices, who are no longer given time to shower, adding to humiliation, a loss of self-worth, stress. It affects mental health and punishes communities. Water is a weapon against Palestinians' lives.

Challenging the description of a region as dry, barren, a terra nullius (the term used by colonial powers to describe a land as barren, unoccupied, and uninhabited in order to justify colonization, genocide, and dispossession) contributes to a decolonial narrative. It is important to insist on the fact that no region was barren, that it had lush gardens, snow, wet mountains, oases where water has long nourished a flourishing agriculture, or deserts where life was sustained. "Water scarcity is not so much about how much water there is and more about what it is being used for."[486] Images of water scarcity, of streets full of discarded plastic bags and refuse, make for compelling headlines. The deliberate poisoning of water by the State of Israel and the Israeli army shows that depriving Palestinians of clean water is a racial weapon.[487]

Occupying Armies and Water Contamination

Occupations by armies have a direct effect on water because of their material needs and the daily needs of soldiers, because of their waste, and because of the racist assumptions underlying occupations. The cholera epidemic that broke out in October 2010 in Haiti, six months after the 2010 deadly earthquake—"one of the most deadly in modern times, with 800,000 sick and at least 10,000 dead" (the official death toll)—embodies the politics of the colonial and imperialist enclosure of water that leads to death. Despite the high death rate, the search for the causes took a very long time, bringing to light complicit links between the military, the politics of neglect of a civilian Black population, racist assumptions, and, in this case, adding the obstacles international institutions created to slow if not forbid inquiry in their chain of management.[488] For nearly two months after the outbreak began, the United Nations, the World Health Organization, and the U.S. Centers for Disease Control and Prevention in Haiti refused to investigate the source of the cholera epidemic, arguing it was more important to treat patients than to find the source of the disease.

If it had not been for the relentless pressure of Haitians themselves—who were convinced that there was an explanation other than the lack of sanitation in Haiti and rejected the racist assumption that since it was Haiti (poor, with corrupted elites and neglect of hygiene), an epidemic was not surprising—the source would likely not have been uncovered. They organized protests and finally, in December, UN Secretary-General Ban Ki-moon relented and called for an investigation. The UN had until then refused to consider what Haitians had suggested: that circumstantial evidence implicated UN peacekeepers. The protection of the institution preceded the protection of the Haitians. The hypothesis of the Haitians had to be proven right by a French doctor from Doctors without Borders, Renaud Piarroux—another sign of racism. Piarroux retraced the path of the vibrio taken from the sick in Nepal, where an epidemic was raging at the same time, to the Nepalese peacekeepers' camp in Haiti, where many soldiers were sick, and then to the towns and villages along the river that feeds a water system where thousands of Haitians drink, bathe, and play. Thus, the hypothesis of the Haitians was proved right. It was the discharge of the septic tanks of the camp in the river that was at the origin of the bacteriological epidemic. Despite the proof, the UN refused to apologize and to consider reparations. Haitian life was considered cheap; it did not matter. A river had been wasted, people had died, but saving a reputation and avoiding having to pay for damages were more important. The search for the causes of the cholera epidemic in Haiti showed that it is necessary to discover the cause of lack, of contamination and pollution, before imagining what action could be taken. Finding the source of the cholera epidemic did not contribute to imagining the kind of action that would concretely lead to a politics of the elemental.

Engineering Water and New Forms of Privatization

Water's scarcity is another opportunity for engineering that serves neoliberal racial capitalism. The rush to artificially produce rain and other technologies to provide water (desalinization, for instance) has mobilized engineers, states, and the military. The United Arab Emirates, a petro-monarchy, one of the hottest and driest regions on Earth, has been leading the effort to seed clouds and increase precipitation. It flies planes that release salt flares into the most promising white clouds, hoping to trigger rain.[489] Another technique is to zap clouds with electricity.[490] However, there are questions over whether seeding clouds in one location might take rain away from another location, and over the long-term environmental impacts of silver iodide. China, Iran, the USA, and India are all experimenting with artificial rain. In India, Kondala Murali Mohan, a scientist with Krishi Vigyan Kendra (Medak), who works on such experimentations, said: "The method can lead to acidification of the oceans, ozone layer depletion and an increase in the levels of atmospheric carbon dioxide. Silver is a heavy, toxic metal and it harms the health of plants, humans and animals. Cloud seeding is also a costly method. A foot of rainfall costs around USD 200."[491] According to engineers, "produced water" found in most oil- and gas-bearing rocks will mitigate lack of water. Produced water is the result of the technique of hydraulic fracturing ("fracking"), which brings "frac fluid" or "flowback water" to the surface. Engineering, closely associated with the military and the economy of extraction, offers technological solutions to social and political problems whose formulation neutralizes short- and long-term consequences.[492] Thinking together technology and race, Ruha Benjamin coins the term "the New Jim Code," by which she means "the use of new technologies that reflect and reproduce existing inequalities, but are promoted and perceived as more objective and progressive than the discriminatory systems of a previous era."[493]

The production of contaminated water and air, of racially and socially segregated public and social space, has not stopped. We cannot expect communizing politics of water from the neoliberal authoritarianism whose objectives have been embraced by the state. Sources of water that feed worthless projects (the swimming pools and lawns of the rich, resorts, and so on) or mining, fast fashion, the military, and the chemical, car, nuclear, and agribusiness industries must be cut and reappropriated. Any privatization of water must be resisted. The discourse of "sobriety," advocated by Western governments, puts the burden on people, whereas industries that consume too much water and reject polluted water continue to do as they want. The way in which imperialism, the military, and capitalism talk about the wars on water is a warning. Their war is a war to protect expropriation and extraction, and armies are mobilized to keep water flowing for their interests and those of capitalists. Engineers and scientists are mobilized to find artificial sources of water rather than contributing to stop climate warming, deforestation, mining, and agribusiness. Against this war of attrition that condemns the majority of humanity and other species to death by thirst, wars of liberation of the commons must be organized. If the enemy cannot be underestimated because it knows nothing else but colonization and extraction, then for those fighting the wars of liberation of the commons, it is a question of life and death for the many.

The denunciation of the fabricated triviality of non-white women's *elementary* needs must be connected to the current crisis around water. The analysis of the hindered access to water and its consequences for health and washing reveals a nexus of diverse interests: the long history of wars around water, and the privatization of water and its transformation into a rare and costly commodity; the role of the chemical, cattle, fashion, agriculture industries in the pollution and contamination of water; the military; and the class of engineers who are trained to treat social and cultural demands with indifference. Communities' opposition to the privatization of water and engineering projects that threaten the sources of water, the constant work of scientists and activists to unveil why and how water is contaminated, and what are the diseases that contamination produces, bring to light the understanding of water as a common that must be collectively managed.

Colonialism Lays Waste

"Hostile nature, obstinate and fundamentally rebellious, is in fact represented in the colonies by the bush, by mosquitoes, natives and fever, and colonization is a success when all this indocile nature has been tamed," wrote Fanon.[494] Colonialism transforms peoples into bodies to exhaust to death and land into a resource to exhaust to extinction. Both are capitalized upon. Colonization moves to a new site to exploit once it has dispossessed and over-worked a people, once it has exhausted a mine, a territory, a forest, a river of their resources. It leaves behind open pits, emptied forests, contaminated soils, legacies of trauma, villages destroyed; it increases the consequences of fires and floods. Waste is the other name of colonialism.

To Liboiron, to make "capitalism and colonialism synonymous, or to conflate environmentalism and anticolonialism, misses [the] complex relations" that Glen Sean Coulthard (Yellowknives Dene) has explained when calling "for scholars to shift their analysis away from capitalist relations (production, proletarianization) to colonial relations (dispossession, Land acquisition, access to Land)." Liboiron cites Coulthard: "Like capital, colonialism, as a structure of domination predicated on dispossession, is not a 'thing', but rather the sum effect of the diversity of interlocking oppressive social relations that constitute it. When stated this way, it should be clear that shifting our position to highlight the ongoing effects of colonial dispossession in no way displaces questions of distributive justice or class struggle; rather, it simply situates these questions more firmly alongside and in relation to the other sites and relations of power that inform our settler-colonial present."[495] In other words, Liboiron wants "to make (more) apparent their ongoing relationships maintaining colonial Land relations as well as to anti-colonial Land relations."[496] Liboiron cites Eve Tuck and K. Wayne Yang, for whom the "homogenization of various experiences of oppression as colonialism" accomplishes "a form of enclosure, dangerous in how it domesticates decolonization. It is also a foreclosure, limiting in how it recapitulates dominant theories of social change."[497] As Tuck and Yang write, among the different forms of colonialism, settler colonialism institutes a relation to land and home that is

rooted in a homesteading worldview where the wild land and wild people were made for his benefit. [The settler colonist] can only make his identity as a settler by making the land produce, and produce excessively, because "civilization" is defined as production in excess of the "natural" world (i.e. in excess of the sustainable production already present in the Indigenous world). In order for excess production, he needs excess labor, which he cannot provide himself. The chattel slave serves as that excess labor, labor that can never be paid because payment would have to be in the form of property (land). The settler's wealth is land, or a fungible version of it, and so payment for labor is impossible. The settler positions himself as both superior and normal; the settler is natural, whereas the Indigenous inhabitant and the chattel slave are unnatural, even supernatural.[498]

As I was reading during the summer of 2023 about the devastating fires in Maui, Hawaii, which destroyed much of the historic city of Lahaina, I guessed colonialism was partly responsible. At a briefing on August 9, 2023, Major Gen. Kenneth Hara, commander general of the Hawaii Army National Guard, said: "We don't know what actually ignited the fires, but we were made aware in advance by the National Weather Service that we were in a red flag situation—so that's dry conditions for a long time, so the fuel, the trees and everything, was dry. That, along with low humidity and high winds set the conditions for the wildfires."[499] Despite this, colonialism was quickly held responsible, along with climate disaster, and explanations appeared about how colonialism had contributed to climate disaster. Posts claiming "the wildfires in Maui are not a 'natural' disaster" started to appear online.[500] Scientists "prominently mentioned the role of non-climate influences in the intensity of the firestorm, such as the introduction of highly combustible nonnative plants, as well as weather patterns that happen naturally."[501] Carmen Lindsey, the board chair of the Office of Hawaiian Affairs, said: "The fires of today are in part due to the climate crisis, a history of colonialism in our islands, and the loss of our right to steward our ʻāina and wai. The same Western forces that tried to erase us as a people now threaten our survival with their destructive practices."[502]

The city of Lahaina was once the seat of the independent Hawaiian Kingdom, where the "waters were so abundant that boats once surrounded the iconic Waiola Church. Kamehameha The Great's palace stood tall at the town's center, keeping watch over the shoreline."[503] Then the USA colonized the island,[504] and 19th-century colonizers seized land from Indigenous hands, disrupted "traditional resources management," and introduced non-native plant species such as guinea grass, whereas plants native to Hawaii were beneficial to limiting wildfires.[505] The colonial objective was to "forcibly snuff out native flora, creating land area for large-scale agriculture and plantations."[506] Cattle ranching and sugar and pineapple plantations (Dole Pineapple Company) laid waste on the island. Large-scale monocropping "led to the rapid loss and degradation of native ecosystems through increasing dominance by non-native plants," which contributed to the frequency and strength of fires. During the "post-plantation era," starting around the 1990s, plantations were abandoned, and easily flammable non-native grass spread. The number of wildfires Hawaii experienced rose drastically in the same era.[507] Maui became an island where "golf courses glisten emerald green, hotels manage to fill their pools and corporations stockpile water to sell to luxury estates. And yet, when it came time to fight the fires, some hoses ran dry."[508] To Kaniela Ing, former Hawaiian legislator and the director

of the Green New Deal Network, the wildfires are "a tragic symbol of the climate emergency and colonial greed."[509] Ing notes that the colonial "ethos of
extraction and destruction persists in Maui's most dominant industries: land
speculation and tourism."[510] Canadian political analyst Naomi Klein and
Hawaiian law professor Kapua'ala Sproat warned about what would unfortunately come if there were no collective organization: more water privatization, more land speculation: "Disaster capitalism—the well-worn tactic
of exploiting moments of extreme collective trauma to rapidly push through
unpopular laws that benefit a small elite—relies on this cruel dynamic," they
wrote, recalling the aftermaths of Hurricane Katrina in New Orleans in 2005,
Puerto Rico after Hurricane Maria in 2017, and the 2004 tsunami in Thailand
and Sri Lanka. Maui was disaster colonial capitalism.[511]

   There are not crimes of colonialism, colonialism is itself a crime.[512] It sets
up a model of extraction and exhaustion whose consequences persist long
after plantations or mines have been abandoned. Today, agribusiness and
other economies of extraction and appropriation such as tourism are the
heirs of the economy of the plantation: the privatization of land, soil and sub-
soil, rivers, and lakes; extraction to the point of exhaustion; destruction of the
environment; exploitation of people of color and Indigenous communities.

Is Colonialism a Direct Cause of Climate Disaster?

The International Panel on Climate Change (IPCC) has recognized in its
sixth report (2022) the responsibility of colonialism in climate disaster.
"Vulnerability of ecosystems and people to climate change differs substan-
tially among and within regions (*very high confidence*), driven by patterns of
intersecting socioeconomic development, unsustainable ocean and land use,
inequity, marginalization, historical and ongoing patterns of inequity such as
colonialism, and governance."[513] Hence, the distinction must be made between
colonial and capitalist wasting because otherwise we "miss the necessary
place of stolen Land in colonizers' and settlers' ability to create sinks for pollution as well as stolen Land's place in alternative economies (via a communal
commons) and environmental conservation (via methylmercury-producing
hydroelectric dams)," as Liboiron has argued.[514] In other words, the question
is: Is it upon stolen land that capitalism dumps its waste, does some greenwashing, or builds its sites of conservation? Colonialism, which has not disappeared with the end of European colonial empires and continues to shape
societies, is stolen land, and that fact must never be forgotten. The discourse
and iconography of waste (bad for health; bad for the environment; bad for

animals, fish, and birds; ugly) feeds the desire to make waste disappear and to preserve protected natural reserves while masking the fact that these programs of conservation are on stolen land, or that *cleaning up* may endanger complex bio-systems. Waste must not be approached in ways that will criminalize the "unclean," support capitalist forms of recycling, and encourage consent to technological fixes. *Cleaning up* to save the planet without dismantling colonial relations and racial capitalism is greenwashing. "When most people refer to waste and pollution today, they are referring to a set of relations that uses Land as a sink for a relatively new form of waste characterized by unprecedented tonnage, toxicity, and heterogeneity, created within industrial political economies premised on growth and profit," Liboiron notes.[515]

Invoking the image of Land as a sink, of Earth as a toilet, will not challenge the Eurocentric ideology of cleanliness. The bourgeoisie considered that what is being dumped is dirty and people who work in the massive dumping sites are unclean, choosing to ignore the ongoing relationships between production, consumption, race, and waste. The distinction between colonialism as pollution and capitalism as production of waste means that we must carefully retrace the history of cleanliness as white supremacy and colonial rule and look at its "formidable shock in return" in the racial treatment of waste under capitalism. The notion of "formidable shock in return" (*un formidable choc en retour*) is taken from Aimé Césaire's 1950 *Discourse on Colonialism*.[516] Translated into English as a "terrific boomerang effect" in the sentence "one fine day the bourgeoisie is awakened by a terrific boomerang effect," it was meant to describe how colonization, "distilled into the veins of Europe," would mean that "slowly, but surely, the continent proceeds towards savagery."[517] A formidable shock in return seems more appropriate here to describe the astonishment and psychological difficulties with which a majority of Western Europeans and North Americans observe how their lands can become sinks and toilets.

As sociologist Gurminder K. Bhambra has argued, "it is not simply a capitalist world that colonialism had facilitated through 'primitive accumulation', but a world in which colonialism is continuous with the reproduction of capitalism."[518] Otherwise, the danger will be to fail "to attend to the historical production or ecocidal impacts of dominant models of extractivism."[519] The end of European empires is not enough, and the rise of "new postcolonial nations is not the final realization of a global, capitalist market economy, it is a return to 'colonialism by corporation', by transnational corporations with assets beyond the scale of all but a few nation states."[520]

Racial capitalism does not replace colonialism, it exists alongside it and adds to the level of devastation. "Instead of treating the Earth like a precious entity that gives us life, Western colonial legacies operate within a paradigm that assumes they can extract its natural resources as much as they want, and the Earth will regenerate itself," said Hadeel Assali, postdoctoral scholar at the Columbia Center for Science and Society.[521] If colonialism cannot be made the sole and direct cause of climate disaster, its economy of extraction, dispossession, exploitation, mining, monoculture, and war has had lasting consequences that have added to the devastation caused by racial capitalism, the fossil fuel industry and mining, and imperialism and its wars. One must also examine how the logic of colonization has been adopted by postcolonial nation-states, authorizing mining, forestry, or road building in minorities' territories without their approval, imposing *a* culture, language, and form of knowledge. The term "settler" has been banalized as if a settler is not the occupier of someone else's land. A decolonial feminist politics of vital needs must insist on the abolition of settler politics, the most brutal and violent expression of which can be seen in occupied Palestine, but that can also be observed in South America, Asia, or Africa against Indigenous peoples.

The Wasting of French Colonialism-Imperialism

To step aside from the hegemony of North American cases, I look at the ways in which French coloniality under the regime of the republic, neoliberal capitalism, and imperialism has been laying waste to land, resources, and peoples' living conditions. I come from Reunion Island (in the Indian Ocean), which became a French colony in the 17th century and is today a French department. I have had a direct experience of how race and colonialism shape the environment and how their consequences not only last centuries, but some of these consequences are felt long after destruction has been effected. I learned early on that we were living in an environment shaped by slavery and colonialism—why cities were built where they were; why poor people of color lived where they did; and how the large sugarcane fields, rivers, mountains, volcanoes, and beaches had been inscribed in the colonial and postcolonial economy; but also how, from the first years of colonization, autonomous territories had been carved out by the maroons in the high mountains of the island. They drew two geographies: the one they fled, under colonial domination; and another where they created alternative ways of living. I studied the combined work of scientists (first botanists, then biologists, oceanographers, and volcanologists), engineers, soldiers, and business executives (whether slave traders, slave owners, bankers, or multinational CEOs) who fabricated "nature" as excess that needed to be tamed and disciplined and, through the tourism industry, enjoyed. I observed how the Cold War and the Green Revolution continued to transform the environment in the Indian Ocean and to consolidate an alliance between the military, engineers, multinationals, and scientists. Understanding what is at stake in the negotiations around "climate change" meant considering the place of these stakeholders in the context of a global counterrevolution—the erosion of rights, the politics of "non-raciality" beneath which, as David Theo Goldberg has argued, lurk more sinister shadows of the racial everyday and persistent institutional and structural racisms[522]—and colonial/racial capitalism.

In the 15th century, European navigators described two islands in the southwest of the Indian Ocean, known today as Mauritius and Reunion, as paradises, with no natives and no dangerous animals but with abundant water and forests, and birds and fish that were so unafraid of humans that they were easily captured. On Reunion and Mauritius, European colonizers met flocks of dodo, a bird strange to their eyes, which they described as a cross between a turkey and a bird. A specimen of the dodo brought by the Dutch, who had taken possession of Mauritius (the European act of "taking possession" being in itself colonial), to Europe in 1599 became an instant fascination and was widely represented in drawings and paintings. Within 80 years, the species was extinct. Ebony forests, whose trees are famous for their high quality and resistance, and which covered Mauritius, were cut en masse for exportation by Dutch settlers. Land was cleared to give way to plantations of sugarcane brought from Java, Indonesia. When they left on July 16, 1658, the Dutch abandoned a mutilated island to move to Java, a move from extraction source to extraction source that would be repeated through colonial history and persists to this day. Ecocide preceded the racial violence of slavery and colonization. On Reunion, coffee then sugar plantations meant clearing forests, deeply transforming the coastal geography. Today, both islands' environment has been reshaped to satisfy tourists' desire for the tropics: access to pristine beaches, to all-inclusive services, to landscapes and an unthreatening multiculturalism that can be shown on Instagram. Making tropical islands Europeans was to make them white, multicultural, and open to white fantasies of the tropics.

Colonization always starts with massacres and destruction (which do not target only a human population; in the case of Reunion and Mauritius, there was in fact no native population), and is followed by control and the construction of a pacified environment. I take the ravaging of forests and birds as a forerunner of what was to come: deforestation, monocultures, enslavement, exploitation, fabrication of lives that do not matter or "matter for the wrong reason—for use value, expendable and disposed of once no longer needed," as Maynard and Simpson have written.[523] There is no colonization without the destruction of the environment. The disappearance of the dodo and of ebony forests brings to light the logic of the colonial economy of exhaustion: exploit a resource until it no longer provides benefits and move further to exploit another source; and to do so, dispossess, exploit, extract, and destroy.

The French bought enslaved Malagasy and Africans to work in the plantations of Reunion, and indentured workers from India, China, Africa, and Madagascar. Roads and cities were built to facilitate the work of the colonial administration and its militia, and the transport of sugar and coffee between plantations and the harbor. Enslaved from Madagascar, East Africa, and other countries of the ocean's rim; indentured workers from the Indian continent, China, East Africa, Madagascar, and Kanaky; migrants from Gujarat, Guangdong, and countries of Southeast Asia made these islands theirs. Slavery was work until death, racism, torture, and constant humiliation.

It is important to understand both the common and different traits of French colonialism to study its politics of dispossession of Indigenous communities, its regimes of enslavement, forced labor, organized migrations and the plantation, its campaigns of sterilization and forced abortion, its penal colonies, its policies of deportation and exile. They reveal how the afterlives of slavery and colonialism live on. More attention has been given to environmental racism in French overseas territories, especially Martinique and Guadeloupe, thanks to the work of Vanessa Agard-Jones, Jessica Oublié, and Malcom Ferdinand.[524] However, we are still missing a comprehensive work that analyzes how the French state practices environmental racism in all its overseas territories (the Indian Ocean, the Pacific, the Caribbean, and South America) from those who experience it: Indigenous peoples, descendants of the enslaved, of migrants, of indentured workers, of refugees and migrants in all the diversity of their practices, memories, and knowledge (in the way that U.S., South American governmental or corporate environmental politics are analyzed by Indigenous peoples and Afro-descendants communities).[525] The racism of French white environmentalism and of the European Community (the French overseas territories are integrated in the EC) plays an important role. It requires that we pay attention to local and regional specificities, class conflicts, racisms, gendering, and anti-migrant policies while tracing what connects these differences under the political frame of French republican coloniality.

The French Army, Science, Stolen Land

In French Guiana, French colonization attacked Indigenous lives, stole their lands, destroyed their conditions of life, deported them, forced them into enclosures, exhibited them in human zoos, and imposed evangelization.[526] "Estimated at between 20 and 30,000 at the time of the arrival of the Europeans, the Indigenous were only 1,200 in 1960. These 1,200 people are the only representatives of some fifty nations that populated Guiana at the time of the first settlement of Europeans," writes geographer Jean Hurault.[527] Colonization meant the genocide of Indigenous peoples, slavery, and the creation of a penal colony. The promise of equality, which was the 1946 demand for the end of the colonial status and for the status as a French department with all the same rights as the French, was never accomplished. Racism persists. Today, Indigenous communities coexist with Bushinenge (descendants of maroons), descendants of enslaved, Hmong, Chinese, and Antillean communities, with migrants and refugees from Haiti, Brazil, Suriname, and other neighboring countries. At the top of the social and racial hierarchy, like in any other French postcolony, are the well-paid and racially privileged French administrators, civil servants, engineers, police, and soldiers. The French state remains the largest landowner in French Guiana, with a landholding of 93.66 percent of the cadastral surface area.[528] Gold mining (gold is the second largest export resource of Guiana and accounted for 83 percent of total exports in 2014), the exploitation of the Amazon forest (which covers 8 million hectares of forest, of which 7.5 million belong to the state), the discovery of offshore oil deposits in 2011 by Total, which possesses an exclusive permit for exploration, cohabit with anti-migrants politics, lack of public services, dependency on France for any decision, and organized poverty. All of this characterizes Guiana under French rule.

The installation in 1964 of Europe's Spaceport in Kourou, in the northeast of the country, represented a source of important revenue for the French state and of prestige with the launching of satellites and rockets, and, in December 2021, the successful launching of the James Webb Space Telescope. A white city was created to house engineers and administrative staff and their families. The creation of Kourou showed the historical links between colonialism, the army (2,100 military personnel from the three armies who are permanently stationed in Guiana), and science. France had "lifted a small satellite into orbit" from Algeria in November 1965.[529] For those who would be surprised that it occurred in independent Algeria, let us remind them that the French state insisted on keeping a presence in the Sahara to continue to exploit oil and test nuclear bombs. But the French-Algerian agreement required France to seek another site. The French institution in charge of the construction of the Spaceport "contracted Colombians to provide manual labor, they were supplemented by workers from elsewhere, particularly Brazil and Surinam."[530] Colonialism requires European expertise, but land and workforce are extracted from the enslaved, forced laborers, or migrants. In Guiana, the workforce was not even local. During the construction of the site, opposition described the "project as a 'cancer,' a 'diabolical plan' that would produce a 'white city' by chasing Guyanese from their land and redistributing it to Europeans."[531] As sociologist and antiracist activist Saïd Bouamama summarizes:

The decision to set up the space centre in Guiana in 1964 was done at the same time and for the same reasons as that to carry out nuclear tests in Polynesia. Algeria's independence simultaneously deprived French colonialism of its nuclear testing ground in the Sahara and the Hammaguir base near Bechar where missile and rocket launch tests were conducted. Two sets of factors contributed to the choice of Guiana. The first related to geographical and climatic factors: Guiana is close to the equator and does not experience seismic and cyclonic hazards. The second was political: Guiana at the time was thinly populated and characterized by low economic development which limited both the risks of human disasters in the event of accidents and those (it was believed) of a consistent medium-term demand for independence.[532]

The state developmentalist ideology was strong among the local conservatives and even the Left Creole elite; Kourou was seen as progress and modernism. The creation of Europe's Spaceport also entailed the expulsion of Indigenous communities, the clearing of forests, and the militarization of the site. In 1971, Marie-José Jolivet, a French social scientist, described Kourou as a "socio-professional hierarchy to be exactly inscribed on the ground."[533] Kourou, according to Jolivet, was carefully constructed to enforce social and racial borders:

For the Boni or Saramaka laborer: salvaged boards and a well-camouflaged shantytown (the landscape must not be disfigured!). For the relocated cultivator: cramped accommodation in a reserved housing project located at the entry of the city. For the skilled worker: an apartment in a standard housing complex at the edge of the town's center, the only place where it is imagined that Creoles and Whites could mix. And then the White town, with its hierarchical gradations almost scrupulously respected . . . Can one have dreamed up a more vivid demonstration of the expertise of Whites to orchestrate the countless hierarchical encounters that allow them to maintain the ideological bases of their domination?[534]

The racialized spatialization that Jolivet outlined in 1971 can be found in any French overseas territory. Producing wasted land and wasted rivers, extracting resources, and exhausting bodies are enterprises protected by the state, which facilitates the installation of private corporations, mining, the leasing of lands, expropriation, and dispossession.

Mining Is Wasting

According to the International Indian Treaty Council, "during the California Gold Rush, miners dug up 12 billion tons of earth, excavating riverbeds and blasting hillsides in their fervor. They also used mercury to extract gold from the ore, releasing an estimated 7,600 tons of the toxic chemical into Northern California rivers and lakes. The amount of mercury required to violate federal health standards today would be equivalent to one gram in a small lake."[535] Mining is waste producing and wasting.[536] There is no threshold of dispossession, exploitation, and extraction in mining. When corporations abandon a mine, they leave the earth open and the soil, air, water, and people contaminated. Coal, oil, nickel, gold, cobalt, anything that can be found deep in the earth or in the ocean to serve growth and profit attracts corporations and states. Around the planet, on land and sea, tools for researching, identifying the sources of minerals, and for their extraction are becoming more and more sophisticated. The tale that justified Spanish conquistadores' devastating colonial conquest in Central and South America, and that remains powerful, goes like this: in the early 1500s, Spaniards heard of "an Amazonian king who regularly coated his body with gold dust, then plunged into a nearby lake to wash it off while being showered with gold and jewels thrown by his subjects. They called the city ruled by this flamboyant monarch *El Dorado*, Spanish for 'gilded one.' "[537] The tale grew into a legend of a whole country paved with gold. To this day, "Eldorados" excite the appetites justifying the openings of the Earth or of the oceans.[538]

The colonial need for silver and gold opened wide the Earth. In Potosi, the modern mine was born, "where the average 'working' life of a miner was six to eight years (on Southern sugar plantations, it was eight to ten years)."[539] According to the International Indian Treaty Council, in California,

over 150,000 Indigenous Peoples lived prior to the Gold Rush with sustainable cultures and economies based primarily on hunting, gathering and fishing. By 1870, the Native population of California had declined to an estimated 31,000 with over 60 percent perishing from diseases introduced by the 49ers [the name given to gold diggers rushing to the west of the USA in 1849]. Tribes were also systematically chased off their lands, forcibly relocated to missions and reservations, enslaved and brutally massacred. In 1851, the California State government paid $1 million for scalping expeditions. $5 was paid for a severed Indian head in Shasta in 1855 and twenty-five cents was paid for a scalp in Honey Lake in 1863.[540]

Mining kills and pollutes. In a now-classic book, Uruguayan journalist and novelist Eduardo Galeano spoke of the *Open Veins of Latin America*.[541]

He retraced the history of plundering since the beginning of colonization, the ransacking by Spanish armies, the infamous mine of Potosi, and the tens of thousands of kilos of gold and silver extracted from the mine that arrived in Spain between 1503 and 1660.[542] European modernity was fed by extraction and wasting. Under postcolonial regimes, extraction remains the production of wasting. In 1977, four women and fourteen children arrived in La Paz and started a hunger strike against the destruction of their lives and environment by mining. They said: "We didn't come to consult, but to inform. Our decision has been made. In the mine, the hunger strike never ends. We're born and it begins. We have to die there too. A slower death, but just as certain."[543] They articulated the racial and class fabrication of death, the inevitable premature death promised by capitalism.

In 2021, the biggest diamond mine in Angola, run by Catoca, a joint venture owned by Endiama, the Angolan state mining company, and the Russian mining giant Alrosa, leaked toxic waste in the Kasai River, a southern tributary of the mighty Congo River. The leak caused "an unprecedented environmental and human disaster" in the Democratic Republic of Congo, where 12 people died.[544] "The river turned red. Then dead fish by the ton floated up to the surface. Then thousands of people started getting sick."[545] Reports from local inhabitants confirmed by scientific studies show that cleaning the waste not only takes years but the polluted site may even never be cleaned. Programs of *cleaning up* extremely rarely take advice from local inhabitants. For instance, in Ogoniland, oil pollution by major oil corporations was said in 2021 to take 30 years to clean up (if cleaning is conceived first by the inhabitants). While the Ogoni people see themselves as "custodians of a borrowed environment— borrowed from their forefathers and from a generation not yet born," cleaning up is in the hands of private interests.[546]

In Guiana, the French state supported the Montagne d'Or mine project, which would have produced tons of waste. Drilling started in 2011 to determine the emplacements of gold resources in an area situated between two biological reserves. In 2015, Alexei Mordashov, a Russian billionaire and owner of the mining company Nordgold and the Canadian company Columbus Gold, constituted a conglomerate to exploit the mines, which received the official support of French president Emmanuel Macron. In 2017, the latter confirmed his support: "Everyone knows my involvement in the early stages of the Gold Mountain project."[547] In the name of economic development and developmentalist ideology, the Creole elite, which monopolize local political institutions and represent French Guiana at the French Parliament, backed the project. The Association des Amérindiens de Guyane française (AAGF, created in 1981), which had been asking for the restitution of their land since 1984, opposed the project.[548] The AAGF was transformed in 1992 into the Federation of Amerindian Organization of Guiana (Fédération d'Organisations Amérindiennes de Guyane), which represented Indigenous groups at the national and international level; finally, it became the Organisation des nations amérindiennes de Guyane (ONAG) in 2011. The French government, true to its colonial conception of the republic, gave its authorization to mine in 2020. The Montagne d'Or would have been one of the largest open-cast gold mine projects not only in French Guiana but in the world. Its installation required the total deforestation of 1,513 hectares, including 575 hectares of primary forests, with high ecological value, on a site where more than 2,000 plant and animal species, including 127 protected species, had been inventoried. The proposed mining site would have been 2.5 kilometers long, 500 to 800 meters wide, and 400 meters deep. The area of deforestation, "including all installations combined, would directly destroy around 10 km² of primary rainforest. Millions and millions of cubic meters of minerals will be transported and treated with cyanide to extract 85 tons of gold that Nordgold intends to find in 15 years."[549] Its cyanide ore–processing plant would consume no less than 20 percent of the power generated in French Guiana.

Industrial sites of this type inevitably destroy wide swathes of surrounding forest, and the likelihood of water pollution due to acid mine drainage is high. The greatest risk lies in the dammed storage of millions of tons of cyanide sludge. Since 2000, at least 25 mine tailings dam breaks have occurred around the world. According to the corporations who would have mined, the extraction of gold would have required thousands of tons of explosives and cyanide and 195 million liters of fuel during the 12 years of the project. The projection was such that, in total, 54 million tons of ore would have been extracted from the mountain, but for only 1.6 grams of precious metal per ton of ore.[550] Opposition became fierce.[551] In a powerful manifesto, *Neither Gold, Nor Master* (*Ni Or Ni Maître*), that describes how French colonization divided communities, destroyed the land and the forests, invoked science to silence the diverse communities living in Guyana, and sold the project of the Gold Mountain, the authors cite the Jeunesse autochtone de Guyane (JAG) (Indigenous Youth of Guiana), who saw a "world driven and animated by greed for wealth and power, a world devoid of respect and honor."[552] They declared, "We'll light your Gold Mountain. We'll burn it, we'll destroy it. Because if we don't, you'll destroy it, our mountain."[553] In French Guiana as elsewhere, colonial settlers saw an uninhabited land; "only settlers perceive the forest as virginal,"[554] only for themselves. They also bring to light the cruel arrogance of the French institutions and tourism. Indigenous activists have also denounced the Creole elite, the descendants of enslaved people who have been educated in the French system and have accessed positions of power.[555]

On November 8, 2017, the International Tribunal for the Rights of Nature, which was created by the Global Alliance for the Rights of Nature in January 2014, heard arguments against the Gold Mountain project, and "Indigenous peoples from Africa, Russia, Bolivia, Ecuador, French Guyana, and the USA/Turtle Island presented testimonies that drew the Tribunal's attention to the sacredness of Earth—dimensions ignored in the COP 23 negotiations."[556] The Tribunal offered a forum for Guianese people to "speak on behalf of nature, to protest the destruction of the Earth—destruction that is often sanctioned by governments and corporations—and to make recommendations about Earth's protection and restoration."[557] Fernando "Pino" Solanas, an Argentinean cinema director and activist, was responsible for determining whether this mega mining project represented a violation of the rights of nature.[558] On December 14, 2018, the UN Committee on the Elimination of Racial Discrimination (CERD) "reprimanded France for its human rights violations against the indigenous peoples of French Guiana related to the controverted mining project 'la Montagne d'Or' ('the Mountain of Gold')."[559] In June 2019, the French government backed off. But it was not because the French state was ready to listen to Indigenous voices, since it still refuses to sign Convention 169 of the International Organization of Labor relative to Indigenous peoples.[560]

The AAGR (Association of Amerindians of French Guiana) led to the creation of the Kolectif Pou-Lagwiyann Dékolé (KPLD), which brought together different communities (Indigenous Bushinenge, Creoles), and for which the right to land became a central demand. Christophe Yanuwana Pierre, member of Indigenous Youth of Guiana, articulates the demand in these terms: "We never had borders. To say that this river's branch marks the end of our territory or that crossing it would mean we no longer are in our territory, this is not our way of thinking."[561] Earth cannot be "the object of appropriation but only of usages and modes of inhabiting."[562] What matters is the relation "to earth, to water, to the living, to the forest, to family, to the basis of what makes us humans."[563] Mining violates Indigenous cosmogonies. Yanuwana Pierre explains: "In Amerindian tradition, we are taught that problems that were resolved by the ancestors have been buried under the earth. By digging, we will reveal what they had succeeded in resolving and that cost them enormous sacrifices."[564] To the Indigenous people of Guiana, what matters is the elemental: land, water, forest, inhabiting a place. Listening to the inhabitants of Guiana does not mean extracting and romanticizing their cosmologies, but deploying solidarity and attacking French imperialism, French militarism, and the corporate class.

When in 2023 a group of young Guyanese created a Zone to Defend (*zone à defendre* in French, or ZAD), which they occupied to prevent the construction of a mega solar factory on Indigenous land that required the destruction of forest, they showed that the struggle continued. The project, supported by the French state with no consultation with the inhabitants, is managed by the Bordeaux-based company Hydrogène de France (HDF) and 60 percent owned by the investment fund Meridiam, headed by Thierry Déau, a black Martinican millionaire who is a close ally of Emmanuel Macron.[565] It is opposed by the Indigenous community of the village Prosperité,[566] which is challenging the argument of the French state about this being an "empty space."[567] "They [the company] consider the site to be empty, dehumanized? But we, Amerindians, have lived for centuries in osmosis with the forest: the latter represents a site of life in the strongest sense, a hunting and fishing ground, a living pharmacy, and more importantly, a space of intergenerational transmission of knowledge. Without the forest, there is no life."[568] The generation engaged in the ZAD operates a "junction between indigenous demands and wider anti-capitalist and ecological struggles"[569] that deeply disturb a French state used to using armed force in its overseas territories to further private or public projects, to neutralize and control sites, and to import its culture of expatriates, French settlers in the 21st century, in the remnants of its colonial empire.

The devastation brought by the mining industry cannot be underestimated, nor the profits the leading 40 companies make (the total revenue worldwide was some 925 billion U.S. dollars in 2021).[570] Satellite images show 21,060 polygons created by mines covering 57,277 km^2.[571] There are more than 6,000 active mining sites across the globe according to visual interpretation of satellite images.[572] Open-pit mines create a significant amount of waste, and almost one million tons of ore and waste rock per day can be moved from the largest mines; a couple of thousand tons per day are moved from small mines.[573] Mining leaves behind wasted lands and bodies that industrial *cleaning up* programs do not alleviate. Mines eject an enormous number of tons of toxic residue. In France, a mine closed in 2004 was still contaminating the environment ten years later.[574] Arsenic, mercury, cadmium, lead, contaminated soil, and other toxic elements do not disappear when the mine is abandoned. A mine kills by poisoning and asphyxiation; it is an important element of what I call the politics of *unbreathing* (more on this later) and poisoning.

Whether mining is open-pit, underground, or both; conventional mining, dredging of placer deposits, or harvesting brine from salt lakes; or the collection of nodules from the sea floor or harvesting minerals from submarine volcanic vents (iron ore, coal, copper, nickel, tin, lithium, gems, potash, kaolin) and the mechanization of deep-sea mining, the availability of cheap labor remains connected to colonialism, capitalism, and imperialism. In Colombia, in the Cerrejón region where the Wayuu people live, the third-largest coal mine in the world (the largest in South America) has been destroying the Indigenous people and their territory.[575] In 2009, the Colombia Supreme Court warned of an imminent risk of destruction of the Wayuu. Besides the destruction of the environment, ways of living, and erasure of Indigenous knowledge and even words, open mining has brought new diseases: 40 children die every year of respiratory disease produced by coal dust. The mining industry brings poverty and hunger, it diverts rivers, contaminates soil and water. There are no longer fish in the Malacas River, from which Indigenous people drew their food. The French state, says Juan Pablo Gutierrez, international delegate for ONIC/Yukpa, bears a responsibility since, for 30 years, it imported coal from that mine so that French people would have electricity in their homes. Mining is war, adds Guterriez, and mining corporations use paramilitary groups to terrorize Indigenous activists. Two hundred Indigenous people have already been assassinated in the Cerrejón region by the paramilitary.[576]

Stopping the mining industry entails weighing up what it means to oppose corporations that use armed militias, the price Indigenous peoples pay for opposing mining. This brings to mind an act by Extinction Rebellion in March 2023 in London that "targeted lobbying firm UK Finance's headquarters at 1 Angel Court near Bank in London. Two people threw pink paint over the glass panelling across the front of the building. Others stuck a large sticker with the word 'CORRUPT' on the window."[577] Gutierrez remarked that as he walked back to the building a little later, he noticed that the building had already been cleaned. To him, change will come from the Indigenous peoples, for whom "activism is not a choice. The discourse on non-violence is violence in the context of Indigenous peoples' survival."[578]

There is no colonialism and capitalist economy of extraction without mining, and this is why the struggle against mining is global. Thus, it is clear why many ecological and environmental movements and institutions focus on illegal mining as posing the most dangerous threat.[579] *Irreparability* is what colonialism and imperialism fabricate. The denunciation of illegal mining also justifies the intervention of a multiplicity of institutions that, declaring the absence of state power or its complicity with illegal actors, decide what the environmental problem is, then fund global and local initiatives that conform to what they define as the best way to tackle the problem by a *cleaning up* that is not cleaning. Green mining practices are tied with conservation and the creation of "natural parks," feeding a green interventionism, which is a branch of imperialism.

In 1996, the World Water Council, whose first directors came from two major French water corporations (Veolia and Suez, formerly Vivendi), was established in Marseille. In 2012, ten water corporations controlled the market, the two first being French.[580] The World Water Council, which declares that "access to water and sanitation is recognized worldwide as a fundamental right by the international community," masters the vocabulary of inclusion and ecology in the declaration "No water security without ecological security / No ecological security without water security."[581] It is a case of what philosopher Olúfẹ́mi O. Táíwò has called "elite capture"—the process by which a radical concept can be stripped of its political substance and liberatory potential—deployed by political, social and economic elites in the service of their own interests.[582]

Criminalization of Activists

In 2023, the struggle against mega-basins in France took a new turn. Mega-basins are gigantic water storage structures designed to meet the needs of the agro-industry, particularly during the summer months. They are huge artificial basins, plastic coated and impermeable. The average mega-basin covers an area of eight hectares; some of the largest are as large as 18 hectares. Contrary to what the French government asserts, they are not filled with rainwater but with groundwater being pumped out, and they do not avoid evaporation of water, which is an important loss. The existence of mega-basins was brought to the public's attention when, on Saturday, March 25, 2023, a protest against a mega-basin in western France's Sainte-Soline was met with incredible police violence. The movement against mega-basins had been launched with "L'appel des Soulèvements de la Terre" ("The call for Earth uprisings")[583] written in early 2021 on the Notre-Dame-des-Landes ZAD,[584] which vowed to fight against infrastructure deemed unnecessary or dangerous for the environment. With its 628,000-square-meter reservoir, Sainte-Soline quickly became a focal point for protesters. Starting on October 30, 2022, several thousand opponents had demonstrated for two days and were met with police violence; one protester was left with a serious head injury. Construction resumed in November 2022, under constant police protection. Organizers then set a new date of protest, March 25, 2023. The Macron government decided to increase the repression, calling the protesters "eco-terrorists." Two hundred protesters were injured, 40 of them "seriously affected" by LBD ("defensive bullet launcher") shots and shrapnel from stun grenades. Two demonstrators fell into a coma, and a young woman's face was severely injured. Three journalists were also injured.[585] Protesters inscribed their actions in a gene-alogy of struggles against mega-projects with no social utility: "There was Larzac, its ten-year struggle and almost 100,000 demonstrators; there were the voluntary reapers and their hectares of land taken over by GMOs; there was the Notre-Dame-des-Landes ZAD and its victory against airborne glo-balization. Not something new, then, but something of a reminder: the need to root struggles in the territories, to defend them, to get in touch with farm-ers and workers, in front of the police and the ecocidal infrastructures they've been ordered to defend."[586] To many, Sainte-Soline marked "our special obli-gation to the land itself, nourishing land, living land. We have a duty to save the peasants who suffer and disappear en masse as they feed us, and we have a duty to save the living creatures who make the land fertile and fit for cultiva-tion, or who inhabit it in forests and wastelands and make up worlds other than our own."[587] "Rage against the Basin," protesters urge. "In the firing line is the export-oriented agro-industry and intensive livestock farming, brimming with subsidies, supported by the state and lobbies, which encourages water grabbing with no regard for the maintenance of ecosystems and other uses," they declare.[588]

The government's response was to criminalize the protest. Against Gérald Darmanin's (Macron's minister of the interior) demand for the dis-solution of Les Soulèvements de la terre (Earth Uprisings), a movement of solidarity grew. At a meeting of solidarity in Paris on April 12, 2023, as Les soulèvements de la terre was being threatened with dissolution by the gov-ernment, I reminded the public that criminalization of leftist activists had a long history, that the state had experimented with environmental destruction since slavery in its colonies, that in the 19th century it had deforested vast areas in Algeria for colonial settlers, that it has externalized nuclear tests first in Algeria then in the Pacific French islands, that it had poisoned Martinique and Guadeloupe with chlordecone, and that there were ZAD everywhere, in the racialized, popular neighborhoods of France.[589]

Earth Uprisings looked at what has happened in Spain, where between the 1950s and 1990s, 1,226 basins were originally built for intensive agricul-ture, nautical tourism, and the hydraulic industry, but in fact the majority (85 to 95 percent) were for intensive agriculture.[590] These basins ended up watering golf courses and large farms without any restriction, and drought increased. In the summer of 2023, the Convoi de l'eau (Convoy of Water) crossed France, planning to arrive in Paris on August 26, stopping in towns and villages where mega-basins threaten the environment. These 2023 strug-gles against mega-basins that benefit private interests and contribute to the destruction of the environment occurred simultaneously with an uprising by young people protesting the murder of 17-year-old Nahel M. by a policeman. The police first accused the young Nahel, who was of Moroccan and Algerian descent, of having tried to run them over, but a smartphone video showed that the vehicle was not directly threatening the police officers. The two young men who were in the vehicle with Nahel testified that the "policeman standing next to Nahel shouted, 'Don't move or I'll put a bullet in your head,' while the second officer then said, 'Shoot him.' "[591]

For days after, the youth of the banlieues, including some as young as 12–14, took to the streets and fought back against the police. They immediately understood that the police would lie. They know that for years, Black and Arab men and children have been killed by the police and these crimes have remained unpunished. They are stopped on their way to school, as young as 11, they are brutally searched and insulted. From murders in 1973 to the racist crimes of the 1980s and of the 1990s, over 700 cases of police murders have been recorded.[592] They had learned that "race kills twice": the first type of violence "affecting a person's physical integrity, the second violence taking place at institutional level, when penal treatment ignores the racist nature of the crimes on trial."[593] Even the Defender of Rights, an independent constitutional authority in France, said that young men of Black or North African origin are 20 times more likely to be subjected to identity checks by the police than the rest of the population.[594] In December 2022, the UN Committee on the Elimination of Racial Discrimination condemned both politicians' racist rhetoric and police ID checks that "disproportionately target specific minorities."[595] But nothing has stopped the violence of the French police.

The revolts, which showed the magnitude of structural racism in France, were unsurprisingly condemned by the government and its allies, among them some academics, journalists, and commentators. I argued then that the ZADs, a term commonly used among environmentalists, were not only in the countryside, sites where agribusiness, the cattle industry, or other polluting industries wanted to settle, but also in the banlieues, where structural racism also meant no green parks, no good food, and bad water.[596] What I will soon be naming the *racial politics of suffocation* are not only about air pollution but also about the violence that racism creates, a place where obstacles to breathing abound.

Antiracist Politics of Breathing

"I can't breathe": these three words uttered by George Floyd as his life was extinguished beneath the knee of a police officer in the U.S. in March 2020 became a rallying cry for racial justice and police reform in the U.S. and across the globe, launching a movement of toppling statues and monuments dedicated to racists, colonialists, and imperialists. These three words had already been cried out in 2014 by Eric Garner as he was killed by police in New York City. As anthropologist Omotayo Jolaosho has written, these "three words have even deeper resonance: they provoke grief and mourning; they urge action; they invoke restorative practices among Black people to mediate repression; and they beseech us, as anthropologists, to investigate racial inequities in the access to breath, the essence of life itself."[597] Blackness here "illuminates social inequity that is specific but not limited to Black African descendants. Similarly, breath has the potential to be a connective force drawing together multiple points of exposure and vulnerability specific to Black experiences, and also marginalization and bodily precarity among those not racialized as Black."[598]

By connecting the ways in which Black and Indigenous breathing has been hindered in industrially polluted urban peripheries and in the areas where capitalism installs its polluting industries, I suggest extending the issue of waste, cleaning, and race to the analysis of the fabrication of *an irrespirable and uninhabitable planet*. Air pollution is a major cause of death among the poor peoples of color, and climate disaster, by intensifying mega fires, is adding to making the world irrespirable, suffocating, deadly, and toxic. In 2015, the United Nations reported that about 9 million people had died because of pollution, confirming toxic contamination as the "single largest source of premature death in the world today,"[599] from "sources such as coal plants, industry, transport, household fires (16% of all deaths globally)."[600] According to the authors of the *Lancet* Commission on pollution and health, "toxic air, water, soils and workplaces are responsible for the diseases that kill one in every six people around the world. The deaths attributed to pollution are equivalent to three times those from Aids, malaria and tuberculosis combined."[601] And unsurprisingly, the majority of these deaths occur in the Global South. When it was made clear that the COVID-19 virus that targets the respiratory system had a disproportionate impact on the poor, the Indigenous, and peoples of color worldwide,[602] and given that deaths from COVID-19 were related to severe structural racial inequalities affecting access to healthcare and vaccines, the crisis of breathing that people of color live within came to light. What I call here *the racial politics of unbreathing* are the air pollution and contamination that colonialism and racial capitalism are producing that cause terrible respiratory diseases and premature death among Indigenous people and peoples of color and make their world uninhabitable. The World Health Organization observed in 2022 that "almost all of the global population

(99%) are exposed to air pollution levels that put them at increased risk for diseases including heart disease, stroke, chronic obstructive pulmonary disease, cancer and pneumonia. WHO monitors the exposure levels and health impacts (i.e. deaths, DALYs) of air pollution at the national, regional and global level from ambient (outdoor) and household air pollution."[603] Speaking of *unbreathing* and *un-inhabitability* in a book about race and cleaning in a world of waste means speaking about the programs of *cleaning up* that states or international institutions are launching and which end up being detrimental to the wellbeing of peoples of color. It also means insisting that fighting for clean air is fighting for an antiracist world. To reach that goal is to raise the question of what decolonial antiracist cleaning is. It is a revolutionary struggle whose goal is to dismantle the structures of domination, dispossession, and exploitation.

It is important to distinguish between levels of the irrespirable according to different situations: "unbreathable" is a situation where the air is not suitable for respiration; "suffocating" is when there is not enough oxygen for breathing; "deadly" is when the air contains harmful gases or substances that can cause death; and "toxic" is when the air is poisonous and poses a danger to life.[604] All these terms refer to conditions that are hazardous to human and nonhuman health and safety, especially in the Global South. To clarify what I have tried to explain here, *unbreathing* refers to the fact that one must hold one's breath under the racialized system. Slavery, colonialism, and racial capitalism are not interested in the fact that people can not only not fully breathe but not breathe clean air. The lungs of the exploited have always been damaged. In the industrial era, respiratory diseases have been the norm rather than the exception;[605] in today's plantations, mines, factories, and housing for the poor and racialized, the lungs are attacked. As Fanon wrote, in colonialism "the *individual's breathing is an observed, an occupied breathing*. It is a combat breathing."[606]

Racial capitalism and colonialism's *politics of unbreathing* bring to light the link between extraction, exhaustion, racism, and suffocation. To map unbreathing is to trace the geographies of extraction, waste, and poverty of Indigenous, Black, and non-white communities in the Global South and North. It is also to look at another element of the imperial mode of living, the promotion and marketing of breathing exercises when that very mode of living is responsible for unclean air and suffocation of the planet. Further, these exercises constitute a case of imperialist cultural appropriation, for example, when in January 2019 the journal *Scientific American* renamed breathing techniques known as *pranayama* in India as "cardiac coherence breathing."[607] The article had "labelled pranayam 'ancient' while simply repackaging its basic methods and principles for a western audience. Some even called it an instance of cultural appropriation and plagiarism."[608] One Twitter (now X) user replied: "Another case of Turmeric Latte. Pranayama of Yoga called as 'Cardiac Coherence Breathing'. Next thing we know, it will be patented and sold back to us terming it as superior way of living. Just saying it existed in ancient cultures is not enough."[609]

The struggle for breathing is an antiracist struggle, which is what I argued in 2019 in my text "Breathing: A Revolutionary Act."[610] Exercises in breathing become acts of resistance, bringing air in the lungs to sing. This is what Jolaosho says about isiZulu-speaking shack dwellers in Durban, South Africa, who practice " 'ukubhodla' (coughing out)" which is "key to mediating the tension of not being able to breathe in an industrially polluted urban periphery."[611] They cite anthropologist Kerry Ryan Chance, who, in *Living Politics in South Africa's Urban Shacklands*, writes that "coughing out is when you clear your lungs of pollution to breathe—whether to sing, pray, or speak—in [collective] ritual space."[612] According to Jolaosho, "ukubhodla therefore facilitates connection and solidarity during collective events by allowing residents besieged in urban peripheries to momentarily change their bodies by expelling pollutants even as they change the air and link with one another through sound."[613]

In *Proletarian Lung*, literary theorist and psychoanalyst Damir Arsenijevic turns to the lungs of those who work in toxic environments: "I must start with the 'proletarian lung' of the metal picker whose lungs get burned by the left-over chlorine in HAK [Chlorine Alkaline Power House] pipes, who succumbs to his injuries and dies. His death is the toll of the extractive logic of predatory capitalism in Bosnia & Herzegovina today."[614] To Arsenijevic, proletarian lungs, proletarian cancer caused by pollution, and proletarian asthma attacks deserve to have their own autobiographies written and shared.

There is no alternative to breathing. If I cannot breathe, I die. The lungs of humans and animals, as well as the lungs of forests, plants, and oceans, have long been under assault. Now, across the globe, breathing has become a privilege of class and race. The Global South cannot breathe. Indigenous, Black, poor, Brown peoples are systematically poisoned with contaminated air produced by mining, chemical, weapons, construction, and car industries, and the consequences on their health are compounded by bad housing, bad food, no access to public health services, stress, poverty, and racism. Exhaustion and suffocation are consubstantial with slavery, colonialism, and capitalism, which mined, and continue to mine, Black and Brown bodies, lands, rivers, and oceans until they have no life energy left. What remains is an uninhabitable and irrespirable world, whose politics of unbreathing deplete its populations, albeit unequally. These are what poet and novelist Dionne Brand has described as "the corpses of the humanist narrative."[615] The politics of unbreathing are historically racist, tied to capitalist industrial growth and environmental degradation. In the 19th century, cities in the Global North were heavily polluted—London was known for its contaminated smog—but today, with much industrial production outsourced to China, India, and countries in the Global South, and with these countries' development, it is Southern/Eastern cities that have dangerously high levels of air pollution. What has become a pressing issue for countries in the North/West, meanwhile, is how to keep externalized pollution from reaching its "clean" areas. What is taken for granted in the Global North and West—running water, electricity, rail travel, open schools and hospitals with staff and medication, cheap fashion, avocados in winter—is the exception rather than the rule. It is a way of life made possible by a regime of exploitation of the many. The "good life" reserved for the few requires, in the words of development scholar Christa Wichterich, a "transnational care extractivism,"[616] organized so that women of the Global South compensate for a crisis of care in the Global North (care for children and the elderly, the labor of cleaning and cooking, sex work), while their own needs, and those of their families, are not respected or fulfilled. The lives of people of color are wasted for the comfort of a few.

The exploitation of cleaning work and ideologies of cleanliness that hold the planetary ecosystem of racial capitalism together are a site where forms of structural violence were at their most blatant during the COVID-19 pandemic, which as we know attacks the respiratory system, the lungs. Governmental responses to the COVID-19 pandemic exacerbated inequalities and injustices. The governmental and health organizations' advice to wash one's hands thoroughly came up against a lack of access to water that was the result of political choices. People of color, who had no choice but to go to their "essential" jobs, were more exposed to the virus. The links between hyper-consumerism, racial capitalism, deforestation and increasing zoonoses, the privatization of health services, and the fabrication of lives that do not matter were again demonstrated.[617] Further, studies showed that hesitancy among Black and Indigenous people toward vaccines was caused by historical racism, and the memories of the legacy of racism in healthcare and medical research, including in vaccinations, has had a lasting impact.[618] Vaccine inequality—which also has historical racial roots, and meant that much of the world's vaccine production and distribution capacity was reserved by wealthier nations—increased the vulnerability of non-Western populations to premature death.[619]

On March 18, 2020, the French government ordered a lockdown. The race/class division between those who could afford to stay inside, who were protected by their class and race status, and those who were not protected and had to work outside so the society would continue to function was made clear. On March 20, 2020, I wrote the following on Facebook:

So now there are the confined and the unconfined who make their daily living from the former—who bring food to the shops, stock shelves, clean, run the till, refuse collectors, postmen, delivery men (I've seen 3 already since this morning), transport drivers, hotel cleaners and waitresses (who stay open and provide room service), and so many others. Class, gender, age, racialization, health cut across both groups but the unconfined are the most exposed . . . There are those who live in 12 m² and those in 150 m², who can have deliveries made or not, who have enough money to subscribe to many streaming platforms or not, who have a lot of bandwidth to ensure lessons at home or not, who can help the children with lessons or not, who have a computer and a printer or not, who are totally isolated or not, who have papers or not, who are financially comfortable or not, women and children who live with violent partners, single women with children, in short, thousands and thousands of situations drowned out by the discourse of national unity in a country where inequality, state violence, racism and sexism have organized social life for years.

I was stressing the permanence of a structure: what makes social life possible in "normal" times as well as during a pandemic is the exploitation of the work of millions of women of color. The pandemic brought the notion of protection to the fore: protection from the virus, from one another, of one another, from sickness. The state was called upon to fulfill its responsibilities. But state protection has never been the same for everyone, neither locally nor at the global level. The differences between those who could be confined because it did not profoundly threaten their living conditions, who could afford, and those who had no other choice than to expose themselves to the virus were magnified in the Global South, and between North and South. What the pandemic made more visible were the deep, violent, deadly, and destructive asymmetries and inequalities produced by racial capitalism. But visibility is only one element in the struggle to change structures. Containment exposed the very conditions of its possibility: invisible and exploited, racialized, gendered labor (with differences obviously occurring within a gender—not all women are equal, and not all men are equal, and there are not only two genders). The importance of those carrying out "essential jobs"—nurses, supermarket employees, deliverers, and cleaners—was suddenly discovered by the bourgeoisie and the media. They were applauded and congratulated, promises were made to ameliorate their working and living conditions, but all this quickly disappeared and went back to "normal." The COVID-19 pandemic revealed the need for clean water, clean air, emission cuts, and public health services in a planet made *uninhabitable* and *irrespirable* for billions of people by racial capitalism. It made visible the threats posed by the multiplication of zoonoses, the increase of air and maritime transport, agribusiness, and the cattle industry, and the inequalities in the access to water and other forms of protection against contamination.

COVID-19 unleashed an economic storm that hit the poor the hardest, with women and marginalized workers facing the most job losses. According to the UN, close to 96 million people were pushed into extreme poverty in 2020, and "for the first time in two decades, the share of the world's workers living in extreme poverty increased, rising from 6.7 per cent in 2019 to 7.2 per cent, pushing an additional 8 million workers into poverty."[620] "Eighty per cent of disaster-related mortality was estimated to be due to the coronavirus," declared the UN Department of Economic and Social Affairs in 2020, adding: "Even without considering significant underreporting (the World Health Organization (WHO) estimates global excess deaths of 4.5 million in 2020), this figure is already in stark contrast to the 2015–2019 period, when the disaster-related mortality rate averaged 0.93 persons per 100,000 population."[621] There was no vaccine equity, nor equity in terms of access to care and prevention.[622] Without surprise, we learned that the mortality rate was, worldwide, higher among Black and Indigenous communities, who have been deliberately marginalized by state privatization policies of public health.[623] Black feminists derided the sudden "discovery" by the white middle class that when the home was functioning as an office, online school, gym, and leisure space, the housework to be done doubled, if not tripled, reminding us that "most care and maintenance work—also known as housework—is done by underpaid and undervalued racialized women."[624] White bourgeois feminists like to think that their problems and the way they perceive them are universal, white ignorance protecting them from learning history. Though they applauded women of color continuing to do the "essential jobs" under lockdown, the latter were quickly forgotten.

In 2020, the UN warned that women in the Global South and women of color in the North would bear the heavier burden of the crisis because nearly 40 percent of *all women employed globally* were working in the four most affected industries by the pandemic: hotels, restaurants, retail, and manufacturing.[625] Further, they account for more than 75 percent of all unpaid care work in the world and constitute the majority of workers in the cleaning industry and 90 percent in social services.[626] Including girls, women dedicate roughly 12.5 billion hours to unpaid work every day, and due to the overload of domestic work, 42 percent of women in the world are excluded from the labor market (compared to 6 percent of men).[627] Globally, 58 percent of employed women work in informal employment, and estimates suggested that during the first month of the pandemic, informal workers globally lost an average of 60 percent of their income.[628] According to 2021 projections of the International Labour Organization (ILO), "fewer women than men would regain employment during the COVID-19 recovery." They also showed that state intervention slowed the impact of COVID-19 on women's employment: Colombia and Senegal "created or strengthened support for women entrepreneurs," and in Mexico and Kenya, "quotas were established to guarantee that women benefited from public employment programmes."[629] The year 2020 also saw Bangladesh under water, a burning Arctic, devastating fires in California, the increasing frequencies of extreme weather events, the consequences of austerity programs imposed by the IMF or the World Bank on public health services, prevention, and education, and growing inequalities on a global scale—all of which added to the gravity of COVID-19. The pandemic highlighted what the movement for environmental justice had argued for a while: the existence of environmental racism, which "refers to the unequal access to a clean environment and basic environmental resources based on race," and the fact that "communities of color are disproportionately victimized by environmental hazards and are far more likely to live in areas with heavy pollution."[630] Indeed, as climate disaster continues to destroy habitats and livelihoods, infectious diseases will spread more easily and rapidly through populations.[631]

But looking only for the consequences of climate change is taking a wrong path, as environmental and social justice campaigner Jeremy Williams has shown.[632] Climate change is structurally racist, disproportionately caused by white people in majority-white countries, with the damage unleashed overwhelmingly on people of color, and the climate crisis reflects, and reinforces racial injustices.[633] The pandemic is not behind us.

The killer was not only the virus, one might say, but the afterlives of slavery and colonialism and the current politics of unbreathing and extraction. The uninhabitable world is not the consequence of natural phenomena, and climate disaster is increasing its uninhabitability. In 2022, parts of India and Pakistan reached 50°C, the Philippines suffered destruction from another strong hurricane season, floods devastated the Durban region of South Africa, and wars continued to ravage countries and peoples. The economy of extractive exhaustion of bodies and minds has been compounded by the economy of suffocation. Even before being born, children in the Global South and in poor, Indigenous, Black, and non-white neighborhoods in the Global North are more vulnerable to premature death. Studies have found that "air pollution [is] linked to harm to children while they are still in the womb": "The Southern California Children's Health study looked at the long-term effects of air pollution on children and teenagers. Tracking 1,759 children who were between ages 10 and 18 from 1993 to 2001, researchers found that those who grew up in more polluted areas face the increased risk of having reduced lung growth, which may never recover to their full capacity."[634] Children exposed to air pollution in the womb are born with more respiratory diseases and less resistance to further respiratory and cardiovascular diseases.

The politics of unbreathing are historically racist. "There is an increase in respiratory diseases due to harmful products emitted in the air and water," said Cri activist Melina Laboucan-Massimo about the extraction of tar sands in her region, where, as of 2010, more than 2,600 oil and gas wells had been drilled.[635] Armies have contributed to pollution and contamination of land, air, and water. The environmental impact of wars begins long before they do and lingers long after. As the Conflict and Environment Observatory summarizes, military forces consume great quantities of resources: common metals and rare earth elements, water, and hydrocarbons. Military vehicles, aircraft, vessels, buildings, and infrastructure all require energy, and frequently this comes from low-efficiency oil.[636] Military bases and facilities, whether on land or at sea, for testing or training, are highly polluting, and in their environment, cancer and respiratory diseases are common. The deadly contamination of bodies and the environment by military activity is intimately tied to racial capitalism and its uneven effects on life span.[637]

The aftermaths of military damage upon breathing persist for generations: one has only to think of the ongoing detriments to health, including respiratory cancers, caused by Agent Orange in Vietnam, Laos, and Cambodia, which I discussed at the outset.[638] The objective of this powerful defoliant, 80 million liters of which were sprayed on Vietnam by the U.S. Army between 1964 and 1975, was to destroy the forest where Vietcong fighters took refuge, and to destroy crops. Between 2.1 and 4.8 million Vietnamese were directly exposed, and to this number must be added Cambodians, Laotians, U.S. civilians and military personnel, and their various allies.[639]

Imagining and practicing strategies of *de-poisoning*—part of what I am calling a decolonial feminist cleaning, as opposed to *cleaning up*—contributes to the struggle for the right to breathe. De-poisoning practices include: Indigenous struggles for the preservation of forests or against the privatization of rivers; Indian peasants fighting against the construction of dams that damage both the natural and cultural environment; or people around the world boycotting or protesting against the polluting industries of weapons, fast fashion, agribusiness, and on-demand e-commerce. Making the right to breathe a revolutionary demand means dismantling the racist economy of exhaustion and suffocation. The revolutionary right to breathe means asserting this vital function, which is hindered by capitalism: if we can breathe, we can talk, shout, and sing; we can express, in words, our anger, sadness, or joy. If we can speak, we must be breathing, and so, we are alive. Fighting for the right to breathe, by striving to reduce air pollution, is fighting for the right to a dignified life.

The Politics of Refusal

During slavery, marooning was a practice of radical refusal. Escaping the plantation meant creating autonomous ways of life in a new environment by learning what that environment was offering (mountains to hide in, rivers for water, forests for food) and by using ancestral knowledge (how to fight, how to grow food, how to commemorate, to mourn, and to celebrate). In Reunion, maroons not only survived the war waged against them by the armed militia of plantation owners, they carved forever their names on the territories they had liberated, and to this day, the mountains in the interior of the island bears their names: Dimitile, Cimendef, Anchaing . . . By leaving their names to the spaces they had conquered and lived in, the maroons won a victory over colonial hegemony, which made every effort to erase their memories and their struggles. Contrary to the official narrative, maroons did not disappear after the abolition of slavery in 1848; they continued to be autonomous from the colonial norms of life, property, and work. To this day, marooning remains a praxis of refusal in the (post)colonial situation where the people of Reunion have no real autonomy over their lives.

In 1979, three brothers, the Adékalom brothers, small-scale farmers, settled near Étang-Salé, in the southwest of the island. Condemned and imprisoned for "squatting" on a plot of the Office National des Forêts (National Forest Organization, a state institution) with their herd, they were given disproportionate sentences, and fined exorbitantly for occupying the state-owned plot of land. On October 25, 1979, gendarmes and agents from the Office National des Forêts surrounded the Adékaloms' *boukan* (the Creole word for maroons' camps). The police operation was extremely violent; the state confiscated their property and auctioned off their animals.[640] They became the focal point of a complex struggle for independence and cultural resistance. Danyel Waro, a *maloyeur*, sang: "Adekalom Adekalom Adekalom paye pas / Adekalom Adekalom Adekalom paye pas l'amende là. Ici la Réunion kartié étang-salé / 3 jeunes Réyonais la partie marron" (Adékalom, Adékalom don't pay the fine / don't pay that fine. In Reunion, at Étang Salé / three young Reunionnese went marooning). Waro extolled the fact that the Adékalom brothers did not pay the fine and that they had followed the long tradition of marooning. The

Adékalom brothers were challenging the law of state property rooted in slavery and colonial law. Their story lived through the song of Danyel Waro, but their practice of marooning as living communism was buried in the past by the repressive state. As we saw in the examples of Guiana, Guadeloupe, and Mayotte, among others, the French state remains a colonial and racial state.

With their action, the Adékalom brothers affirmed that the land belonged to those who worked it, not to the colonial settlers. Their struggle joined the vast range of fights against colonial state violence so clearly expressed by an Indian reserve commissioner in 1876, on an Indian reserve on Vancouver Island in the region currently known as Canada. He "addressed members of 'a Native audience' (Nation unspecified), who were being moved to reserves that were a fraction of the size of their previous Land bases. He explained, 'The Land was of no value to you. The trees were of no value to you. The Coal was of no value to you. The white man came he improved the land you can follow his [*sic*] example.'"[641] For this settler commissioner, "until Europeans arrived, most of the land was waste, or, where native people were obviously using it, [their] uses were inadequate."[642]

We can expand that remark to land without a native population, such as Reunion. The absence of a native population when the French colonized the island has fed a narrative that claims that since there was no native population, the land belongs equally to "all" (to descendants of enslaved, of settlers, of plantation owners, of French civil servants who work there). That narrative adopted by conservative politicians and media is also supported by a fringe of local historians, such as Olivier Fontaine, for whom a colony is "a territory on which there's already a population, which is conquered militarily or by treaty, and on which a dominant country settles and organizes the colony according to its interests."[643] To him, the "aim was to make Reunion, and therefore the Reunion population, look like victims of colonization, on a par with the Algerians, Indochinese and Cameroonians, so as to be able to demand reparations and claim autonomy. It has therefore become an ideological and political issue."[644] The island becomes an exception, an example of multicultural France. But the land belongs first to those who escaped slavery and created on the territory itself, from what had been a land of unfreedom, a space of freedom. It belongs to those who work the land. By seizing the land, the natural resources (forest, water, air), and wealth stolen from the people by slavery and capitalism, the Adékalom brothers worked in the service of revolution.

I share here the ethical imperatives that Maynard and Simpson propose in their conversation about decolonization and the right to land when the claims of African Americans and Indigenous peoples of the Americas are considered. "To fully understand the post-Columbus world, I believe we must think through Indigenous genocide in the Americas and in African contexts along the commencement of the African transatlantic slave trade," says Simpson, adding that "land is of unquestionable importance to Indigenous peoples and land is of unquestionable importance to Black peoples."[645] But to Black peoples deported in the colonies, "there's really nowhere else to go back to."[646] Hence, "what if Black and Indigenous relationality refuses settler logic and centres the dismantling in a grounding of the very best practices of Indigenous and Black radical politics?"[647] With the "deep sharing that comes with being part of the land"[648] that they propose, the potential for a decolonial global ethics emerges that respects different contexts. Hence, if I apply their propositions to the case of Reunion, I argue that decolonial justice and restitution of land are not about native rights but about the right to land built by struggles against slavery and anticolonialism, about the ways oppressed Reunionnese created Creole ways of cultivating the land, refusing the logic of plantation extraction and exhaustion of the land with their Creole gardens and their knowledge of medicinal plants that their ancestors brought from their native lands (Madagascar, East Africa, India, China)—but also from 17th-century poor rural France.

Collectives answer to the violence of the state and corporations' violence with the occupation of sites, protests, taking the state and corporations to court, answering to violence with anti-violence strategies. It means overcoming how "we have been so programmed into believing that violence doesn't accomplish anything, that it only begets other violence, that we fail to take steps to defend ourselves, because we believe that we will lose," as Black Panther Dhoruba Bin Wahad has said.[649] We cannot wait for reforms in the production of waste, racialization, gendering, and over-exploitation of cleaners. Cleaners have shown that interventions, occupation, and strikes "can generate the quick wins needed to sustain and grow" social revolutionary movements.[650]

Anti-Cleaning Politics

What I call *a decolonial feminist politics of cleaning* entails, as I have said above, cleaning liberated from racism and white patriarchal bourgeois norms, while paying attention to the need for cleaning oneself—vital, *elemental* needs that must be attended to. Decolonial feminist cleaning is a strategy of resistance in a time of ruination. Since cleaning, as I have argued, is rooted in the racialized, bourgeois, and colonial ideologies of clean/dirty, in the whitening of cleanliness, in assigning cleaning to women (and to men) of color, and in considering cleaning a job without great importance, reform will not dismantle its racial-class-gender structure. Cleaning must be imagined outside of bourgeois norms (immaculate, germ-free environment) or industrial *cleaning up* (business for capitalists), which is like pushing dust from one place to another. A decolonial feminist politics of cleaning looks at the originary technology of breathing and smell in the slave ship. "Slave ships had air ports carved out of the hull above the water line so that the living human cargo could breathe," and "slave ships were instantly recognizable by the stench they emitted, caused by various kinds of human excreta: urine, feces, vomit, or pungent, fear-filled sweat. It was said in Charleston, South Carolina, when the wind was blowing in off the water, that one could smell a slave ship before one could see it."[651] It is not that there is no cleaning up to do; rather, one must look at programs of rehabilitation and restoration developed by Indigenous people and peoples of color; and there again, one must distinguish these from punitive programs of rehabilitation based on the criminalization of Blacks, Arabs, Indigenous peoples, Brown peoples.[652]

A decolonial feminist cleaning is not anti-technology, though it is aware that numerous technologies have served to reinforce domination and racism,[653] but we also know that colonialism and capitalism did not need advanced technology to deforest, practice genocides, create plantations. The exploitation of enslaved Blacks and what could be considered rudimentary technologies (sailing ships) compared to today fed the emerging capitalism. In the speculative fiction book *Everything for Everyone*, the authors imagine themselves as recording the people who, by the middle of the 21st century, have faced war, famine, economic collapse, and climate catastrophe and have forged a collective alternative after insurrections reached the nerve center of global capitalism—New York City. The members of the post-catastrophe commune turn to technology to design "a new ecosystem partially from scratch" and to hold "major debates about how to balance autonomy, accountability, and sovereignty in land use decisions."[654] The objective is not to save, because "it's too late to *save*, but we might repurpose. Suturing, jerry-rigging, cobbling together."[655] Currently, the objective is to find "unexpected resources in the muck, using them in new ways. A strategy for ruination."[656]

Cleaning in the parlance of white supremacy is *cleaning up*, getting rid of the inhabitants of a site it wants to preserve. Its understanding of preservation and conservation is connected to bourgeois patriarchal notions of patrimony and heritage: things must be kept in their "original" state for its heirs, they must remain in the family untouched by non-whites family members and non-whites in general. This idea of conservation as preservation can be observed in the incredible number of looted objects that are kept in Western museums.[657] It is the most blatant example of conservation as an obsession for a rigid and fixed past and for heritage as private property passed from white father to white son—and thus for humanity, since they stand for humanity and they are the only "humans," as we saw earlier with Wynter. That ideology has pervaded white bourgeois environmentalism, which often propagates the dispossession of Indigenous peoples and peoples of color for the common good of the world.[658] In this utopia as dystopia, green enclaves and natural parks are created to offer the rich and powerful the image of a world cleaned of everything that could disturb its enjoyment. The museification of the environment mirrors the structure of the museum: appropriating memories, knowledge, objects, plants, animals, and hiring some people as décor to project an idea of beauty.

The ideology of a Malthusian environment can be found in the current association between migrants and a threat to the environment that Hage, cited above, has analyzed. The current rise of "eco-minded white supremacy follows a direct line from the powerful attorney, conservationist and eugenicist Madison Grant—a friend of trees, Teddy Roosevelt, and the colonial superiority of white land stewardship. Grant, along with the influential naturalist John Muir and other early Anglo-Saxon conservationists, was critical in preserving the country's wildlands for white enjoyment."[659] Muir, who founded the well-admired Sierra Club in 1892, was disturbed by the "uncleanliness of the Native Americans," whom he wanted removed from Yosemite.[660] Published in 1968, *The Population Bomb* by Stanford University biology professor Paul Ehrlich predicted that overpopulation would fuel worldwide famine and global upheaval. Indeed, white environmentalism became linked with crude Malthusianism, the idea that the birth rates in the Global South were threatening the environment; vast programs of sterilization were organized—an ideology that has not disappeared. As Miéville writes: "In the combative variant called Deep Ecology, the tweeness of that vision can morph into brutality, according to which the problem is overpopulation, humanity itself. At its most cheerfully eccentric lies the Voluntary Human Extinction Movement, advocating an end to breeding: at the most vicious are the pronouncements of David Foreman of Earth First!, faced with the Ethiopian famine of 1984: '[T]he worst thing we could do in Ethiopia is to give aid—the best thing would be to just let nature seek its own balance, to let the people there just starve.' "[661] Programs of birth control, of forced abortion and sterilization,[662] the lack of water for women and girls, and climate catastrophe all combine to maintain the racial fabrication of stress, mental health problems, exhaustion, and premature death. "Environmentalists were hardcore eugenicists. They were as committed to racial thinking as they were to protecting the great redwoods in California," said Heidi Beirich, intelligence project director at the Southern Poverty Law Center.[663]

But "faced with the scale of what's coming," Miéville writes, it is tempting to turn to "a self-shackling green politeness. 'Anything', the argument goes, 'is better than nothing.'"[664] It is that ideology of "better than nothing" that allows capitalism to continue. We are sold a dream: that small gestures and goodwill will stop the devastation of the planet. True, the reading of reports can easily produce despair, but "despair without fear, without resignation, without a sense of defeat, makes for a stance towards the world here such as I have never seen before," as John Berger wrote about the situation of the Palestinians.[665] He quotes a Palestinian former prisoner:

You learn how to struggle together and become inseparable. Certain conditions have improved over the last forty years—improved thanks to us and our hunger strikes. The most I did was twenty days. We won a quarter of an hour more exercise time each day. In the long-sentence prisons they used to mask the windows so there was no sunshine in the cells. We won back some sunshine. We got one body search removed from the daily routine . . . . In the streets it's the language of bullets and stones between us. Inside it's different. They're in prison just as we are. The difference is we believe in what's got us there, and they mostly don't, because they're just there to earn a living. I know of some friendships that began like that.[666]

This is what the cleaners' strikes do. They reject the "swathes of ecological thinking (that) are caught up with a nebulous, sentimentalized spiritualist utopia" in "what the ecofeminist Chaia Heller calls 'Eco-la-la.'"[667] The strike, "as it has been reinvented by contemporary feminism, shows how precarity is a common condition, but also one differentiated through class discrimination, sexism, and racism."[668] Gago, speaking of the women's strike in Argentina, has argued that "the strike has allowed for mapping, from the perspective of insubordination, the forms of labor exploitation" to "map the unrecognized and unpaid ways in which we produce value and to elaborate a diverse collective image of what we call *work, territory* and *conflict.*"[669] The internationalism of cleaners' strikes brings to light the fact that it is a global struggle.

In Aubervilliers (Greater Paris) in June 2023, a group of women of color told me that what they aspired to for their neighborhood was trees, gardens (and not "green spaces" conceived by designers), clean streets, and safety. They understood that the environment in which they live was fabricated by race and class, that the state did not think they deserve to create and manage

their own environment.[670] The uncleanliness and the lack of trees and gardens were designed to express racial and class contempt.

The daily gestures of resistance and of humanization of the world belie
the dreary tone of reports. A woman interviewed by the French radio France
Inter on August 20, 2023, who takes care of the sick and the elderly—knowing
that, in institutions, overworked staff only pass a humid glove over the face,
under the armpits, and between the legs of patients—has decided to give one
hour to each person she washes and then styles their hair, shaves men, and
gives them some perfume.[671] She knows it matters.

It is important, however, to speak as I conclude this book about a decolonial feminist politics of cleaning of how Canadian-American feminist writer
and activist Shulamith Firestone resolved in *The Dialectics of Sex* the issue of
women's drudgery work, in which she included reproduction.[672] To Firestone,
"cybernation would take care of most domestic chores."[673] Firestone wanted
a total liberation from drudgery and material contingencies, the end of labor
and reproduction. She dreamed of cybernetic socialism, of a feminist revolution that would give women control over technology. And we recall Davis's
view of cleaning as so unproductive and irredeemable that no one of any gender should waste their precious time on it. She pleaded rather for a universal income for all and for a hi-tech socialization of housework. Even if a job
is repetitive and invisible, it would get women out of the home and into the
workplace, where they would discover collective action and escape the atom-
ization and privatization associated with domesticity. Even if work is brutal, it
is a site of social, racial, and gendered struggle, where the possibility of class,
race, and gender consciousness arises.

In a 2017 article, "Promethean Labors and Domestic Realism," tech-
nofeminism and social reproduction theorist Helen Hester argued that "the
idea that automation in the home might eradicate many of the daily burdens
of housekeeping is one that has long been promoted by consumer capitalism,
and Firestone's techno-optimism here affirms her critics' suspicions that she
neglects the socio-political."[674] Though Hester acknowledges there are limits
to Firestone's theory (especially racism, colonialism, and imperialism, which
are not "details"), she argues for a "Promethean feminism," where "love,
work, leisure, the family, science, art, and sexual reproduction are all equally
mutable, contestable, and available for species-wide re-engineering." She
adds: "The home can be reconceived of as a site of Promethean potentiality
rather than as an example of stubbornly embedded material hegemony; that
is to say, it is a space that can be mutated to facilitate a Promethean politics
rather than a site of risk aversion inherently obstructive to the development of
the solidarities that such a politics demands," and concludes that "feminism

should be Promethean, and Prometheanism *must* be feminist."[675] I thought it was important to quote these two responses to the drudgery of cleaning, even though both look exclusively at housework and do not address the industrialization and marketisation of cleaning, where the work is not unpaid, but underpaid, exploited, and the site of systemic sexual and racial violence. I don't think that cybernation or trained and well-paid workers fully answer the questions I raised at the beginning, notably: What is a decolonial feminist cleaning?

What I have tried to do in this book has been to look at the colonial-racial fabrication of clean/unclean, at corporate *cleaning up* as washing the untold damages colonialism and capitalism have produced, and to analyze how genders, race, and class intervene. I made clear that if women of color constitute the majority of cleaners worldwide (in private or public spaces), men assigned by race and caste to cleaning are also exposed to contamination and pollution. Colonialism is pollution, capitalism is waste producing, people of color are dying of fatigue and disease: these are concrete facts that neither green colonialism nor green capitalism can stop, because they rest on racialization and the fabrication of premature death.

A decolonial feminist and antiracist politics of cleaning acknowledges cleaning as a vital need but *imagines cleaning out of drudgery*. There will be no return to a pristine state, no clean slate, but a world where cleaning will be *imagined out of cleaning up* as erasure and dispossession. It means attacking the structures of violence rather than lamenting their effects. As abolitionist activists Day and McBean, cited earlier, have said, the struggle requires "intervention" because intervention "builds the confidence needed to harness class power," and because intervention "can generate quick wins needed to sustain and grow"[676] movements of resistance. These interventions create multiple "[archipelagos] of solidarity."[677] This is not solidarity as it has been conceived by liberalism (a private economic connection between a creditor and a debtor), but communally conceived solidarity, an internationalism from below.[678]

The ways people conceive of what cleaning is, what smells are delicious, must be considered. What matters is to get rid of the racialized hierarchy that leads to concrete politics that affect housing, access to water, to toilets. It is also about the freedom to arrange green spaces and refuse norms imposed by the state. Struggles change people and their environment. A decolonial feminist and antiracist cleaning cannot not be exclusively associated with care because "care is not inherently good," as "Natasha Myers (settler), and Ana Viseu (unmarked)" have pointed out, writing that "practices of care are always shot through with asymmetrical power relations. . . . Care organizes, classifies, and disciplines bodies. Colonial regimes show us precisely how care can become a means of governance."[679] As an internationalist politics, this theory of care acknowledges a genealogical connection between race, waste, gender, and class but does not consider them analogical. By building "(life)affirming institutions,"[680] struggles against the whitening of cleaning create sites of freedom. What matters is "to learn to stop appealing to the system itself for redress, to stop believing the forces that are killing you can or will save you,"[681] to look with open eyes at "the hideous smile of gold-toothed capitalism, a green gold smile with the breath of a jackal."[682] Resistance is global.

Notes

i   Teele Rebane and Allegra Goodwin, "Israel Has Dropped the Same Number of Bombs on Gaza in Six Days as during the Entire 2014 Conflict," CNN, October 13, 2023, https://edit ion.cnn.com/middleeast/live-news/israel-news-hamas-war-10-13-23/h_2cb99ccbc0e06 4342a74eb7cbad0fb8f.

ii Hanna Duggal, Mohammed Hussein, and Shakeeb Asrar, "Israel's Attacks on Gaza: The Weapons and Scale of Destruction," *Al Jazeera*, November 9, 2023, https://www.aljaze era.com/news/longform/2023/11/9/israel-attacks-on-gaza-weapons-and-scale-of-dest ruction.

iii Ariel Salleh, *Ecofeminism as Politics: Nature, Marx and the Postmodern* (Zed Books, 2017), 2nd ed., pp. 288, 289.

iv Studs Terkel, *Working: People Talk about What They Do All Day and How They Feel about What They Do* (New Press, 1974), p. 225.

Is Cleaning a Decolonial Struggle?

1 See for instance Robert Dorfman "Incidence of the Benefits and Costs of Environmental Programs," *American Economic Review* 67, no. 1 (1977): 333–340; Total Energy, "Our Climate, Coastal Areas and Oceans Actions," https://fondation.totalenergies.com/en/our-actions/our-climate-coastal-areas-and-oceans-actions; Shell Foundation, "Focus Areas," https://shellfoundation.org/focus-areas/.

2 Shell Foundation, "Gender," https://shellfoundation.org/gender/. One sees similar moves by TotalEnergies and BP.

3 U.S. Department of Defense, "Environmental Programs," 2004, https://comptroller.defe nse.gov/Portals/45/Documents/defbudget/fy2004/budget_justification/pdfs/01_Operat ion_and_Maintenance/Overview_Book/25_Environmental_Programs.pdf, pp. 133–134.

4 See the U.S. Army Environmental Command, Army Clean Up Program, at https://aec. army.mil/restore/cleanup; and Army Restoration Program at https://aec.army.mil/rest ore/IRP.

5 Anne Nguyen, "L'Agent Orange au Vietnam: La violence lente de la guerre à travers la destruction des écosystèmes," *Grip*, July 25, 2023, https://www.grip.org/lagent-ora nge-au-vietnam-la-violence-lente-de-la-guerre-a-travers-la-destruction-des-ecosyste mes/. Unless otherwise stated, all translations from the French are mine. See also David Zierler, *The Invention of Ecocide: Agent Orange, Vietnam, and the Scientists Who Changed the Way We Think about the Environment* (University of Georgia Press, 2011); David Biggs, *Footprints of War: Militarized Landscapes in Vietnam* (University of Washington Press, 2018).

6 Nguyen, "L'Agent Orange au Vietnam," p. 199.

7 Scott R. Anderson, "Walking Away from the World Court," *Lawfare*, October 5, 2018, https://www.lawfaremedia.org/article/walking-away-world-court.

"Slow Violence"

8 Rob Nixon, *Slow Violence and the Environmentalism of the Poor* (Harvard University Press, 2011).

9 Ibid., p. 6.

10 "No Clean Up, No Justice: Shell's Oil Pollution in the Niger Delta," Amnesty International, June 18, 2020, https://www.amnesty.org/en/latest/news/2020/06/no-clean-up-no-justice-shell-oil-pollution-in-the-niger-delta.

11 John Vidal, "Niger Delta Oil Spills Clean-Up Will Take 30 Years, Say UN," *Our World*, May 8, 2011, https://ourworld.unu.edu/en/niger-delta-oil-spills-clean-up-will-take-30-years-says-un.

12 Godwin Ojo, cited in "Shell's Oil Pollution: Niger Delta People 'Sick of Waiting' for Justice," Friends of the Earth Europe, June 18, 2020, https://friendsoftheearth.eu/press-release/shells-oil-pollution-niger-delta-people-sick-of-waiting-for-justice/.

13 "Shell in Nigeria: Polluted Communities Can 'Sue in English Courts,'" *BBC News*, February 23, 2021, https://www.bbc.com/news/world-africa-56041189.

14 Personal notes from Gilmore's online intervention for the international conference "Capitalism, Anticapitalism and Social Sciences Engaged on a Global Scale: Around the Works of Immanuel Wallerstein," Fondation Maison des Sciences de l'Homme, Paris, September 11–12, 2023.

15 The phrase "benign neglect," Moynihan said in a telephone interview, came from an 1839 report on Canada by the British Earl of Durham. The Durham report, he said, described Canada as having grown more competent and capable of governing itself "through many years of benign neglect" by Britain. Peter Kihss, " 'Benign Neglect' on Race Is Suggested by Moynihan," *New York Times*, March 1, 1970, https://www.nytimes.com/1970/03/01/archives/benign-neglect-on-race-is-proposed-by-moynihan-moynihan-urges.html. " 'Salutary neglect' was the unwritten, unofficial stance of benign neglect by England toward the American colonies. On the whole, the colonists were relatively autonomous and were allowed to govern themselves with minimal royal and parliamentary interference. The colonies, in turn, fulfilled their role in the mercantilist system as the suppliers of raw materials for manufacture in England and as markets for those finished goods." See "Salutary or Benign Neglect," https://community.weber.edu/weberreads/salutary_or_benign_neglect.htm.

16 Daniel Patrick Moynihan, Memorandum for the President, the White House, January 16, 1970, https://www.nixonlibrary.gov/sites/default/files/virtuallibrary/documents/jul10/53.pdf, p. 3.

17 Ibid., p. 5.

18 Ibid., p. 7.

19 Ibid., p. 5.

20 Kihss, " 'Benign Neglect' on Race."

21 Moynihan, Memorandum for the President, p. 7.

22 Moynihan is also known for his infamous 1965 report, *The Negro Family: The Case for National Action* (Office of Policy Planning and Research, US Department of Labor, 1965). The report argued that the matriarchal structure of Black culture weakened the ability of Black men to function as authority figures. The report, which has had a lasting impact, was immediately attacked by Black scholars and activists and it continues to be the object of critical studies. Black feminists have denounced its inextricable racism, sexism, and defense of capitalism. See for instance, Hortense Spillers, "Mama's Baby, Papa's Maybe: An American Grammar Book," *Diacritics* 17, no. 2 (1987): 64–81; Saidiya V. Hartman and Frank B. Wilderson, "The Position of the Unthought," *Qui Parle* 13, no. 2 (2003): 183–201.

23 Ruth Wilson Gilmore, *Abolition Geography: Essays towards Liberation* (Verso, 2022), p. 229.

24 Ibid, p. 230.

25 Ibid, pp. 227–228.

26 "Guilherme Boulos: Struggles of the Roofless," interview by Mario Sergi Conti, *New Left Review*, July–August 2021, https://newleftreview.org/issues/ii130/articles/struggles-of-the-roofless. See also Sue Branford and Jan Rocha, eds., *Cutting the Wire: The Story of the Landless Movement in Brazil* (Latin American Bureau, 2002).

27 "Guilherme Boulos."

28 Helena Varkker, *The Forests for the Palms: Essays on the Environment in Southeast Asia* (ISEAS, 2021).

29 Arne Hector, Luciana Mazeto, Vinicius Lopez, and Minze Tummescheit, dirs., *Urban Solutions* (Germany-Brazil, 2022).

30 Personal notes from *Urban Solutions*.

Radical Hope

31 Robyn Maynard and Leanne Betasamosake Simpson, *Rehearsals for Living* (MIT Press, 2021), p. 25.

32 Ruth Wilson Gilmore, "Foreword," in Maynard and Simpson, *Rehearsals for Living*, p. 9.

33 Ibid., p. 10.

34 Aviah Sarah Day and Shanice Octavia McBean, *Abolition Revolution* (Pluto Books, 2022), p. 203.

35 On abolitionism, see Wilson Gilmore, *Abolition Geography*.

36 Françoise Vergès, *Program de désordre absolu. Décoloniser la musée* (La Fabrique, 2023), forthcoming in English as *A Program of Absolute Disorder: Decolonising the Museum* (Pluto Press, 2024).

37 Mierle Laderman Ukeles, *Manifesto for Maintenance Art*, 1969, available at https://queen smuseum.org/wp-content/uploads/2016/04/Ukeles-Manifesto-for-Maintenance-Art-1969.pdf.

38 The performance was part the 2018 exhibition "Bell Invites" in collaboration with Emory Douglas and the HIPHopHuis, the University of Color, which took place in Stedelijk Museum Bureau Amsterdam. See https://www.pkaersenhout.com/copy-of-installations-2017-1.

39 For instance, see *La Cérémonie* (1995) and *Diary of a Chambermaid* (1964) for the first approach, and *The Help* (2011) or the Lifetime series *Devious Maids* for a whitewashing patronizing approach that makes racism and class mere details.

The Elemental

40 Being a trivial matter means being "ordinary," or "insignificant, trifling" (1590s); it comes from the Latin *trivialis*, which means "common, commonplace, vulgar." https://www.etymonline.com/word/trivial.

41 "La police harcèle, tente d'intimider et agresse violemment les personnes qui aident les réfugiés," Amnesty International, June 5, 2019, https://www.amnesty.org/fr/latest/press-rele ase/2019/06/france-police-harassing-intimidating-and-even-using-violence-against-peo ple-helping-refugees/.

42 Personal communication with a collective of volunteers based in the northwest of France, September 18, 2023.

43 Simon Louvet, "La police accusée de voler les tentes de migrants à Paris, en plein trêve hivernale," ActuParis, December 22, 2021, https://actu.fr/ile-de-france/paris_75056/vid eos-la-police-accusee-de-voler-les-tentes-de-migrants-a-paris-en-pleine-treve-hivernale_ 47417201.html.

44 Thomas Berry, *The Great Work: Our Way into the Future* (Crown, 2000).

45 Ashe, "Qu'est-ce que la théorie du colibri?," *ConsoFutur*, January 16, 2023, https://www.con sofutur.com/c-quest-ce-que-la-theorie-du-colibri-7851/.

46 Ibid.

Cleaning, Cleanliness, Cleansing

47 Max Liboiron and Josh Lepawsky, *Discard Studies: Wasting, Systems, and Power* (MIT Press, 2022), p. 26.

48 Ibid, p. 3.

49 Bernice Yeung, "Under Cover of Darkness, Janitors Face Rape and Sexual Assault," *Reveal*, June 23, 2015, https://revealnews.org/article/under-cover-of-darkness-female-janitors-face-rape-and-assault/.

50 This is the refrain of "Dur dur ménage!," a song written in solidarity with the strikers by Bobbyodet, an Ivoirian singer and composer. For the video of the song and further information, see Tyshka Rostov, " 'Dur, dur ménage!' Le clip entraînant des femmes de chambre en grève de l'hôtel Ibis Batignolles," *Révolution permanente*, November 4, 2020, https:// www.revolutionpermanente.fr/Dur-dur-menage-le-clip-entrainant-des-femmes-de-cham bre-en-greve-de-l-hotel-Ibis-Batignolles.

Water, an Elemental

51 See Frank Westerman, *Les ingénieurs de l'âme*, translated by Danielle Losman (Christian Bourgeois, 2004).

52 "Water Scarcity," WWF, https://www.worldwildlife.org/threats/water-scarcity.

53 "1 in 4 People in the World Do Not Have Access to Clean Drinking Water, the UN Says," NPR, March 22, 2023, https://www.npr.org/2023/03/22/1165248040/1-in-4-people-in-world-lack-clean-drinking-water-u-n-says.

54 In 2020, the UN declared that "everyone on the planet has a right to a healthy environment, including clean air, water, and a stable climate." Climate and Clean Water Coalition, August 2, 2022, https://www.ccacoalition.org/news/un-declares-healthy-environment-includ ing-clean-air-human-right.

Women as a Praxis

55 I borrow this phrase from Max Liboiron, *Pollution Is Colonialism* (Duke University Press, 2021).

56 Françoise Vergès, "Capitalocene, Waste, Race, and Gender," *e-flux* 100 (May 2019), https:// www.e-flux.com/journal/100/269165/capitalocene-waste-race-and-gender/.

57 Yoga belongs to this industry, developing from an "underground practice to a multibillion-pound industry driven by celebrity such as Gwyneth Paltrow and Jennifer Aniston. In 2019, the global yoga industry was worth an estimated $37.46bn (£30.53bn)." Nadia Khomani,

"Cultural Appropriation: Discussion Builds over Western Yoga Industry," *Guardian*, December 12, 2022, https://www.theguardian.com/lifeandstyle/2022/dec/12/cultural-appropriation-discussion-builds-over-western-yoga-industry.

Exiting Colonial Dystopia

58 China Miéville, "A Strategy for Ruination," *Boston Review*, January 8, 2018, https://bosto nreview.net/literature-culture-china-mieville-strategy-ruination.

59 "An Open Letter to Extinction Rebellion," *Red Pepper*, May 3, 2019, https://www.redpepper. org.uk/an-open-letter-to-extinction-rebellion/. Wretched of the Earth is "a grassroots collective for Indigenous, black, brown and diaspora groups and individuals demanding climate justice and acting in solidarity with our communities, both here in the UK and in Global South." Wretched of the Earth, Facebook page, https://www.facebook.com/wotearth/.

60 Ibid.

61 Juan Pablo Gutierrez, @juan_pablo_gutierrez_official, Instagram, November 20, 2022. Capitals in the original.

62 Ibid.

63 Gilmore, "Foreword," in Maynard and Simpson, *Rehearsals for Living*, p. 10.

Polluting, Contaminating, Cleaning Up

64 Fred Magdoff and Chris Williams, "Capitalist Economies Create Waste, Not Social Value," *Monthly Review Press*, August 17, 2017, https://truthout.org/articles/capitalist-economies-create-waste-not-social-value/.

65 See the emerging field of energetic humanities with Sheena Wislon, Adam Carlson, and Imre Szeman, *Petrocultures: Oil, Politics Cultures* (Mac-Gill Queen University Press, 2017).

66 Laurie L. Dove, "Has Online Shopping Changed How Much Cardboard We Use?" HowStuffWorks, June 9, 2023, https://science.howstuffworks.com/environmental/green-science/online-shopping-cardboard-consumption-industry-amazon.htm; "What A Waste 2.0," World Bank, https://datatopics.worldbank.org/what-a-waste/.

67 "Trends in Solid Waste Management," World Bank, https://datatopics.worldbank.org/what-a-waste/trends_in_solid_waste_management.html.

68 "Construction created an estimated third of the world's overall waste, and at least 40% of the world's carbon dioxide emissions." Norman Miller, "The Industry Creating a Third of the World's Waste," BBC, Future Planet, December 16, 2021, https://www.bbc.com/fut ure/article/20211215-the-buildings-made-from-rubbish. Per the EC, "construction and demolition waste (CDW) accounts for more than a third of all waste generated in the EU." "Construction and Demolition Waste," European Commission, https://environment.ec.eur opa.eu/topics/waste-and-recycling/construction-and-demolition-waste_en.

69 Joshua Frank, "The South China Sea's Resources War: It's Not Only about Fossil Fuels," *CounterPunch*, September 15, 2023, https://www.counterpunch.org/2023/09/15/the-south-china-seas-resource-wars-its-not-only-about-fossil-fuels/.

70 "Trends in Solid Waste Management."

71 See the full text of the agreement at https://avalon.law.yale.edu/20th_century/den001.asp.

72 Victoria Herrmann, "Unearthing the Arctic's Toxic Past: Camp Century and Cold War Secrets," *High North News*, August 11, 2018, https://www.highnorthnews.com/nb/unearth ing-arctics-toxic-past-camp-century-and-cold-war-secrets.

73 Hege Eilertsen, "More Toxic Waste Than Expected on American Base in Greenland," *Arctic Today*, August 25, 2017, https://www.arctictoday.com/more-toxic-waste-than-expected-on-american-base-on-greenland/.

74 Andréa Poiret, "The Policy of Danization of the Local Greenlandic Populations as Viewed by Inhabitants of Ilulissat," *Géoconfluences*, November 1, 2022, http://geoconfluences.ens-lyon.fr/programmes/dnl/dnl-hg-anglais/danization-groenland.

75 Ede Ijjasz-Vasquez, Sameh Wahba and Silpa Kaza, "Here's What Everyone Should Know about Waste," World Bank Blogs, September 20, 2018, https://blogs.worldbank.org/sustainablecities/here-s-what-everyone-should-know-about-waste.

76 Hauke Engel, Martin Stuchtey, and Helda Vanthournout, "Managing Waste in Emerging Markets," McKinsey Sustainability, https://www.mckinsey.com/capabilities/sustainability/our-insights/managing-waste-in-emerging-markets.

77 Ibid.

78 "10 Things You Didn't Know about the World Bank Group's Work on Climate Change," World Bank, October 29, 2021, https://www.worldbank.org/en/news/factsheet/2021/10/29/10-things-you-didn-t-know-about-the-world-bank-group-s-work-on-climate.

79 Emily Field, Alexis Krivkovich, Sandra Kügele, Nicole Robinson, and Lareina Yee, "Women in the Workplace, 2023," McKinsey, https://www.mckinsey.com/featured-insights/diversity-and-inclusion/women-in-the-workplace; and "Race in the Workplace: The Frontline Experience," McKinsey, https://www.mckinsey.com/featured-insights/diversity-and-inclusion/race-in-the-workplace-the-frontline-experience; "The World Bank Group: Addressing Racism and Racial Discrimination," World Bank, November 11, 2021, https://www.worldbank.org/en/news/factsheet/2021/11/11/the-world-bank-group-addressing-racism-and-racial-discrimination; "The World Bank in Gender," World Bank, https://www.worldbank.org/en/topic/gender; Martin Cihak, Montfort Mlachila, and Ratna Sahay, "Race and Racism in Economics," September 2020, https://www.imf.org/en/Publications/fandd/issues/2020/09/race-and-racism-in-economics-IMF; "Race Forward," Bill and Melinda Gates Foundation, https://www.gatesfoundation.org/about/committed-grants/2021/05/inv028280; "Gender Equality," Bill and Melinda Gates Foundation, https://www.gatesfoundation.org/our-work/programs/gender-equality.

80 Larry Summers, cited in Jim Valette, "Larry Summers' War against the Earth," *CounterPunch*, June 1999, https://www.counterpunch.org/1999/06/15/larry-summers-war-against-the-earth/.

81 In *Pollution Is Colonialism*, Max Liboiron discusses at length the notion of threshold and its limits.

The Racial Politics of Wasting and Cleaning Up

82 Jim Wheeler, "Madison Grant and the Dark Side of the Conservation Movement," *Public Historian* 45, no. 3 (2023): 75–82; Dina Gilio-Whitaker, *As Long as Grass Grows: The Indigenous Fight for Environmental Justice from Colonization to Standing Rock* (Beacon Press, 2019); Dorceta Taylor, *The Rise of the American Conservation Movement: Power, Privilege, and the Environmental Protection* (Duke University Press, 2016).

83 Joseph Lee, "How the World's Favorite Conservation Model Was Built on Colonial Violence," *Grist*, April 13, 2023, https://grist.org/indigenous/30x30-world-conservation-model-colonialism-indigenous-peop/.

84 Ibid.

85 Cited in ibid.

86 Ibid.

Race, Gender, Capital, and Cleaning

87 Françoise Vergès, *A Decolonial Feminism*, translated by Ashley J. Bohrer (Pluto Press, 2021), first published as *Un féminisme décolonial* (La Fabrique, 2019); Vergès, "Capitalocene, Waste, Race, and Gender."

88 Regarding the term "civilizational feminism," see Vergès, *A Decolonial Feminism*, ch. 2.

89 Marco D'Eramo, "Darning the Planet," *Sidecar*, August 8, 2023, https://newleftreview.org/sidecar/posts/darning-the-planet.

90 Ibid.

91 Ibid.

92 "One in Five People in the EU at Risk of Poverty or Social Exclusion," Eurostat, October 15, 2021, https://ec.europa.eu/eurostat/web/products-eurostat-news/-/edn-20211015-1; "Poverty and Inequalities Surge across Europe in the Wake of Covid-19," University of Oxford, October 19, 2020, https://www.ox.ac.uk/news/2020-10-29-poverty-and-inequality-surge-across-europe-wake-covid-19; Oxfam, "This Is What Inequality Looks Like in 2022," https://www.weforum.org/agenda/2022/01/inequality-in-2022-oxfam-report/.

93 The World Counts, "A World of Waste," https://www.theworldcounts.com/challenges/planet-earth/state-of-the-planet/world-waste-facts, emphasis mine.

94 Stéphane Mandard, "Pollution Is Responsible for 9 Million Deaths Each Year Worldwide," *Le Monde*, May 18, 2022, https://www.lemonde.fr/en/environment/article/2022/05/18/pollution-is-responsible-for-9-million-deaths-each-year-worldwide_5983946_114.html; "Global Pollution Kills 9 Million People a Year," European Commission, https://ec.europa.eu/newsroom/intpa/items/612355/en.

The Elemental of Cleaning

95 Cristen Hemingway Jaynes, "UAE to Triple Renewable Energy Output amid COP28 Controversy," *EcoWatch*, July 6, 2023, https://www.ecowatch.com/uae-renewable-energy-production.html.

96 Abu Hail, "Solar Panel Cleaning Services in Dubai," https://abuhail.ae/solar-panel-cleaning-services-in-dubai/. See the gallery of photos on their website.

97 Martin Croucher, "Robot 'Maid' Keeps Solar Panels Clean," *The National*, June 6, 2014, https://www.thenationalnews.com/business/technology/robot-maid-keeps-solar-panels-clean-1.304204.

98 Liboiron and Lepawsky, *Discard Studies*, p. 7.

99 K. Tijdens and M. van Klaveren, "Domestic Workers: Their Wages and Work in 12 Countries," WageIndicator data report, University of Amsterdam, 2011, http://www.wageindicator.org/documents/publicationslist/publications-2011/DFL-WageIndicatorReportDomestic%20workers_2011.pdf.

100 "Cleaning Industry in France: Mainly the Domain of Women and Migrants without Any Other Options," ETUI, https://www.etui.org/about-etui/news/cleaning-industry-in-france-mainly-the-domain-of-women-and-migrants-without-any-other-options. In the industry of sanitation and waste handling, Black and Brown men constitute 90 percent of the workers.

101 "Who Are Domestic Workers," ILO, https://www.ilo.org/global/topics/domestic-workers/who/lang--en/index.htm.

102 Kim Kelly, "How Black Washerwomen in the South Became Pioneers of American Labor," *Washington Post*, April 17, 2022, https://www.washingtonpost.com/history/2022/04/17/black-washerwomen-strike/.

The Distribution of Time according to Class and Race

103   Jacques Rancière, *Modern Times* (Multimedia Institute, 2017), p. 61.
104   From "Sisters Are Doin' It for Themselves," 1985, performed by Aretha Franklin and Annie Lennox of Eurythmics.
105   Vergès, "Capitalocene, Waste, Race, and Gender."
106   Ibid.
107   Ibid.
108   Vergès, *A Decolonial Feminism*, pp. vi, 1–3.
109   Louise Rocabert, "Après huit mois de grève et deux de confinement, les travailleuses en lute de l'hôtel Ibis ne lâchent rien," *Basta!*, May 25, 2020, https://basta.media/greve-hotel-Ibis-femmes-de-chambre-CGT-HPE-discriminations.
110   David Dufresne, Melina Laboucan-Massimo, Rudy Wiebe, Nancy Huston, and Naomi Klein, *Brut* (Lux, 2015), p. 86.
111   Ibid.

Why Must Cleaners Be Invisible?

112   Liboiron, *Pollution Is Colonialism*, pp. 104, 106, emphasis in the original.
113   Grace Abena Akese, "Electronic Waste (e-Waste) Science and Advocacy at Agbogblloshie: The Making and Effects of 'the World's Largest e-Waste Dump,'" PhD diss., University of Newfoundland, 2019, p. 95.
114   Vergès, "Capitalocene, Waste, Race, and Gender."
115   Ibid.
116   Ibid.

The Denial of Vital Needs

117   Liboiron and Lepawsky, *Discard Studies*, p. 27.
118   Angela Davis, *Women, Race and Class* (Vintage Books, 1981), p. 223.
119   Ibid.
120   Ibid.
121   "National Overview: Facts and Figures on Materials, Wastes and Recycling," Environmental Protection Agency, https://www.epa.gov/facts-and-figures-about-materials-waste-and-recycling/national-overview-facts-and-figures-materials.
122   Jordane Burnot and Lina Cardenas, "Caméra aux poings. Images dans la grève: Des usages pluriels dans la lutte syndicale," *Images du travail, travail des images* 12 (2022): 4.
123   Ibid, p. 20.
124   Hugo Bret, "Éboueurs, un métier essentiel mais souvent méprisé," *The Conversation*, May 17, 2023, https://theconversation.com/eboueurs-un-metier-essentiel-mais-souvent-meprise-204377.
125   Ibid.
126   Ibid.
127   Megan Clément, "La grande victoire des femmes de chambre qui ont lutté contre l'industrie hôtelière," *Les Glorieuses*, August 29, 2021, https://lesglorieuses.fr/il-faut-payer/.
128   "Grève des éboueurs: À Paris, 10 000 tonnes de déchets non ramassés et une situation confuse," *Le Monde*, March 17, 2023, https://www.lemonde.fr/politique/article/2023/03/17/greve-des-eboueurs-a-paris-10-000-tonnes-de-dechets-non-ramasses-et-une-situation-confuse_6165909_823448.html.

129 From "Dur, dur ménage!"

130 While I am speaking here about cleaners' own narratives, the issues I address are also tackled by artists. See for instance the work of South African artists Mary Sibande (https://www.sahistory.org.za/people/mary-sibande) and Zanele Muholi (https://www.sahistory.org.za/people/zanele-muholi; https://www.artsy.net/gene/the-domestic-and-domesticity), and Surinamese Dutch artist Patricia Kaersenhout, whose work has been described above (https://www.pkaersenhout.com/bio).

131 See, for instance, Françoise Éga, *Lettre à une noire. Récit antillais* (L'Harmattan, 1978), or Sembène Ousmane's film *La Noire de* (1972).

How to Name the Age of Waste and Wasting

132 Henrik Ernston and Erik Swyngedouw, *Urban Political Ecology in the Anthropo-Obscene: Interruptions and Possibilities* (Routledge, 2019).

133 Paul J. Crutzen and Eugene F. Stoermer. "The 'Anthropocene,'" *International Geosphere-Biosphere Programme* 41 (2000): 17–18.

134 "Anthropocene," British Geological Survey, https://www.bgs.ac.uk/geology-projects/anthropocene/.

135 Anna Lowenhaupt Tsing, *The Mushroom at the End of the World: On the Possibility of Life in Capitalist Ruins* (Princeton University Press, 2015), p. 19.

136 Jason W. Moore, "The Capitalocene Part I: On the Nature and Origins of Our Ecological Crisis," *Journal of Peasant Studies* 44, no. 3 (2017): 595. See also Jason W. Moore, "The Capitalocene Part II: Accumulation by Appropriation and the Centrality of Unpaid Work/Energy," *Journal of Peasant Studies* 45, no. 2 (2018): 237–239.

137 Moore, "The Capitalocene Part I," p. 593.

138 Ibid., p. 595.

139 Ibid., p. 600.

140 Ibid., p. 607. See also "Names and Locations of the Top 100 People Killing the Planet," Decolonial Atlas, April 27, 2019, https://decolonialatlas.wordpress.com/2019/04/27/names-and-locations-of-the-top-100-people-killing-the-planet/.

141 Moore, "The Capitalocene Part II," p. 22.

142 Kathryn Yusoff, *A Billion Black Anthropocenes or None* (University of Minnesota Press, 2018), e-book, loc. 161.

143 Ibid., loc. 180.

144 Ibid., loc. 223.

145 Ibid., loc. 308.

146 Andreas Malm, *The Progress of the Storm: Nature and Society in a Warming World* (Verso, 2020), p. 181.

147 Ibid., p. 182.

148 Ibid., pp. 26–27.

149 Ibid., p. 178.

150 Cited in ibid., p. 46.

151 Cited in ibid., p. 97.

152 Donna Haraway, "Anthropocene, Capitalocene, Plantationocene, Chthulucene: Making Kin," *Environmental Humanities* 6 (2015): 160.

153 Ibid., p. 160.

154 Ibid, p. 160.

155 Ibid., p. 161.

156 Malm, *The Progress of the Storm*, p. 186.

157 Ibid., p. 187.

158 Françoise Vergès, "Racial Capitalocene," in *Futures of Black Radicalism*, edited by Gaye Theresa Johnson and Alex Lubin (Verso, 2017), pp. 72–82.

159 Joachim Randkau, *Power and Nature: A Global History of the Environment* (Cambridge University Press, 2008), p. 153.

160 Andreas Malm, *Fossil Capital: The Rise of Steam Power and the Roots of Global Warming* (Verso, 2016), p. 9.

161 Donna M. Orange, *Climate Crisis, Psychoanalysis and Radical Ethics* (Routledge, 2017), p. 39.

162 Françoise Vergès, *Abolir l'esclavage: Une utopie coloniale. Les ambiguités d'une politique humanitaie* (Albin Miche, 2001).

163 Ibid.

164 Robyn D. G. Kelley, "What Did Cedric Robinson Mean by Racial Capitalism?" *Boston Review*, January 12, 2017, https://www.bostonreview.net/articles/robin-d-g-kelley-intro duction-race-capitalism-justice/.

165 Ibid.

166 Gargi Bhattacharyya, *Rethinking Racial Capitalism: Questions of Reproduction and Survival* (Rowman and Littlefield, 2018), p. ix.

167 Paul Gilroy, "The 2019 Holberg Lecture," https://holbergprize.org/en/news/holberg-prize/ 2019-holberg-lecture-laureate-paul-gilroy.

168 Ibid.

169 Commission for Racial Justice, United Church of Christ, "Toxic Wastes and Race in the United States: A National Report on the Racial and Socio-Economic Characteristics of Communities with Hazardous Waste Sites," 1967, https://www.nrc.gov/docs/ML1310/ ML13109A339.pdf.

170 Delegates to the First People of Color Environmental Leadership Summit, "Principles of Environmental Justice," 1991, https://www.ejnet.org/ej/principles.html.

171 Vergès, "Racial Capitalocene."

172 Aurore Chaillou, Louise Roblin, and Malcom Ferdinand, "Why We Need a Decolonial Ecology," *Green European Journal*, June 4, 2020, https://www.greeneuropeanjour nal.eu/why-we-need-a-decolonial-ecology/. See also Malcom Ferdinand, *Decolonial Ecology: Thinking from the Caribbean World*, translated by Anthony Paul Smith (Wiley, 2022).

173 Chaillou, Roblin, and Ferdinand, "Why We Need a Decolonial Ecology."

174 Ibid.

175 Ibid.

176 Haraway, "Anthropocene, Capitalocene, Plantationocene, Chthulucene."

177 Tsing, *The Mushroom at the End of the World*, p. 38.

178 Ibid., p. 38.

179 Ibid., p. 39.

180 Sydney Mintz, *Sweetness and Power: The Place of Sugar in Modern History* (Penguin Books, 1986), p. 47.

181 Marco Armiero, *Wasteocene: Stories from the Global Dump* (Cambridge University Press, 2021), pp. 1–2.

182 Ibid., p. 2.

183 Ibid.

184 Ibid., p. 10.

185 Ibid., p. 20.

186 Ibid.

187 Ibid., p. 29.

188 Ibid., p. 10.

189 Liboiron and Lepawsky, *Discard Studies*, p. 5.

190 Ibid., pp. 2, 7.

191 It is impossible to do justice to the growing literature on climate disaster, race, class, and environmental racism. Here, and only in English, which considerably restricts the field, Catherine Coleman Flowers, *Waste: America's Dirty Secret* (The New Press, 2020); Gilio-Whitaker, *As Long as Grass Grows*; Nick Estes, *Our History Is the Future: Standing Rock versus the Dakota Access Pipeline, and the Long Tradition of Indigenous Resistance* (Verso, 2019); Luke W. Cole and Sheila R. Foster, *From the Ground Up: Environmental Racism and the Rise of Environmental Justice Movement* (NYU Press, 2001); Michel Mascarenhas, ed., *Lessons in Environmental Justice: From Civil Rights to Black Lives Matter and Idle No More* (Sage, 2020); Carl A. Zimring, *Clean and White: A History of Environmental Racism in the United States* (NYU Press, 2016); Carolyn Finney, *Black Faces, White Spaces: Reimagining the Relationship of African-American to the Great Outdoors* (University of Carolina Press, 2014); Robert D. Bullard, *Unequal Protection: Environmental Justice and Communities of Color* (Sierra Club Books, 1996); and Harriet A. Washington, *A Terrible Thing to Waste: Environmental Racism and Its Assault on the American Mind* (Little, Brown Spark, 2019).

192 Françoise d'Eaubonne, *Le féminisme* (Éditions A. Moreau, 1972).

193 René Dumont, *L'Utopie ou la mort!* (Seuil, 1973).

194 Françoise d'Eaubonne, *Le féminisme ou la mort* (Pierre Horay Éditeur, 1974).

195 See Pierre Desrochers and Christine Hoffbauer, "The Post War Intellectual Roots of the Population Bomb Fairfield Osborn's *Our Plundered Planet* and William Vogt's *Road to Survival* in Retrospect," *Electronic Journal of Sustainable Development* 1, no. 3 (Summer 2003).

196 Ibid.

197 Alexis Vrignon, "René Dumont ou le socialisme 'de l'arbre et du jardin,'" *Cahiers d'histoire. Revue d'histoire critique* 130 (2016): 63–78.

198 Serge Moscovici, *La société contre nature* (Seuil, 1972), p. 42.

199 Jean-Pierre Nandrin, "Serge Moscovici, *La société contre nature,*" *Revue interdisciplinaire d'études juridiques* 10, no. 1 (1983): 189.

200 Gandon, "L'écoféminisme," p. 6.

201 Simone de Beauvoir, *The Second Sex* (Gallimard Poche, 1973).

202 D'Eaubonne, *Le féminisme*.

203 Gandon, "L'écoféminisme," p. 6.

204 D'Eaubonne, *Le féminisme*; cited in Gandon, "L'écoféminisme," p. 9.

205 D'Eaubonne, cited in Gandon, "L'écoféminisme," p. 9.

206 Ibid., p. 11.

207 Ibid., p. 21.

208 Jules Falquet with Solange Goma, Céline Ostyn, Fatou Sow, and Marie-Dominique de Suremain, *Écologie: Quand les femmes comptent* (L'Harmattan, 2002); Rosi Braidotti, Ewa Charkiewicz, Sabine Hausler, and Saskia Wieringa, *Women, the Environment and Sustainable Development* (Zed Books, 1994); Azzedine Mekoua, "Les savoirs sanitaires des femmes à l'épreuve du développement durable," in *Femmes et développements durables et solidaires*, edited by Fatou Sarr and Georges Thill (Presses universitaires de Namur, 2006), pp. 67–77; Mary Mellor, *Feminism and Ecology* (New York University Press, 1997); Mary Mellor, *Breaking the Boundaries: Towards a Feminist Green Socialism* (Virago Press, 1992); Maria Mies and Vandana Shiva, *Ecofeminism* (Fernwood Publications,1993); Judith Plant, ed., *Healing the Wounds: The Promise of Ecofeminism* (Green Print, 1989); Val Plumwood,

"Androcentrism and Anthropocentrism," in *Ecofeminism: Women, Culture, Nature*, edited by Karen J. Warren (Indiana University Press, 1997), pp. 327–355; Ariel Salleh, "Sustaining Marx or Sustaining Nature? An Ecofeminist Response to Foster and Burkett," *Organization and Environment* 14, no. 4 (2001): 443–450; Ariel Salleh, "Les femmes entre nature, travail et capital au cœur de la plus forte des contradictions. Les défis de l'écoféminisme," *Écologie politique* (1996): 107–128; Catriano Sandilands, "Raising Your Hand in the Council of All Beings: Ecofeminism and Citizenship," *Ethics and the Environment* 2 (2004): 219–233.

209   Selma Jones, *Our Time Is Now: Sex, Race, Class, and Caring for People and Planet* (Pm Press, 2021), p. 43.

210   Ibid., p. 60.

211   Ibid., p. 68.

212   Ibid., p. 66.

213   Ibid., p. 68.

214   See Philippe Descola, whose *Par delà nature and culture* has been very influential: *Beyond Nature and Culture*, translated by Janet Lloyd (University of Chicago Press, 2013).

215   Khayaat Fakier, Diana Mulnari, and Nora Räthzel, eds., *Marxist-Feminist Theories and Struggles Today: Essential Writings on Intersectionality, Labour and Ecofeminism* (Zed Books, 2020).

216   Great Gaard, *Ecofeminism: Women, Animals, Nature* (Temple University Press, 1993).

217   Laury-Anne Cholez, "Cultiver, nettoyer…: L'écoféminisme valorise ces tâches vitales,'" interview with Jeanne Burgart Goutal, *Reporterre*, March 8, 2022, https://reporterre.net/Nettoyer-cultiver-L-ecofeminisme-valorise-ces-taches-vitales. See also Jeanne Burgart Goutal, *Être écoféministes: théories et pratiques* (L'Échappée, 2020).

218   Cholez, "Cultiver, nettoyer."

219   Ibid.

220   Veronica Gago, *Feminist International: How to Change Everything*, translated by Liz Mason-Deeze (Verso, 2020), pp. 185–186.

221   Ibid., p. 186.

Racism and Waste

222   Mike Davis, "The Case to Let Malibu Burn," *Environmental History Review* 19, no. 2 (Summer 1995): 4.

223   Ibid., p. 4.

224   Gary Nunn, "Australian Fires: Aboriginal Planners Say the Bush 'Needs to Burn,'" *BBC News*, January 12, 2020, https://www.bbc.com/news/world-australia-51043828.

225   Ibid.

226   Ibid.

227   Davis, "The Case to Let Malibu Burn," p. 21.

228   Ibid., p. 33.

The Racial Stain of Cleanliness

229   See for instance, Octavia Butler's *Kindred* (Doubleday, 1979); *Parable of the Sower* (Four Walls, Eight Windows, 1993); *Parable of the Talents* (Seven Stories Press, 1998).

230   See her page: https://www.tjcuthand.com/biography/. There is also the AfroFuturist genre (literature, cinema, music, art): see for instance Ytasha L. Womack, *Afrofuturism: The*

World of Black Sci-Fi and Fantasy Culture (Lawrence Hill Books, 2013); Isah Lavender III, *Afrofuturism Rising: The Literary Prehistory of a Movement* (Ohio State University Press, 2019), the films *Black Panther: Wakanda Forever* (2022) and *Get Out* (2017), and the films and music of Sun Ra.

231 Thirza Jean Cuthand, "Thirza Jean Cuthand: Reclamation," *Maat*, April 30, 2021, https:// ext.maat.pt/cinema/thirza-jean-cuthand-reclamation.

232 Ibid.

233 Ibid.

234 Ibid.

235 Samantha McBride, *Recycling Reconsidered: The Present Failure and Future Promise of Environmental Action in the United States* (MIT Press, 2012), cited in Liboiron and Lepawsky, *Discard Studies*, p. 11; Samantha McBride, "Does Recycling Actually Conserve or Preserve Things?," *Discard Studies*, February 11, 2019, https://discardstudies.com/2019/02/11/12755/.

236 McBride, "Does Recycling Actually Conserve."

237 Ibid., emphasis in the original.

238 "World Clean Up Day 2020: What Does 'A World without Waste' Mean to You?," September 2020, https://www.positiveluxury.com/2020/09/18/a-world-without-waste/.

239 "World Clean Up Day 2020."

240 Ibid.

241 Liboiron and Lepawsky, *Discard Studies*, p. 12.

242 "Fast Fashion Produces over 92 Million Tonnes of Waste a Year, Study Finds," *Circular*, April 9, 2020. The same number is given by Earth.org: "10 Concerning Fast Fashion Waste Statistics," Earth.org, August 21, 2023, https://earth.org/statistics-about-fast-fashion-waste/. See also Kirsi Niinimäki, Greg Peters, Helena Dahlbo, Patsy Perry, Timo Rissanen, and Alison Gwilt, "The Environmental Price of Fast Fashion," *Nature Reviews Earth and Environment* 1 (2020): 189–200.

243 Vijay Prashad, "The Death of Over a Thousand Garment Workers in Bangladesh: The Sixteenth Newsletter," Tricontinental, April 20, 2023, https://thetricontinental.org/newsletterissue/bangladeshi-garment-workers/.

244 Ibid.

245 Ibid.

246 Lamia Karim, "Disposable Bodies: Garment Factory Catastrophe and Feminist Practices in Bangladesh," *Anthropology Now* 6, no. 1 (April 2014): 52.

247 Ibid.

248 Ibid. For the history of the World Trade Organization and of the General Agreement on Tariffs and Trade (GATT) from 1948 to 1994 see WTO, "The GATT Years: From Havana to Marrakesh," https://www.wto.org/english/thewto_e/whatis_e/tif_e/fact4_e.htm. GATT has been criticized for giving the West power over international trade.

249 Kristina Strachov, Saydia Gulrukh, Mushrefa Mishu, and Amin Amirul, "Ten Years after Rana Plaza," *Rosa Luxembourg Stiftung*, https://www.rosalux.de/en/news/id/50300/ten-years-after-rana-plaza.

250 "Six Years On from Bangladesh's Rana Plaza Tragedy, One in Five Survivors' Health Is Deteriorating," ActionAid, April 24, 2019, https://actionaid.org/news/2019/six-years-bangladeshs-rana-plaza-tragedy-one-five-survivors-health-deteriorating.

251 Thaslima Begum, "'A Nightmare I Couldn't Wake Up From': Half of the Rana Plaza Survivors Unable to Work 10 Years after Disaster," *Guardian*, April 28, 2023, https://amp.theguardian.com/global-development/2023/apr/28/a-nightmare-i-couldnt-wake-up-from-half-of-rana-plaza-survivors-unable-to-work-10-years-after-disaster.

252 Ibid.

253 "Eight Years On from the Rana Plaza Tragedy," Oxfam Canada, April 23, 2021, https://www. oxfam.ca/story/eight-years-on-from-the-rana-plaza-tragedy-the-women-who-make-our-clothes-are-still-stuck-in-poverty/.

254 Quoted in Prashad, "The Death of Over a Thousand Garment Workers."

The Politics of the Elemental

255 Elif Shafak, "After the Terrifying Earthquakes, It's Women and Girls in Turkey Feeling the Aftershocks," *Guardian*, March 8, 2023, https://www.theguardian.com/commentisfree/ 2023/mar/08/earthquakes-women-girls-turkey-abuse-misogynist-society.

256 Fatima Bhutto, "There's No Greater Feminist Cause Than the Climate Fight—and Saving Each Other," *Guardian*, March 26, 2023, https://www.theguardian.com/commentisfree/ 2023/mar/26/climate-change-crisis-women-feminism-pakistan-floods.

257 "Women and Girls among Most Affected by Turkey Syria Earthquake, Says Humanitarian Organisation ActionAid," ActionAid, February 7, 2023, https://actionaid.org/news/2023/ women-and-girls-among-most-affected-turkey-syria-earthquake-says-humanitarian.

258 Haroon Janjua, "A Year On, the Devastating Long-Term Effects of Pakistan's Floods Are Revealed," *Guardian*, August 5, 2023, https://www.theguardian.com/global-developm ent/2023/aug/05/a-year-on-the-devastating-long-term-effects-of-pakistans-floods-are-revealed.

259 Islamic Relief, *Towards a Resilient Pakistan: Moving from Rhetoric to Reality* (2023), p. 13.

260 Shafak, "After the Terrifying Earthquakes," 2023.

261 Disha Shetty, "Do Women Really Make Up 80 Percent of All Climate Migrants?," *Undark*, June 6, 2023, https://undark.org/2023/06/14/do-women-really-make-up-80-percent-of-all-climate-migrants/.

262 Ibid.

263 "Climate Change Exacerbates Violence against Women and Girls," UNHR, July 12, 2022, https://www.ohchr.org/en/stories/2022/07/climate-change-exacerbates-violence-agai nst-women-and-girls.

264 Camille Schmoll, *Les damnées de la mer* (La Découverte, 2020), pp. 146, 182. Schmoll's title, which translates as "The Wretched of the Sea," intentionally echoes Frantz Fanon's *Les damnés de la terre* (The Wretched of the Earth), but the feminine form "damnées" signifies that she is speaking of the "wretched" or "damned" as female.

265 Naomi Michelson, "The Impact of Climate Change on Black Girls' and Women's Health: Using Theory to Mitigate and Organize," *Undergraduate Journal of Public Health* 6 (2022): 79–89, https://doi.org/10.3998/ujph.2314.

266 Ibid.

267 Ibid.

268 Swedish International Development Cooperative Agency (SIDA), "Water and Sanitation. Anti-Corruption in Water and Sanitation," August 2019, https://www.sida.se/en/publicati ons/water-and-sanitation-4. See also Georgia L. Kayser, Namratha Rao, Rupa Jose, and Anita Raj, "Water, Sanitation and Hygiene: Measuring Gender Equality and Empowerment," *Bulletin of the World Health Organization* 97 (2019): 438–440.

269 "Gender, Water and Sanitation: A Policy Brief," United Nations, May 26, 2006, https://www. unwater.org/publications/gender-water-and-sanitation-policy-brief.

270 See the bibliography annotated by Jess MacArthur, Naomi Carrard and Juliet Willetts, "WASH and Gender: A Critical Review of the Literature and Implications for

Gender-Transformative WASH Research," *Journal of Water, Sanitation and Hygiene for Development* 10, no. 4 (2020): 818–827.

271 J. R. McNeil, *Something New under the Sun: An Environmental History of the Twentieth-Century World* (Norton, 2000), pp. 191, 190.

272 Rasandeep Kaur Phull, "Mass Womb-Icide: Why Are Maharashtra's Female Sugarcane Labourers Paying for Expensive Hysterectomies?," Organization for Regional and Inter-regional Studies, December 7, 2016, p. 25, https://www.waseda.jp/inst/oris/assets/uplo ads/2023/07/jisedaironshu6note.pdf.

273 Ibid., p. 32.

274 "India's Female Cane Cutters Face Child Marriage and Hysterectomy," Climate Home News, December 20, 2022, https://www.climatechangenews.com/2022/12/20/indias-fem ale-cane-cutters-face-child-marriage-and-hysterectomy/.

275 Priya Varadarajan, "Bitter Reality: Mass Hysterectomy of Women in Beed's Sugarcane Fields," *Feminism in India*, March 8, 2021, https://feminisminindia.com/2021/03/08/hyste rectomy-beed-women-sugarcane-field/.

276 Kristyna R. S. Hulland, Rachel P. Chase, Bethany A. Caruso, Rojalin Swain, Bismita Biswal, Krushna Chandra Sahoo, Pinaki Panigrahi, and Robert Dreibelbis, "Sanitation, Stress, and Life Stage: A Systematic Data Collection Study among Women in Odisha, India," *Plos One*, November 9, 2015, p. 2, https://journals.plos.org/plosone/article?id=10.1371/journal.pone.0141883, in A. Wutich and K. Ragsdale, "Water Insecurity and Emotional Distress: Coping with Supply, Access, and Seasonal Variability of Water in a Bolivian Squatter Settlement," *Social Science and Medicine* 67, no. 12 (2008): 2116–2125.

277 Ibid, p. 8.

278 Ibid, p. 12.

279 Ibid, p. 1.

280 Samantha Winter, Robert Dreibelbis, and Francis Barchi, "Context Matters: a Multicountry Analysis of Individual- and Neighbourhood-Level Factors Associated with Women's Sanitation Use in Sub-Saharan Africa," *Tropical Medicine and International Health* 23, no. 2 (2017): 174.

281 Ibid., p. 173.

282 Prathiba Singh, "How Female Toilet Builders Are Taking on Menstrual Hygiene Management in India: A Programme to End Open Defecation in Jharkhand Ends Up Transforming Gender Roles," UNESCO, May 28, 2019, https://www.unicef.org/stories/how-female-toilet-builders-are-taking-menstrual-hygiene-management-india; "The Unexpected Link between Access to Toilets and Women's Rights," iD4D, November 14, 2019, https://ideas4development.org/en/unexpected-link-access-toilets-womens-rights/.

283 "Gates Foundation Launches Effort to Reinvent the Toilet," Bill and Melinda Gates Foundation, https://www.gatesfoundation.org/ideas/media-center/press-releases/2011/07/gates-foundation-launches-effort-to-reinvent-the-toilet.

284 Ibid.

285 Ruth Wilson Gilmore, "In the Shadow of the Shadow State," *Scholar and Feminist Online* 13, no. 2 (Spring 2016), https://sfonline.barnard.edu/ruth-wilson-gilmore-in-the-shadow-of-the-shadow-state/.

286 Ibid.

287 Ibid.

288 S'bu Zikode, in Richard Pithouse, "Resist All Degradations and Divisions. S'bu Zikode in Interview with Richard Pithouse," *Interface: A Journal for and about Social Movements* (November 2009): 39.

289 Ibid., p. 27.

290 Ibid., pp. 39, 40.

291 Ibid., p. 39.

292 Gilmore, cited in Nik Heynen and Megan Ybarra, "On Abolition Ecologies and Making 'Freedom as a Place,'" *Antipode* 53, no. 1 (2021): 22.

293 Ruth Wilson Gilmore, "Fatal Couplings of Power and Difference: Notes on Racism and Geography," *Professional Geographer* 54, no. 1 (2002): 22.

294 Monica White, "A Pig and a Garden: Fanny Lou Hamer's Freedom Farm Cooperative," in *Freedom Farmers: Agricultural Resistance and the Black Freedom Movement* (University of North Carolina Press, 2018), pp. 65–87.

295 Leah Wang, "Prisons Are a Daily Environmental Injustice," *Prison Policy Initiative*, April 20, 2022, https://www.prisonpolicy.org/blog/2022/04/20/environmental_injustice/.

296 See Gilmore, *Abolition Geography*.

297 Wang, "Prisons Are a Daily Environmental Injustice."

298 Abby Outterson, "Polluted Prisons," *Public Health Post*, https://www.publichealthpost.org/research/polluted-prisons/.

299 Pierre Bienvault, "Des conditions de vie 'dégradantes' dans les prisons en France," *La Croix*, January 31, 2020, https://www.la-croix.com/France/conditions-detention-degradantes-pris ons-France-2020-01-31-1201075423.

300 Ali Rocha, "The Chronic Crisis of Brazil's Prisons," International Bar Association, https://www.ibanet.org/article/92748934-3237-44EB-B537-332198617B14.

301 Study and Struggle, Fall 2021 Curriculum, "October: Green," https://static1.squarespace.com/static/5a354481a9db0961249f52ec/t/613a55f22c83d848a216f226/1631213043030/Green+Discussion+Guide+%28GF+Final%29.pdf. See also Akinyele Umoja, "Why We Say 'Free the Land,'" in *Remaking Radicalism: A Grassroots Documentary Reader of the United States, 1973–2001*, edited by Dan Berger and Emily K. Hobson (University of Georgia Press, 1984), pp. 449–450.

The Marxist Feminist Theory of Social Reproduction

302 Silvia Federici, "Social Reproduction Theory. History, Issues and Present Challenges," *Radical Philosophy* 2, no. 4 (Spring 2019), p. 55.

303 Davis, *Women, Race and Class*, p. 9. See also Hazel Carby, "Policing the Black Woman's Body in an Urban Context," *Critical Inquiry* 18, no. 4 (1992): 738–755; Jacqueline Jones, *Labor of Love, Labor of Sorrow: Black Women, Work, and the Family, from Slavery to the Present* (Basic Books, 2000); Leah Lakshmi Piepzan-Samarasihna, *Care Work: Dreaming Disability Justice* (Arsenal Pulp Press, 2018); Audre Lorde, *A Burst of Light and Other Essays* (Ixia Press, 2017); Mary Jeanne Larrabee, ed., *An Ethic of Care: Feminist and Interdisciplinary Perspectives* (Routledge, 1992); Jennifer C. Nash, "Practicing Love: Black Feminism, Love-Politics, and Post-Intersectionality," *Meridians* 11, no. 2 (2011): 1–24; Gloria T. Hull, Patricia Bell-Scott, and Barbara Smith, *But Some of Us Are Brave*, 2nd ed. (Feminist Press at CUNY, 2015).

304 Davis, *Women, Race and Class*, p. 9.

305 Ibid., p. 90.

306 Ibid., pp. 223, 229, 223.

307 Selma James, *Sex, Race, and Class—The Perspectives of Winning: A Selection of Writings 1952–2021* (PM Press, 2012).

308 Selma James, "Time Off Women (1985–1990)," in *Our Time Is Now: Sex, Race, Class and Caring for People and the Planet* (PM Press, 2021), p. 6.

309 "Legacy and International Impact of the 1975 Icelandic Women's Day Off," University of Iceland, https://english.hi.is/news/legacy_and_international_impact_of_the_1975_icela ndic_womens_day_off.

310 Louise Toupin, "The History of Wages for Housework," Pluto Press blog, https://www.plu tobooks.com/blog/wages-housework-campaign-history/; the blog is a summary of her book *Wages for Housework: A History of an International Feminist Movement, 1972–77* (Pluto, 2018).

311 Ibid.

312 Ibid.

313 James, *Our Time Is Now*, p. 34.

314 Ibid., p. 23.

315 Ibid.

316 Ibid., p. 30.

317 Ibid., p. 40.

318 Ibid., p. 60.

319 Federici, "Social Reproduction Theory," p. 56. The Wages for Housework campaign is still active. On the Marxist feminist theory of social reproduction, see Tithi Bhattacharya, ed., *Social Reproduction Theory: Remapping Class, Recentering Oppression* (Pluto Press, 2017); Lise Vogel, *Marxism and the Oppression of Women: Toward a Unitary Theory* (Rutgers University Press, 1983); Giovanna Franca Dalla Costa and Mariarosa Dalla Costa, *The Work of Love: Unpaid Housework, Poverty and Sexual Violence in at the Dawn of the 21st Century* (Automedia, 2010); Maria Mies et al., *Patriarchy and Accumulation on a World Scale: Women in the International Division of Labour* (Zed Books, 2014); Susan Ferguson, *Women and Work: Feminism, Labour and Social Reproduction* (Pluto Press, 2019); Selma James, *A Woman's Place* (1952); Selma James, *The Global Kitchen: The Case for Counting Unwaged Work* (1985, 1995).

320 Sophie K. Rosa, "The Wages for Housework Campaign Is as Relevant as Ever," *Novara Media*, March 21, 2022, https://novaramedia.com/2022/03/21/the-wages-for-housework-campaign-is-as-relevant-as-ever/.

321 See Silvia Federici, *Revolution at Point Zero: Housework, Reproduction and Feminist Struggle* (PM Press, 2020).

322 Dorothy Roberts, "Spiritual and Menial Housework," *Yale Journal of Law and Feminism* 9 (1997): 51.

323 Ibid.

324 Ibid., p. 59.

325 Ibid, p. 60.

326 Janette Dill and Mignon Duffy, "Structural Racism and Black Women's Employment in the US Health Care Sector," *Health Affairs* 41, no. 2 (2022): 266.

327 Roberts, "Spiritual and Menial Housework," p. 61.

328 Dill and Duffy, "Structural Racism," p. 371.

329 Evelyn Nakano Glenn, "From Servitude to Service Work: Historical Continuities in the Racial Division of Paid Reproductive Labor," *Signs: Journal of Women in Culture and Society* 18, no. 1 (1992): 1–43.

330 Glenn, "From Servitude to Service Work," p. 20.

331 "Black Women for Wages for Housework," https://globalwomenstrike.net/blackwomenf orwagesforhousework/, emphasis in the original. See also Beth Capper and Arlen Austin,

" 'Wages for Housework Means Wages *against* Heterosexuality': On the Archives of Black Women for Wages for Housework and Wages Due Lesbians," *GLQ: A Journal of Lesbian and Gay Studies* 24 no. 4 (2018): 445–466.

332 Jacqui Germain, "The National Welfare Rights Organization Wanted Economic Justice for Black Americans," *Teen Vogue*, December 24, 2021, https://www.teenvogue.com/story/national-welfare-rights-organization-black-women.

333 Ibid.

334 Ibid.

335 Mathilde Dorcadie, "The Precarious Status of Domestic Workers in Brazil," *Equal Times*, March 14, 2018, https://www.equaltimes.org/the-precarious-status-of-domestic.

The Whitening of Cleanliness

336 See for instance Fabienne Chevallier, *Le Paris moderne: Histoire des politiques d'hygiène, 1855–1898* (Presses universitaires de Rennes, 2010); Sun-Young Park, *Ideals of the Body: Architecture, Urbanism and Hygiene in Postrevolutionary Paris* (University of Pittsburgh Press, 2018); Lee Jackson, *Dirty Old London: The Victorian Fight Against Filth* (Yale University Press, 2015).

337 See Elizabeth Williams, "Baths and Bathing Culture in the Middle East: The *Hammam*," October 2012, Heilbrunn Timeline of Art History, Metropolitan Museum of Art, http://www.metmuseum.org/toah/hd/bath/hd_bath.htm; Marwan Haddad, "Water Supply, Sanitation, Hygienic Considerations and Practices in Muslim Civilizations," *Muslim Heritage*, April 9, 2021, https://muslimheritage.com/water-supply-sanitation/.

338 Shafik Mandhai, "Vikings, Human Sacrifice and Bad Hygiene: Islamic Descriptions of Russia and Ukraine," *Middle East Eye*, March 7, 2022, https://www.middleeasteye.net/discover/russia-ukraine-ibn-fadlan-muslim-descriptions-vikings-hygiene.

339 David Wahl, *Le Sale discours ou Géographie des déchets pour tenter de distinguer au mieux ce qui est propre de ce qui ne l'est pas* (Premier Parallèle, 2018), p. 138.

340 Wahl, *Le Sale discours*, p. 100.

Olfactory Racism

341 Alain Corbin, *The Foul and the Flagrant: Odour and the French Social Imagination* (Picador, 1994). See also Constance Classen, David Howes, and Anthony Synnott, *Aroma: The Cultural History of Smell* (Routledge, 1994).

342 William Tullet, "Grease and Sweat: Race and Smell in Eighteen Century English Culture," *Cultural and Social History* 13, no. 3 (2016): 308.

343 See *South Africa a Century Ago: Letters Written from the Cape of Good Hope (1798–1801) by the Lady Anne Barnard. Edited with a memoir and brief notes by W. H. Wilkins* (Smith, 1901).

344 Quoted by Tullet, "Grease and Sweat," p. 311. Yet, Anne Lindsay Barnard is also described by Esther Esmyol, curator of the Social History Collections, William Fehr Collection and Research and Exhibitions, Iziko Museums of South Africa, as such: "Lady Anne's usage of names and terminologies reflect colonial sentiments and expressions of the time, yet she was interested in and had great empathy with people from all walks of life. She most loved doing portraits of ordinary people, including enslaved and indigenous people, women and children. She represented Black people in a dignified manner; not abstracted or fetishized." "The Unknown Lady Anne Lindsay Barnard," Iziko, March 17, 2023, https://www.iziko.org.za/news/the-unknown-lady-anne-lindsay-barnard/.

345 Comte de Buffon, *Buffon's Natural History* (London, 1797), vol. 4, p. 276.

346 Andrew Kettler, *The Smell of Slavery: Olfactory Racism and the Atlantic World* (Cambridge University Press, 2022).

347 Mark Smith, *How Race Is Made: Slavery, Segregation and the Senses* (University of North Carolina Press, 2006), p. 153.

348 Marco d'Eramo, "Odourless Utopia," *Sidecar New Left Review*, August 17, 2022, https://newleftreview.org/sidecar/posts/odourless-utopia.

349 Kristin Ross, *Fast Cars, Clean Bodies: Decolonization and the Reordering of French Culture* (MIT Press, 1995).

350 Ross, *Fast Cars*, p. 108.

351 Ross, *Fast Cars*, p. 215.

352 Samia Henni, "Architecture of Counterrevolution: The French Army in Algeria, 1954–1962," *ABE Journal* 9-10 (2016), https://journals.openedition.org/abe/10965#quotation. See also Samia Henni, *Architecture of Counterrevolution: The French Army in Northern Algeria* (Taylor & Francis, 2017).

353 "Discreet Violence: Architecture and the French War in Algeria," Architectural Exhibitions International, https://www.architecture-exhibitions.com/en/het-nieuwe-instituut/discreet-violence-architecture-and-the-french-war-in-algeria.

354 Frantz Fanon, "Concerning Violence," in *The Wretched of the Earth*, translated by Constance Farrington (Penguin Books, 1990).

355 See Fanon, "Concerning Violence" p. 39; for a Fanonian approach to the current context, see Stephen Sheehi and Lara Sheehi, "The Settler's Town Is a Strongly Built Town: Fanon in Palestine," *Applied Psychoanalytic Studies* 17, no. 2 (2020): 183–192.

356 Victor Considérant, *Destinée sociale*, vol. 1, *Au bureau de la phalange* (1834), p. 462.

357 The Goutte d'or is a popular neighborhood in the 20th arrondissement of Paris where many migrant workers from the African continent have been living since the 1950s and where many still live. It was a stronghold of the Algerian Front of Liberation during the Algerian war of independence.

358 "Chirac et l'immigration: 'Le bruit et l'odeur,'" https://www.ina.fr/ina-eclaire-actu/video/cab91027484/chirac-et-l-immigration-le-bruit-et-l-odeur.

359 Zebda, "Le bruit et l'odeur" (1995).

360 See Bridget V. Osborne, "A Nose for Trouble," *British Journal of General Practice* 62, no. 605 (2012): 652–653.

361 Colleen Walsh, "What the Nose Knows," *Harvard Gazette*, February 27, 2020, https://news.harvard.edu/gazette/story/2020/02/how-scent-emotion-and-memory-are-intertwined-and-exploited/.

362 Walsh, "What the Nose Knows."

363 See, for example, S. Senthalir, "Photos: In Tamil Nadu, Dalit Sanitation Workers Are Told to Help Doctors Perform Autopsies," Scroll.in, March 17, 2019, https://scroll.in/magazine/915568/photos-in-tamil-nadu-dalit-sanitation-workers-are-told-to-help-doctors-perform-autopsies.

Wasting and Protecting under Racial Capitalism

364 See Gavin P. Smith and Dennis Wenger, "Sustainable Disaster Recovery: Operationalizing an Existing Agenda," in *Sustainable Development and Disaster Risk Reduction*, edited by J. Uittoand and R. Shaw (Springer Tokyo, 2016), pp. 234–257; Global Platform for Greater Risk Reduction, https://globalplatform.undrr.org/2022/practical-information/sustainability.html; "Disaster Risk Reduction," UN, https://sustainabledevelopment.un.org/topics/disasterriskreduction; the Green Agenda of the UAE, Ministry of Climate Change and Environment, moccae.gov.ae.

365 Sameh Wahba and Silpa Kaza, "What a Waste: An Updated Look into the Future of Solid Waste Management," World Bank, September 20, 2018, https://www.worldbank.org/en/news/immersive-story/2018/09/20/what-a-waste-an-updated-look-into-the-future-of-solid-waste-management.

366 "Uganda: New Forests Company—FSC Legitimizes the Eviction of Thousands of People from Their Land and the Sale of Carbon Credits," World Rainforest Movement, October 30, 2011, https://www.wrm.org.uy/other-information/uganda-new-forests-company-fsc-legitimizes-the-eviction-of-thousands-of-people-from-their-land-and-the.

367 Tania Page, "Pine Trees: A Force for Good or Bad in the Climate Change Fight?," *1news*, July 23, 2023, https://www.1news.co.nz/2023/07/23/pine-trees-a-force-for-good-or-bad-in-the-climate-change-fight/.

368 "Pine Tree Pollution," Carnegie Mellon University, https://www.cmu.edu/homepage/environment/2012/summer/pine-trees.shtml.

369 "Guaraqueçaba Climate Action Project in Traditional Communities in Paraná, Brazil," EJAtlas, https://ejatlas.org/conflict/carbon-offset-project-creates-pressure-on-indigenous-communities-in-parana-brazil.

370 "Forest Carbon Project in Panraná, Brazil: Reduction of Deforestation and Persecution of Local Communities," World Rainforest Movement, August 30, 2011, https://www.wrm.org.uy/bulletin-articles/forest-carbon-project-in-parana-brazil-reduction-of-deforestation-and-persecution-of-local-communities.

371 China Miéville, "The Limits of Utopia," *Salvage*, 2014, https://salvage.zone/mieville_all.html.

372 Edward Broughton, "The Bhopal Disaster and Its Aftermath: A Review," *Environmental Health* 4 (2005), https://www.ncbi.nlm.nih.gov/pmc/articles/PMC1142333/.

373 Rhitu Chatterjee, "How the 1984 Bhopal Tragedy in India Has Hurt Multiple Generations," NPR, June 16, 2023, https://www.npr.org/2023/06/16/1182853996/how-the-1984-bhopal-gas-tragedy-in-india-has-hurt-multiple-generations.

374 Cited in Miéville, "The Limits of Utopia."

375 "World Urbanization Prospects 2018," UNDESA, Population Dynamics, http://esa.un.org/unpd/wup/.

376 On dumpsites and waste, see "Waste Atlas: The World's 50 Biggest Dumpsites, 2014 Report," https://www.nswai.org/docs/World%27s%20Fifty%20biggest%20dumpsites,Waste%20Atlas%202014.pdf.

377 Jan Iler Hansen, "The Graveyard of Giants: A History of Ship Breaking in Bangladesh," *Captain*, February 28, 2012, a https://gcaptain.com/graveyard-giants-history-ship/.

378 "Be Waste Wise," BioEnergy Consult, November 7, 2021, https://www.bioenergyconsult.com/author/bewastewise/.

379 See Nate Millington and Mary Lawhon, "Geographies of Waste: Conceptual Vectors from the Global South," *Progress in Human Geography* 43, no. 6 (2018), https://journals.sagepub.com/doi/10.1177/0309132518799911; C. Alexander and J. Reno, eds., *Economies of Recycling: The Global Transformation of Materials, Values and Social Relations* (Zed Books, 2012); A. Baabereyir, S. Jewitt, and S. O'Hara, "Dumping on the Poor: The Ecological Distribution of Accra's Solid-Waste Burden," *Environment and Planning A* 44, no. 2 (2012): 297–314; J. Beall, "Dealing with Dirt and the Disorder of Development: Managing Rubbish in Urban Pakistan," *Oxford Development Studies* 34, no. 1 (2006): 81–97; S. Chari, "Detritus in Durban: Polluted Environs and the Biopolitics of Refusal," in *Imperial Debris: On Ruins and Ruination*, edited by A. L. Stoler (Duke University Press, 2013).

380 Ghassan Hage, *Is Racism an Environmental Threat?* (Polity, 2017), e-book.

381   Ibid., loc. 104.
382   Ibid., loc. 701.
383   Ibid., loc. 710.
384   Ibid., loc. 841.
385   Ibid., loc. 1074.

The Pleasure of Water

386   Christie Pearson, "A People's History of Bathing," *Literary Hub*, November 10, 2020, https://lithub.com/a-peoples-history-of-bathing/.
387   "How Much Water Is There on Earth?," USGS, November 13, 2019, https://www.usgs.gov/special-topics/water-science-school/science/how-much-water-there-earth.
388   "What Is the Average Percentage of Water in the Human Body?," MedicalNewsToday, https://www.medicalnewstoday.com/articles/what-percentage-of-the-human-body-is-water.
389   Casey Walsh, *Virtuous Waters: Mineral Springs, Bathing and Infrastructure in Mexico* (California University Press, 2018), p. 17.
390   Ibid., p. 19.
391   Shamira Ibrahim, "What Spiritual Baths Mean for Black Wellness," *Allure*, September 17, 2021, https://www.allure.com/story/spiritual-bathing-black-community.
392   Ibid.
393   Ibid.

The Enclosure of Water

394   Charles H. Lee, "Water Resources in Relation to Military Operations," *Military Engineer* 12, no. 63 (May–June 1920): 285.
395   Danny Haiphong, "War Is a Racist Enterprise," *Black Agenda Report*, September 1, 2021, https://www.blackagendareport.com/war-racist-enterprise.
396   Alan Holland, "Nature and Our Sense of Loss," in *Restoring Layered Landscapes: History, Ecology, and Culture*, edited by Marion Hourdequin and David G. Havlick (Oxford Academic, 2015).
397   Haiphong, "War Is a Racist Enterprise."
398   Ibid.
399   Ibid.
400   "Improving Access to Water, Sanitation and Hygiene Can Save 1.4 Million Lives per Years, Says New WHO Report," WHO, June 28, 2023, https://www.who.int/news/item/28-06-2023-improving-access-to-water--sanitation-and-hygiene-can-save-1.4-million-lives-per-year--says-new-who-report.
401   "Trachoma," WHO, October 5, 2022, https://www.who.int/news-room/fact-sheets/detail/trachoma.
402   "Clearing the Waters: A Focus on Water Quality Solutions," UNEP, 2010, https://pacinst.org/wp-content/uploads/2010/03/clearing_the_waters3.pdf, p. 7.
403   "Secretary-General Warns Two Thirds of Global Population Could Face Water-Stressed Conditions within Next Decade, in Message for International Forests Day," UN, March 18, 2016, https://press.un.org/en/2016/sgsm17610.doc.htm.
404   "Water Scarcity: Overview," WWF, https://www.worldwildlife.org/threats/water-scarcity.
405   Cited in "Clearing the Waters," p. 11.

406 David Castelvecchi, "Rampant Groundwater Pumping Has Changed the Tilt of Earth's Axis," *Scientific American*, June 21, 2023, https://www.scientificamerican.com/article/rampant-groundwater-pumping-has-changed-the-tilt-of-earths-axis/.

407 Saul Elbein, "Human Society Is Shifting the Tilt of the Earth," *The Hill*, June 30, 2023, https://thehill.com/policy/equilibrium-sustainability/4075087-human-society-is-shifting-the-tilt-of-the-earth/; Mindy Weisberger, "Humans Pump So Much Groundwater That Earth's Axis Has Shifted, Study Finds," CNN, June 26, 2023, https://edition.cnn.com/2023/06/26/world/pumping-groundwater-earth-axis-shifting-scn/index.html.

408 Warren Cornwall, "Humanity's Groundwater Pumping Has Altered Earth's Tilt," *Science*, June 16, 2023, https://www.science.org/content/article/humanity-s-groundwater-pumping-has-altered-earth-s-tilt.

409 Elbein, "Human Society Is Shifting the Tilt of the Earth."

410 "Clearing the Waters," p. 13.

411 "Top 5 Industries with the Highest Water Consumption," Smart Business, January 13, 2020, https://smarterbusiness.co.uk/blogs/the-top-5-industries-that-consume-the-most-water/.

412 Food and Water Watch, "Water Privatization: Facts and Figures," August 2, 2015, https://www.foodandwaterwatch.org/2015/08/02/water-privatization-facts-and-figures/.

413 Silvia Federici, *Caliban and the Witch: Women, the Body and Primitive Accumulation* (Autonomedia, 2004).

414 Silvia Federici, *Re-enchanting the World: Feminism and the Politics of the Commons* (PM Press, 2018).

415 Derek Wall, *The Commons in History: Culture, Conflict and Ecology* (MIT Press, 2014), p. 8.

416 Ibid., pp. 9, 84.

Weaponizing Water

417 All these examples were found at "Water Conflict Chronology," Pacific Institute, https://www.worldwater.org/conflict/list/. Currently the database lists 1,634 cases of water being weaponized, and new cases are being added. At the time of writing, the latest entry for Israel/Palestine was added in 2023, at the beginning of retaliatory attacks on Gaza by Israel; therefore, numerous further cases are not yet included, but it is already clear that the State of Israel, which has always weaponized water, has decided to totally and fully destroy the water system in Palestine.

418 Raja Nazakat Ali, "Indus Water Treaty: A Geo Political Survey," PhD. diss., University of Kashmir, 2013, pp. 76, 77.

419 Shozab Raza, "Flooding Has Devastated Pakistan—and Britain's Imperial Legacy Has Made It Worse," *Guardian*, August 31, 2022, https://www.theguardian.com/commentisfree/2022/aug/31/flooding-pakistan-britains-imperial-legacy.

420 Katlyn Schulz, "Gender, Race, and Class at Love Canal: Women as Leaders in Environmental Activism," *Drake Undergraduate Social Science Journal* (Spring 2019), https://www.drake.edu/media/departmentsoffices/dussj/2019documents/Schulz%20DUSSJ%202019.pdf. See also Elisabeth D. Blum, *Love Canal Revisited: Race, Class, and Gender in Environmental Activism* (University of Kansas Press, 2008).

421 Jordan Kleiman, "Love Canal: A Brief History," SUNY Geneseo, https://www.geneseo.edu/history/love_canal_history.

422 Kleiman, "Love Canal."

423 Hay, "Everyone's Backyard."

424 See Merritt Kennedy, "Lead-Laced Water in Flint: A Step-by Step Look at the Makings of a Crisis," NPR, April 20, 2016, https://www.npr.org/sections/thetwo-way/2016/04/20/465545378/lead-laced-water-in-flint-a-step-by-step-look-at-the-makings-of-a-crisis.

425 The term "Green Revolution" was coined by William S. Gaud of the United States Agency for International Development (USAID) in 1968 for the introduction of new technology and policies implemented in the developing nations, with aid from industrialized nations, to increase the production and yield of food crops. For a critique of the lasting legacies of the Green Revolution, see Raj Patel, "The Long Green Revolution," *Journal of Peasant Studies* 40, no. 1 (2013): 1–63.

426 Daisy A. John and Giridhara R. Babu, "Lessons from the Aftermaths of Green Revolution on Food System and Health," *Frontiers in Sustainable Food Systems* 5 (February 22, 2022): 2.

427 A. R. L. Eliazer Nelson, K. Ravichandran, and U. Antony, "The Impact of the Green Revolution on Indigenous Crops of India," *Journal of Ethnic Food* 6, no. 8 (2019): 2–10.

428 Olivier Petitjean, "The Misdeeds and Misfortunes of Water Multinationals in the Cities of the World," Partage des eaux, October 2, 2009, https://www.partagedeseaux.info/The-Misdeeds-and-Misfortunes-of-Water-Multinationals-in-the-Cities-of-the-World. See also Larbi Bouguerra, *Les batailles de l'eau; pour un bien commun de l'humanité* (Enjeux Planète, 2003), pp. 126–151; "The Water Barons" (case-studies of privatization processes in the world), https://www.icij.org/investigations/waterbarons/.

429 Petitjean, "The Misdeeds and Misfortunes of Water Multinationals in the Cities of the World."

430 For instance, in 2010, the city of Paris successfully regained control over water distribution and management after privatization in 1984. See "L'histoire de l'eau à Paris," https://www.eaudeparis.fr/lhistoire-de-leau-paris. See Andrea Muehlebach, *A Vital Frontier: Water Insurgencies in Europe* (Duke University Press, 2023), pp. 167–174, for the history of that struggle.

431 Juana Vera Delgado and Margreet Zwarteveen, "Modernity, Exclusion and Resistance: Water and Indigenous Struggles in Peru," *Development* 51 (2008): 115.

432 Ibid., p. 115.

433 Ibid., p. 118. The authors cite studies showing that "colonial attempts to annihilate this water culture or 'diabolic practices' as they used to be called, have been without success" (p. 118).

434 Ibid.

435 Muehlebach, *A Vital Frontier*, pp. 12–29.

436 Ibid., p. 26.

437 Ibid., p. 13.

438 Ibid., p. 177.

439 Bernard Barraqué, "The Three Ages of Engineering for the Water Industry," *Anuari de la Societat Catalaan d'Economia, Anuari de la Societat Catalana d'Economia*, no. 18 (2004): 135–152, https://raco.cat/index.php/AnuariEconomia/article/view/264585; cited in *Le Monde diplomatique*, June 2023, p. 17.

440 Ibid.

441 "Proud Flesh Inter/Views: Sylvia Wynter," *Proud Flesh: New Afrikan Journal of Culture, Politics and Consciousness* 4 (2006): 5. See also David Scott, "The Re-Enchantment of Humanism: An Interview with Sylvia Wynter," *Small Axe* 8 (September 2000): 119–207; Bedour Alagraa, "What Will Be the Cure?: A Conversation with Sylvia Wynter," *Offshoot*, January 7, 2021, https://offshootjournal.org/what-will-be-the-cure-a-conversation-with-sylvia-wynter/.

442 "Proud Flesh," p. 15.

443 Ibid; emphasis in the original.

444 Delgado and Zwarteveen, "Modernity, Exclusion and Resistance," p. 119.

445 See Philipe Verdol, *Le chlordécone aux Antilles françaises. Politique publique et gestion de la crise* (L'Harmattan, 2020); Jessica Oublié, *Tropiques toxiques* (Les Escales, 2022); *Tropicomania, la vie sociale des plantes*, Galerie Bétonsalon, 2012. For scientific studies, see "Exposition aux pesticides et au chlordécone," Pôle Expertise collective Inserm, February 2019, https://www.inserm.fr/wp-content/uploads/2019-06/inserm-rapportexpositionauxpe sticidesetauchlordecone-2019.pdf; "L'exposition pré et postnatale au chlordécone pourrait impacter le développement cognitif et le comportement des enfants," Inserm, February 27, 2023, https://presse.inserm.fr/lexposition-pre-et-postnatale-au-chlordecone-pourrait-impacter-le-developpement-cognitif-et-le-comportement-des-enfants/66616/.

446 Malcom Ferdinand, "De l'usage du chlordécone en Martinique et en Guadeloupe: l'égalité en question," *Revue française des affaires sociales* 1–2 (2015): 167, https://www.cairn.info/revue-francaise-des-affaires-sociales-2015-1-page-163.htm.

447 Ibid.

448 Ibid., p. 168.

449 Ibid., p. 171.

450 See Nathalie Guibert, "La décision de non-lieu dans l'affaire du chlordécone n'épargne ni l'État ni les industriels," *Le Monde*, January 14, 2023, https://www.lemonde.fr/societe/arti cle/2023/01/14/chlordecone-l-ordonnance-de-non-lieu-n-epargne-ni-l-etat-ni-les-indus triels_6157850_3224.html.

451 "What Is Ecocide?," End Ecocide on Earth, https://www.endecocide.org/en/what-is-ecocide/.

452 Malcom Ferdinand, "Avec le chlordécone, on touche à la structure des sociétés antillaise, interview by Ocrave Larmagnac-Matheron," *Philosophie Magazine*, January 24, 2023, https://www.philomag.com/articles/avec-le-chlordecone-touche-la-structure-histori que-des-societes-antillaises.

453 "En Guadeloupe, le scandale de l'eau est un désastre écologique," *Reporterre*, April 24, 2021, https://reporterre.net/En-Guadeloupe-le-scandale-de-l-eau-est-un-desastre-ecologique.

454 Julien Lecot, "Chlordécone aux Antilles: 'Il y a enfin une reconnaissance du malheur de nos territoires et de la responsabilité de l'Etat français,'" *Libération*, March 1, 2024, https://www.liberation.fr/environnement/pollution/chlordecone-aux-antilles-il-y-a-enfin-une-reconnaissance-du-malheur-de-nos-territoires-et-de-la-responsabilite-de-letat-francais-20240301_YKPT3C5DKFHOZH3F3ZBEEO7DAM/.

455 From the slavery empire: Martinique, Guadeloupe, Guyana, Reunion; from the post-slavery empire: Kanaky New Caledonia, French islands of the Pacific, Mayotte.

456 See Pierre Camade, *Comores-Mayotte: Une histoire néocoloniale* (Contrefeux, 2010); Alain Ruscio, "Comores, Mayotte, néo-colonialisme: Petit cours d'histoire récente," *Médiapart*, November 12, 2022, https://blogs.mediapart.fr/histoire-coloniale-et-postcoloniale/blog/061222/comores-mayotte-neo-colonialisme-francais-petit-cours-d-histoire-recente; Alain Ruscio "15 juin 1973: Aux racines nécoloniales de la crise à Mayotte," *L'Humanité*, June 10, 2023, https://www.humanite.fr/culture-et-savoirs/comores/15-juin-1973-aux-racines-neocoloniales-de-la-crise-mayotte-797852.

457 Fabrice Floch, "Océan Indien: Un gisement de pétrole et de gaz découvert au Zimbabwe," Reunion1, May 10, 2023, https://la1ere.francetvinfo.fr/reunion/ocean-indien-un-gisem ent-de-petrole-et-de-gaz-decouvert-au-zimbabwe-1394070.html.

458 Robin Prudent, "A Mayotte, une crise de l'eau 'inédite' en raison du manque de pluie et d'infrastructure," Radio France, June 24, 2023, https://www.francetvinfo.fr/france/mayo tte/reportage-a-mayotte-une-crise-de-l-eau-inedite-en-raison-du-manque-de-pluies-et-d-infrastructures_5906105.html.

459 Quentin Menu, "Crise de l'eau à Mayotte: 'Cela fait 20 ans que le gouvernement promet des investissements', dénonce Estelle Youssouffa," FranceInfo, July 15, 2023, https://la1ere. francetvinfo.fr/crise-de-l-eau-a-mayotte-cela-fait-20-ans-que-le-gouvernement-promet-des-investissements-denonce-estelle-youssouffa-1414139.html.

460 "Eau à Mayotte: le gouvernement annonce des mesures d'urgence pour les plus fragiles," Europe 1, September 2, 2023, https://www.europe1.fr/societe/eau-a-mayotte-le-gouve rnement-annonce-des-mesures-durgence-pour-les-plus-fragiles-4201507.

461 "Crise de l'eau à Mayotte: Plusieurs établissements scolaires contraints de fermer," *Libération*, September 21, 2023, https://www.liberation.fr/societe/education/crise-de-leau-a-mayotte-plusieurs-etablissements-scolaires-contraints-de-fermer-20230921_BEB KH2VAQ5FDPLGPFVVS5DH5VU/.

462 Alexis Duclos, "Gestion de l'eau: 'Les Mahorais souffrent avant même le début de la période critique,'" *Mayotte Hebdo*, November 7, 2022, https://www.mayottehebdo.com/actual ite/politique/gestion-eau-mahorais-souffrent-avant-debut-periode-critique/.

463 Claude Serfati, *L'État radicalisé. La France à l'ère de la mondialisation armée* (La Fabrique, 2022), https://lafabrique.fr/letat-radicalise/. Total is a French oil company, and Bolloré is a right-wing billionaire with a history of investing in West Africa who in 2023 made headlines for buying up media and publishing houses to impose his extremist and racist agenda.

Palestine under Colonial Water Politics

464 "The Occupation of Water," Amnesty International, November 29, 2017, https://www.amne sty.org/en/latest/campaigns/2017/11/the-occupation-of-water/.

465 Ibid.

466 "Palestinians Still Struggle to Get Enough Water," *Al Jazeera*, August 27, 2023, https://www. aljazeera.com/gallery/2023/8/27/photos-palestinians-still-struggle-to-get-enough-water.

467 Ibid.

468 Ibid.; "Parched: Israel's Policy of Water Deprivation in the West Bank," May 31, 2023, https://reliefweb.int/report/occupied-palestinian-territory/parched-israels-policy-water-deprivation-west-bank.

469 Isabel Debre, "As Israeli Settlements Thrive, Palestinian Taps Run Dry. The Water Crisis Reflects a Broader Battle," AP, August 23, 2023, https://apnews.com/article/water-climate-change-drought-occupation-israel-palestinians-30cb8949bdb45cf90ed14b6b992b5b42.

470 Ramzy Baroud, "Palestinians Fight for Survival amid Israel's War on Gaza's Water," *Arab News*, March 28, 2022, https://www.arabnews.com/node/2052321.

471 Debre, "As Israeli Settlements Thrive."

472 Z. Brophy and J. Isaac, "The Environmental Impact of Israeli Military Activities in the Occupied Palestinian Territory," Applied Research Institute—Jerusalem, 2014, https:// www.arij.org/wp-content/uploads/2014/01/The-environmental-impact-of-Israeli-milit ary.pdf.

473 Brophy and Isaac, "The Environmental Impact." See also Uri Gordon, "Olive Green: Environment, Militarism and the Israel Defense Forces," in *Between Ruin and Restoration: An Environmental History of Israel*, edited by Daniel E. Orenstein, Alon Tal, and Char Miller (University of Pittsburgh Press, 2019), pp. 242–261.

474 Sharona Weiss, "As Crackdown Intensifies, Palestinian Prisoners Gear Up for Ramadan Protest," *+972 Magazine*, March 16, 2023, https://www.972mag.com/palestinian-prison ers-ramadan-protest/. See also Toi Staff, "Ben Gvir Said to Order Reduced Shower Time for Terror Inmates," *Times of Israel*, February 14, 2023, https://www.timesofisrael.com/ben-gvir-said-to-order-reduced-shower-time-for-terror-inmates/.

475 Weiss, "As Crackdown Intensifies."

476 See "The Occupation of Water;" Mohammed Najib, "Palestine Runs Dry: 'Our Water They Steal and Sell to Us," *Al Jazeera*, July 15, 2021, https://www.aljazeera.com/news/2021/7/15/water-war-palestinians-demand-more-water-access-from-israel; Baroud, "Palestinians Fight for Survival."

477 Zina Rakhamilova, "Israel Made the Desert Bloom—This Is Fact Not Racism," *Jerusalem Post*, May 2, 2023, https://www.jpost.com/opinion/article-741801.

478 "Failing Gaza: Undrinkable Water, No Access to Toilets and Little Hope on the Horizon," Oxfam, https://www.oxfam.org/en/failing-gaza-undrinkable-water-no-access-toilets-and-little-hope-horizon.

479 Ibid.

480 "Parched."

481 Nidal Atallah, "Palestine: Solid Waste Management under Occupation," Heirich Böll Stiftung, October 7, 2020, https://ps.boell.org/en/2020/10/07/palestine-solid-waste-management-under-occupation.

482 Jaclynn Ashly, "Israel Turns West Bank into a 'Garbage Dump,' " *Al Jazeera*, December 5, 2017, https://www.aljazeera.com/news/2017/12/5/israel-turns-west-bank-into-a-garbage-dump.

483 Atallah, "Palestine."

484 " 'Slow Poisoning': 97% of Gaza's Water Undrinkable," TRT World, 2020, https://www.trtworld.com/middle-east/slow-poisoning-97-of-gaza-s-water-undrinkable-50500. The beaches of Gaza, which had been deliberately used as a dumping site for toxic pollution by the Israeli state, were said to have been cleaned in 2022 with the help EU funds. Jill Poole, "People of Gaza Swim in 'Crystal Blue' Sea Again, as Sewage Pollution Finally Clears," *Euronews*, June 9, 2022, https://www.euronews.com/green/2022/06/09/people-of-gaza-swim-in-crystal-blue-sea-again-as-sewage-pollution-finally-clears.

485 David Cronin, "Israel Destroys and Steals $2 Million Worth of EU Aid," *Electronic Intifada*, December 16, 2020, https://electronicintifada.net/blogs/david-cronin/israel-destroys-and-steals-2-million-worth-eu-aid.

486 Jessica Barnes, "Water in the Middle East," MERIP, September 2020, p. 3.

487 "Water in Gaza: Scarce, Polluted and Mostly Unfit for Use," ReliefWeb, August 21, 2020, https://reliefweb.int/report/occupied-palestinian-territory/water-gaza-scarce-polluted-and-mostly-unfit-use.

Occupying Armies and Water Contamination

488 See Rony Brauman, "A propos de 'Choléra, Haïti, 2010–2018, Histoire d'un désastre' de Renaud Piarroux," *Crash*, December 23, 2019, https://msf-crash.org/fr/blog/medecine-et-sante-publique/propos-de-cholera-haiti-2010-2018-histoire-dun-desastre-de-renaud.

Engineering Water and New Forms of Privatization

489 Abir Ahmar, "Parched UAE Turns to Science to Squeeze More Rainfall from Clouds," Reuters, August 30, 2022, https://www.reuters.com/world/middle-east/parched-uae-turns-science-squeeze-more-rainfall-clouds-2022-08-30/.

490 Stephanie Bailey, "Scientists Are Zapping Clouds with Electricity to Make Rain," CNN, May 21, 2021, https://edition.cnn.com/2021/05/27/middleeast/clouds-electricity-rain-spc-intl/index.html.

491 Kakoli Mukherjee, "Rising Temperature, Dry Spells: How Dubai Created Artificial Rain with Cloud Seeding," *News 18*, July 28, 2021, https://www.news18.com/news/buzz/read-how-dubai-created-fake-rain-with-cloud-seeding-3999557.html.

492 Further, engineering training is not neutral but class-, gender-, and race-biased and these biases impact the ways projects are conceived. See Kalynda C. Smith, Cristina Poleacovschi, Scott Feinstein, and Stephanie Luster-Teasle, "Ethnicity, Race, and Gender in Engineering Education: The Nuanced Experiences of Male and Female Latinx Engineering Undergraduates Targeted by Microaggressions," Psychological Reports 126, no. 5 (January 27, 2022), https://journals.sagepub.com/doi/epub/10.1177/00332941221075766; Katherine Rainey, Melissa Dancy, Roslyn Mickelson, Elizabeth Stearns, and Stephanie Moller, "Race and Gender Differences in How Sense of Belonging Influences Decisions to Jajor in STEM," *IJ STEM Ed* 5, 10 (2018): 1–14; Rinat B. Rosenberg-Kima, E. Ashby Plant, Celeste E. Doerr, and Amy L. Baylor, "The Influence of Computer-Based Model's Race and Gender on Female Students' Attitudes and Beliefs Towards Engineering," *Journal of Engineering Education* 99, no. 1 (January 2020): 35–44.

493 Ruha Benjamin, *Race after Technology: Abolitionist Tools for the New Jim Code* (Polity Press, 2019), p. 5. See also her site https://www.ruhabenjamin.com/ and different projects related to that objective at https://colorcoded.la/.

Colonialism Lays Waste

494 Fanon, *The Wretched of the Earth*, p. 200.

495 Glen Sean Coulthard, *Red Skin, White Masks: Rejecting the Colonial Politics of Recognition* (University of Minnesota Press, 2014), p. 15. Cited in Liboiron, *Pollution is Colonialism*, p. 14.

496 Liboiron, *Pollution is Colonialism*, p. 19.

497 Eve Tuck and K. Wayne Yang, "Decolonization Is Not a Metaphor," *Decolonization: Indigeneity, Education and Society* 1, no. 1 (2012): 17, 3. Cited in Liboiron, *Pollution Is Colonialism*, p. 15.

498 Ibid, p. 6.

499 Emily Mae Czachor, "How Did the Maui Fire Start? What We Know about the Cause of the Lahaina Blaze," CBS News, August 17, 2023, https://www.cbsnews.com/news/how-did-maui-fire-start-cause-lahaina-hawaii-wildfire/.

500 weareneutral (@weareneutral), Instagram, August 17, 2023, https://www.instagram.com/p/CwDJiBhMz7J/?igsh=MWxncmlvZzl3aGUxYQ==.

501 Scott Dance, "Maui Fires Not Just Due to Climate Change but a 'Compound Disaster,' " *Washington Post*, August 12, 2023, https://www.washingtonpost.com/weather/2023/08/12/hawaii-fires-climate-change-maui/.

502 "Native Hawaiian Official Blames Colonisation, Climate Change for Maui Wildfires," RNZ, August 18, 2023, https://www.rnz.co.nz/international/pacific-news/496046/native-hawaiian-official-blames-colonisation-climate-change-for-wildfires.

503 Kaniela Ing, "The Climate Crisis and Colonialism Destroyed My Maui Home. Where We Must Go From Here," *Time*, August 17, 2023, https://time.com/6305817/maui-wildfires-climate-change-colonialism-essay/.

504 See J. Kehaulani Kauanui, *Hawaiian Blood: Colonialism and the Politics of Sovereignty and Indigeneity* (Duke University Press, 2008); Noenoe K. Silva, *Aloha Betrayed: Native Hawaiian Resistance to Colonialism* (Duke University Press, 2004).

505 See Kasey E. Barton, Andrea Westerband, Rebecca Ostertag, Elizabeth Stacy, Kawika Winter, Donald R. Drake, Lucas Berio Fortini, Creighton M. Litton, Susan Cordell, Paul Krushelnycky, Kapua Kawelo, Kealoha Feliciano, Gordon Bennett, and Tiffany Knight, "Hawai'i Forest Review: Synthesizing the Ecology, Evolution, and Conservation of a Model System," *Perspectives in Plant Ecology, Evolution and Systematics* 52 (2021): 1–32.

506 Henry Carnell, "How Colonialism Contributed to the Maui Wildfires," *Mother Jones*, August 11, 2023, https://www.motherjones.com/environment/2023/08/how-colonialism-contributed-to-the-maui-wildfires/.

507 Carnell, "How Colonialism Contributed to the Maui Wildfires." See also "Maui Wildfires Expose the Legacy of Colonialism," *People Dispatch*, August 17, 2023, https://peoplesdispatch.org/2023/08/17/maui-wildfire-devastation-exposes-the-legacy-of-colonialism/.

508 Naomi Klein and Kapua'la Sproat, "Why Was There No Water to Fight the Fire in Maui?," *Guardian*, August 17, 2017, https://www.theguardian.com/commentisfree/2023/aug/17/hawaii-fires-maui-water-rights-disaster-capitalism.

509 @kanielaIng, Instagram, August 11, 2023 https://www.instagram.com/p/CvzCVKiOEST/?igsh=NjBhM3l1ZjVvbTdj.

510 Kaniela Ing, "The Climate Crisis and Colonialism Destroyed My Maui Home. Where We Must Go from Here," *Time*, August 17, 2023, https://time.com/6305817/maui-wildfires-climate-change-colonialism-essay/.

511 Klein and Sproat, "Why Was There No Water."

512 See Jacques Vergès, "Le crime de colonialisme," speech given at the 1962 meeting of solidarity with the Algerian people, Rome, personal archives.

Is Colonialism a Direct Cause of Climate Disaster?

513 IPCC, "Climate Change 2022: Impacts, Adaptation and Vulnerability," IPCC Sixth Assessment Report, 2022, https://www.ipcc.ch/report/ar6/wg2/.

514 Liboiron, *Pollution Is Colonialism*, p. 15.

515 Ibid., p. 41.

516 Aimé Césaire, *Discours sur le colonialisme* (Éditions Présence Africaine, 1955 [1950]), p. 77.

517 Aimé Césaire, *Discourse on Colonialism*, translated by Joan Pinkham (Monthly Review Press, 2000), p. 36.

518 Gurminder K. Bhambra, "More Than a Metaphor: 'Climate Colonialism' in Perspective," *Global Social Challenges Journal* 2, no.2 (2023), p. 180, https://bristoluniversitypressdigital.com/gsc/view/journals/gscj/2/2/article-p179.xml.

519 Ibid.

520 Ibid., p. 181.

521 Cited in Carnell, "How Colonialism Contributed to the Maui Wildfires."

The Wasting of French Colonialism-Imperialism

522 David Theo Goldberg, *The Racial State* (Willey Blackwell, 2001); and David Theo Goldberg, *Are We Postracial Yet?* (Willey Blackwell, 2015). These are two essential readings.

523 Maynard and Simpson, *Rehearsals for Living*, p. 77.

524 Jessica Oublié (story), and Nicola Gobbi (drawings), Kathrine Avraam (coloring), Vinciane Lebrun (photos), *Tropiques toxiques. Le scandale du chlordécone* (Steinkis, 2020); Malcom Ferdinand, *Decolonial Ecology: Thinking from the Caribbean World* (Polity Press, 2021);

Vanessa Agard-Jones, *Body Burdens: Toxic Endurance and Decolonial Desire in the French Atlantic* (forthcoming).

525 One of the aims of the NGO Observatoire Terre-Monde (Earth-World Observatory) (https://terremonde.org) is to fill this gap. See the Observatoire Terre-Monde's journal *Plurivers: Revue d'écologies décoloniales / Pluriverse: A Journal of Decolonial Ecologies* (available open access at https://plurivers.net).

The French Army, Science, Stolen Land

526 See Yves Géry, Alexandra Mathieu, and Christophe Gruner, *Les abandonnés de la République. Vie et mort des Amérindiens de Guyane française* (Albin Michel, 2014); Organisations Amérindiennes de Guyane Française, https://gitpa.org/Coordination%20GITPA%20400/ GITPA%20500-2_org.htm; Organisation des nations autochtones de Guyane, 2020, https:// www.ohchr.org/sites/default/files/Documents/Issues/IPeoples/EMRIP/Session13/ submissions/LAC/2020-12-03-organisationdesnations-autochones-de-guyane-nag.pdf.

527 Jean Hurault, "Les Indiens Oayana de la Guyane française," *Journal de la société des Américanistes* 50 (1961): 141, cited in Saïd Bouamama, "French Guiana: The Negative Legacy of French Colonialism," *International Viewpoint*, August 21, 2018, https://interna tionalviewpoint.org/spip.php?article5664.

528 This situation, resulting from the decree of November 15, 1898, was enshrined in the "Code du domaine de l'État," which stipulated that "vacant and unowned land in the department of French Guiana, as well as land that has not been recognized as individual or collective private property under the provisions of decree n° 46-80 of January 16, 1946, forms part of the State domain." See Agence d'urbanisme et de développement de la Guyane, *Observatoire foncier de la Guyane, Propriété foncière. Atlas Cartographique 2020 GeoGuyane,* https://www.geoguyane.fr/accueil/actualites/actualites_generales/12_287/ atlas_cartographique_de_la_propriete_fonciere_2020 and https://carto.geoguyane.fr/1/ Observatoire_foncier.map, p. 6.

529 Peter Redfield, *Space in the Tropics: From Convicts to Rockets in French Guiana* (University of California Press, 2000), p. 125.

530 Ibid., p. 129.

531 Ibid., p. 133.

532 Bouamama, "French Guiana."

533 Marie-José Jolivet, *La question créole: Essai de sociologie sur la Guyane française* (Éditions de l'Office de la Recherche Scientifique et Technique Outre-Mer, 1982), pp. 470–474. See also Clémence Léobal, *Ville noire, pays blanc. Habiter et lutter en Guyane française* (Presses universitaires de Lyon, 2022).

534 Ibid. Boni and Saramaka are Indigenous communities.

Mining Is Wasting

535 International Indian Treaty Council, "Gold, Greed and Genocide," https://www.iitc.org/ gold-greed-genocide/.

536 Whether in ancient Greece, in the Roman Empire, or the Chinese empire, mines already meant enslavement.

537 *Merriam-Webster Dictionary*, s.v. "El Dorado," https://www.merriam-webster.com/diction ary/El%20Dorado.

538 See for instance, the barely contained excited tone of François-Xavier Freland: "Mines: Madagascar, une île aux trésors à fort potentiel. Or, nickel, cobalt, chrome, saphirs, rubis... Madagascar a déjà tout de l'eldorado. Et son potentiel reste considérable, avec de nouveaux projets, notamment dans l'uranium," *Jeune Afrique*, November 2016, https:// www.jeuneafrique.com/mag/373146/economie/mines-madagascar-ile-aux-tresors-a-fort-potentiel/. For a nuanced approach, see Rosaleen Duffy, "Global Environmental Governance and the Challenge of Shadow States: The Impact of Illicit Sapphire Mining in Madagascar," *Development and Change* 36, no. 5 (2005): 825–843.

539 Yusoff, *A Billion Black Anthropocenes*, loc. 875.

540 International Indian Treaty Council, "Gold, Greed and Genocide."

541 Eduardo Galeano, *Les veines ouvertes de l'Amérique latine* (Terre humaine, 1981).

542 Ibid., p. 37.

543 Elena McGrath, "Housewives against Dictatorship: The Bolivian Hunger Strike of 1978," *Nursing Clio*, December 29, 2016, https://nursingclio.org/2016/12/29/housewives-against-dictatorship-the-bolivian-hunger-strike-of-1978/. See also Reynaldo Tapia, "The Evolution of Indigenous Resistance in Bolivia," PhD diss., Rutgers University, 2019.

544 Gilberto Neto and Ruth Maclean, "Waste from Mine in Angola Kills 12 Downstream in Congo, Minister Says," *New York Times*, September 3, 2021, https://www.nytimes.com/ 2021/09/03/world/africa/mine-waste-angola-congo.html.

545 Ibid.

546 Ruth Maclean, "The Nigerian Activist Trying to Sell Plants to the Oil Company That Destroyed Them," *New York Times*, September 3, 2021, https://www.nytimes.com/2021/ 09/03/world/africa/nigeria-delta-pollution-mangroves-agbani.

547 Hélène Ferrarini, "Emmanuel Macron confirme son soutien au désastreux projet de mine en Guyane," *Reporterre*, October 28, 2017, https://reporterre.net/Emmanuel-Macron-confi rme-son-soutien-au-desastreux-projet-de-mine-en-Guyane.

548 For a chronology of AAGF actions, see "Crise au sein des organisations autochtones amé-rindiennes représentatives," https://gitpa.org/Peuple%20GITPA%20500/GITPA%20500-9WEBDOCGUYANESONG.htm.

549 "Gold Mining in Montagne d'Or, French Guyana," EJAtlas, https://ejatlas.org/print/monta gne-dor-guyane-france.

550 "Montagne d'Or: Le gouvernement annonce l'abandon du projet," WWF, https://www.wwf. fr/sengager-ensemble/relayer-campagnes/montagne-dor.

551 See Ferrarini, "Emmanuel Macron confirme son soutien au désastreux projet de mine en Guyane."

552 Goldoracle, QuedlaGold, and Goldebois, *Ni Or Ni Maître. Montagne d'or et consorts* (Les éditions du couac, 2019), p. 20.

553 Ibid, p. 26.

554 Ibid, p. 40.

555 See for instance the Press communique of Indigenous Associations of Guiana, "Les asso-ciations autochtones de Guyane exigent des excuses publiques," March 29, 2018, https:// fondationdaniellemitterrand.org/associations-autochtones-de-guyane-exigent-excuses-publiques/.

556 See 4th International Rights of Nature Tribunal, https://www.rightsofnaturetribunal.org/ tribunals/bonn-tribunal-2017/?lang=fr.

557 Ibid.

558 "Le projet 'Montagne d'Or' de la compagnie canadienne Columbus Gold devant le Tribunal International des droits de la nature," GaïaPresse, https://gaiapresse.ca/2017/ 11/le-projet-montagne-dor-de-la-compagnie-canadienne-columbus-gold-devant-le-tribu nal-international-des-droits-de-la-nature/.

559 "Gold Mining in Montagne d'Or, French Guyana."

560 Géry, Mathieu, and Gruner, *Les abandonnés de la République*, pp. 193–194.

561 Sophie Gosselin, "Décoloniser nos liens à la terre," *Socialter* (Winter 2022–2023): 115.

562 Ibid., p. 114.

563 Ibid.

564 Ibid., p. 115.

565 "Qui est Thierry Déau 'le nouveau maître de l'eau'?," *France-Antilles*, April 27, 2021, https://www.martinique.franceantilles.fr/actualite/economie/qui-est-le-martiniquais-thierry-deau-le-nouveau-maitre-de-leau-914314.php. Thierry Déau was a member of the Socialist Party before joining Emmanuel Macron.

566 Emile Boutelier, "Le Non à la centrale marque t'il un tournant dans la structuration des luttes autochtones?," *Boukan: Le courrier ultramarin*, February 2023, p. 11.

567 I remind the readers that the French state owns 90 percent of land in Guiana.

568 Cited in Boutelier, "Le Non à la centrale," p. 11.

569 Ibid., p. 12.

570 "Revenue of the leading mining companies worldwide from 2005 to 2022," Statista, https://www.statista.com/statistics/208715/total-revenue-of-the-top-mining-companies/.

571 V. Maus, S. Giljum, J. Gutschlhofer, D. M. da Silva, M. Probst, S. L. B. Gass, S. Luckeneder, M. Lieber, and I. McCallum, "A Global-Scale Data Set of Mining Areas," *Scientific Data* 7, no. 289 (2020).

572 Victor Maus, Stefan Giljum, Jakob Gutschlhofer, Sebastian Luckeneder, and Mirko Lieber, "Worldwide Mining Activities Use More Than 57,000 km2 of Land. Results from a Global Assessment of Mining Land Areas Based on Satellite Data," FINEPRINT Brief 2020, no. 12, Vienna University of Economics and Business.

573 *Encyclopedia Britannica*, s.v. "Mining," 2019.

574 Goldoracle, QuedlaGold, and Goldebois, *Ni Or ni Maître*, p. 112.

575 Juan Pablo Gutierrez, international delegate for ONIC/Yukpa, personal communication with author, June 2023. See also his social media accounts @juan_pablo_gutierrez_official on Instagram and @juanpablogutier on X (formerly Twitter).

576 Gutierrez, personal communication.

577 "Breaking: Extinction Rebellion Targets 'Corrupt' UK Finance HQ in London," Extinction Rebellion, March 2, 2023, https://extinctionrebellion.uk/2023/03/02/breaking-extinction-rebellion-targets-corrupt-uk-finance-hq-in-london/.

578 Gutierrez, personal communication.

579 See, for instance, "Illegal Mining and Trafficking in Precious Metals," UN Office on Drugs and Crimes, https://www.unodc.org/unodc/en/environment-climate/illegal-mining.html; "The Devastating Impact of Illegal Gold Mining," Interpol, April 28, 2022, https://www.interpol.int/en/News-and-Events/News/2022/The-devastating-impact-of-illegal-gold-mining-in-Latin-America.

580 "World's 10 Largest Water Companies," ETC Group, January 18, 2012, https://www.etcgroup.org/content/worlds-10-largest-water-companies.

581 "Water Security/Ecological Security," World Water Council, https://www.worldwatercouncil.org/en/water-securityecological-security.

582 Olufemi O. Taiwo, *Elite Capture: How the Powerful Took over Identity Politics (and Everything Else)* (Pluto Press, 2023).

Criminalization of Activists

583 See *On ne dissout pas un soulèvement. 40 voix pour les Soulèvements de la terre* (Seuil, 2023). To understand the circulation of water through the planet, see *Les veines de la*

terre. Une anthologie des bassins-versants, edited by Marin Schaffner, Mathias Rollot, and François Guerroué (Wildproject, 2021).

584 The French State uses the term ZAD for a *zone d'aménagement différé* (deferred-development zone). Designed for long-term development operations, the ZAD designation is a preemption tool that can be used for a wide range of development operations. Activists changed the meaning to a "zone to defend." For an English-speaking introduction to the ZAD de Notre-Dame-des-Landes, see Kristin Ross, " 'The Sweetness of Place': Kristin Ross on the Zad and NoTAV struggles," *Verso Blog*, June 14, 2017, https://www.versobooks. com/en-gb/blogs/news/3262-the-sweetness-of-place-kristin-ross-on-the-zad-and-notav-struggles.

585 See Antoine Albertini, Abel Mestre, Samuel Laurent, Stéphane Mandard, Arthur Carpentier, Sandra Favier, and Rémi Barroux, "What Happened at Violent Protest against Water Reservoirs in Western France?," *Le Monde*, April 4, 2023, https://www.lemonde.fr/ en/environment/article/2023/04/04/what-happened-at-violent-protest-against-water-res ervoirs-in-western-france_6021641_114.html.

586 Philippe Vion-Durt, "Les terres plutôt que la Terre," *Socialter*, December 5, 2023, https:// www.socialter.fr/article/edito-hors-serie-15-les-terres-plutot-que-la-terre.

587 Ibid.

588 Clémant Quintard, "Rage against the Basins," *Socialter*, January 3, 2023, https://www.social ter.fr/article/rage-against-the-mega-bassines-manifestation.

589 Françoise Vergès, "État (toujours) colonial," in *On ne dissout pas un soulèvement*, pp. 59–62. For a video recording of the event and numerous speakers, see Blast, Le souffle d'info, "Nous sommes les soulèvements de la terre, grande soirée de soutien," YouTube, April 12, 2023, https://www.youtube.com/watch?v=VjzUQDHUz1k. See also Françoise Vergès, "Il y a des zones à défendre dans ces quartiers populaires," *Reporterre*, July 1, 2023, https://rep orterre.net/Francoise-Verges-Il-y-a-des-zones-a-defendre-dans-ces-quartiers-populaires.

590 Instagram, @la_releve_et_la_peste, August 10, 2023, https://www.instagram.com/p/Cvwb Al4NAJb/?igsh=MWZzb292bDhiaHhmaw==.

591 "After the Death of Nahel, the Other Two Passengers in the Car Give Their Versions of What Happened," *Le Monde*, July 4, 2023, https://www.lemonde.fr/en/france/article/2023/07/ 04/after-the-death-of-nahel-the-other-two-passengers-in-the-car-give-their-version-of-what-happened_6043000_7.html.

592 Rachida Brahim, *La race tue deux fois* (Éditions Syllepse, 2021).

593 Ibid., back cover.

594 "Décision 2021-054 du 9 mars 2021 relative à des observations devant une Cour d'appel dans le cadre d'une procédure en responsabilité de l'État pour contrôles d'identité dis-criminatoires," Défenseur des droits, October 18, 2018, https://juridique.defenseurdesdro its.fr/index.php?lvl=notice_display&id=39429&opac_view=-1; Fabien Leboucq, "Contrôle au faciès, LBD et violence: la défenseure des droits contre les forces de l'ordre," *Libération*, July 5, 2022, https://www.liberation.fr/societe/police-justice/controle-au-facies-lbd-et-violences-les-griefs-de-la-defenseure-des-droits-contre-les-forces-de-lordre-20220705_ HMHW3YDN5BEMRALPPRPEABGSLA/.

595 Yasemin Inceoglu, "The Murder of Nahel Merzouk, Police Violence and the Media in France," *Wire*, July 14, 2023, https://thewire.in/world/france-murder-nahel-merzouk-pol ice-violence-media.

596 Vergès, "État (toujours) colonial"; Vergès, "Il y a des zones à défendre dans ces quartiers populaires." Indeed, there are equivalents of ZADs in Guyana, Martinique, Reunion. They are not always called ZAD but they are initiated around the same principles: against state megaprojects and around collective forms of working.

Antiracist Politics of Breathing

597 Omotayo T. Jolaosho, "The Enduring Urgency of Black Breath," Anthropology News, April 16, 2021, https://www.anthropology-news.org/articles/the-enduring-urgency-of-black-breath/.

598 Ibid.

599 Stéphane Mandar, "Pollution Is Responsible for 9 Million Deaths per Year Worldwide," *Le Monde*, May 18, 2022, https://www.lemonde.fr/en/environment/article/2022/05/18/pollution-is-responsible-for-9-million-deaths-each-year-worldwide_5983946_114.html.

600 "Global Pollution Kills 9 Million People a Year," European Commission, January 15, 2018, https://ec.europa.eu/newsroom/intpa/items/612355/en.

601 As summarized in "Global Pollution Kills 9 Million People a Year."

602 See "COVID-19 and Indigenous Peoples," UN Departments of Economic and Social Affairs, https://www.un.org/development/desa/indigenouspeoples/covid-19.html. For the U.S.: Riis L. Williams, "Native American Deaths from COVID-19 Highest among Racial Groups," Princeton School of Public and International Affairs, December 2, 2021, https://spia.princeton.edu/news/native-american-deaths-covid-19-highest-among-racial-groups. For Brazil: Paulo Ricardo Martins-Filho, Brenda Carla Lima Araújo, Karyna Batista Sposato, Adriano Antunes de Souza Araújo, Lucindo José Quintans-Júnior, and Victor Santana Santos, "Racial Disparities in COVID-19-Related Deaths in Brazil: Black Lives Matter?," *Journal of Epidemiology* 5, no. 31 (December 2020): 239–240. For Africa: "Number of Coronavirus (COVID-19) Deaths in the African Continent as of November 18, 2022, by Country," Statista, https://www.statista.com/statistics/1170530/coronavirus-deaths-in-africa/.

603 "Air Pollution," WHO, Global Health Observatory, https://www.who.int/data/gho/data/themes/theme-details/GHO/air-pollution.

604 Thesaurus.net, s.v. "irrespirable," https://www.thesaurus.net/irrespirable.

605 See Alexis Zimmer, *Brouillards toxique. Vallée de la Meuse, 1931. Contre-enquête* (Zone sensible, 2017); and Judith Rainhorn, *Blanc de plomb. Histoire d'un poison légal* (Presses de Sciences Po, 2019).

606 Frantz Fanon, *A Dying Colonialism*, translated by Haakon Chevailier (Grove Press, 1965), p. 65.

607 "Pranayama or 'Cardiac Coherence Breathing'? US Magazine Earns Indian Ire for Cultural Appropriation," Qrius, January 31, 2019, https://qrius.com/pranayama-or-cardiac-coherence-breathing-us-magazine-earns-indian-ire-for-cultural-appropriation. See also Anna Gunstone, "Breathing Deep and Diving In: Yoga and Cultural Appropriation," *Oxford Student*, August 26, 2023, https://www.oxfordstudent.com/2020/07/11/breathing-deep-and-diving-in-yoga-and-cultural-appropriation/.

608 "Pranayama or 'Cardiac Coherence Breathing'?"

609 Renuka Govind, cited in ibid.

610 Françoise Vergès, "Breathing: A Revolutionary Act," in *Climate: Our Right to Breathe* (L'Internationale, 2022), pp. 22–27.

611 Jolaosho, "The Enduring Urgency of Black Breath."

612 Kerry Ryan Chance, *Living Politics in South Africa's Urban Shacklands* (University of Chicago Press, 2018), p. 64.

613 Jolaosho, "The Enduring Urgency."

614 Damien Arsenijevic, " 'The Proletarian Lung': The Struggle for the Commons as Memory Politics in Bosnia and Herzegovina," *Springerin* 1 (2019), https://www.springerin.at/en/2019/1/die-proletarische-lunge/.

615 Dionne Brand, *The Blue Clerk* (Duke University Press, 2018), p. 91.

616 Christa Wichterich, "Who Cares about Healthcare Workers? Care Extractivism and Care Struggles in Germany and India," *Social Change* 50, no. 1 (March 2020): 121–140, https://journals.sagepub.com/doi/10.1177/0049085719901087.

617 See Neil Brenner and Swarnabh Ghosh, "Between the Colossal and the Catastrophic: Planetary Urbanization and the Political Ecologies of Emergent Infectious Disease," *Environment and Planning A: Economy and Space* 54, no. 5 (2022): 867–910; Vupenyu Dzingirai, Salome Bukachi, Melisa Leach, Lindiwe Mangwanya, Ian Scoones, and Annie Wilkinson, "Structural Drivers of Vulnerability to Zoonotic Disease in Africa," *Royal Society London Biology Science*, July 19, 2017, https://royalsocietypublishing.org/doi/full/10.1098/rstb.2016.0169; Nancy Fraser, "Climates of Capital, *New Left Review*, no. 27 (January–February 2021), https://newleftreview.org/issues/ii127/articles/nancy-fraser-climates-of-capital.

618 "Racism Is 'Fundamental Cause' of COVID-19 Vaccine Hesitancy among Ethnic Minorities," University of Manchester, December 15, 2022, https://www.manchester.ac.uk/discover/news/racism-is-fundamental-cause-of-covid-19-vaccine-hesitancy-among-ethnic-minorities/.

619 Richard L. Oehler and Vivian R. Vega, "Conquering COVID: How Global Vaccine Inequality Risks Prolonging the Pandemic," *Open Forum* 8, no. 10 (October 2021); Moosa Tatar, Jalal Montazeri Shoorekchali, Mohammad Reza Faraji, Mohammad Abdi Seyyedkolaee, José A. Pagán, and Fernando A. Wilson, "COVID-19 Vaccine Inequality: A Global Perspective," *Journal of Global Health* 12 (2022), https://www.ncbi.nlm.nih.gov/pmc/articles/PMC9559176/; Philippa Kelly, Ashley Kirk, and Kaamil Ahmed, "Covid Vaccine Figures Lay Bare Global Inequality as Global Target Missed," *Guardian*, July 21, 2022, https://www.theguardian.com/global-development/2022/jul/21/covid-vaccine-figures-lay-bare-global-inequality-as-global-target-missed.

620 "End Poverty in All Its Forms Everywhere," UN, Statistics Division, https://unstats.un.org/sdgs/report/2022/goal-01/.

621 Ibid.

622 "Vaccine Equity," WHO, 2022, https://www.who.int/campaigns/vaccine-equity.

623 Tiffany N. Ford, Sarah Reber, and Richard V. Reeves, "Race Gaps in Covid-19 Deaths are Even Bigger Than They Appear," Brookings, June 16, 2020, https://www.brookings.edu/blog/up-front/2020/06/16/race-gaps-in-covid-19-deaths-are-even-bigger-than-they-appear/.

624 Nicole Frolo, "The Pandemic Housework Dilemma Is Whitewashed," *Medium*, October 2, 2020, https://zora.medium.com/the-pandemic-housework-dilemma-is-whitewashed-7b41d5f60789.

625 "Fewer Women Than Men Will Regain Employment during the COVID-19 Recovery Says ILO," International Labour Organization, July 19, 2021, https://www.ilo.org/global/about-the-ilo/newsroom/news/WCMS_813449/lang--en/index.htm.

626 Jorge Moreira da Silva, "Why Should We Care about Unpaid Care Work," OECD, *Development Matters* (blog), https://oecd-development-matters.org/2019/03/18/why-you-should-care-about-unpaid-care-work/.

627 "Not All Gaps Are Created Equal: The True Value of Care Work," Oxfam, https://www.oxfam.org/en/not-all-gaps-are-created-equal-true-value-care-work.

628 "COVID-19 and Its Economic Toll on Women: The Story behind the Numbers," UN Women, September 16, 2020, https://www.unwomen.org/en/news/stories/2020/9/feature-covid-19-economic-impacts-on-women.

629 "Fewer Women Than Men Will Regain Employment."

630 Aneesh Patnaik, Jiahn Son, Alice Feng, and Crystal Ade, "Racial Disparities and Climate Change," *PSC*, August 15, 2020, https://psci.princeton.edu/tips/2020/8/15/racial-disp arities-and-climate-change. See also Beth Gardiner, "Unequal Impacts: The Deep Links between Racism and Climate Change," Yale Environment 360, June 9, 2020, https://e360. yale.edu/features/unequal-impact-the-deep-links-between-inequality-and-climate-change.

631 Emily K. Shuman, "Global Climate Change and Infectious Disease," *New England Journal of Medicine*, March 25, 2010, https://www.nejm.org/doi/10.1056/NEJMp0912931; Emma Sacks, Sonam Yangchen, and Robert Marten, "COVID-19, Climate Changes and Communities," *The Lancet* 5, no. 10 (October 2021), https://www.thelancet.com/journals/lanplh/article/PIIS2542-5196(21)00257-6/fulltext.

632 Jeremy Williams, *Climate Change Is Racist: Race, Privilege and the Struggle for Climate Justice* (Icon Books, 2021).

633 See Aja Barber, *Consumed: The Need for Collective Change: Colonialism, Climate Change and Consumerism* (Brazen, 2021); Dorceta E. Taylor, *Toxic Communities: Environmental Racism, Industrial Pollution and Residential Mobility* (NYU Press, 2014).

634 W. James Gauderman, Edward Avol, Frank Gilliland, Hita Vora, Duncan Thomas, Kiros Berhane, Rob McConnell, Nino Kuenzli, Fred Lurmann, Edward Rappaport, Helene Margolis, David Bates, and John Peters, "The Effect of Air Pollution on Lung Development from 10 to 18 Years of Age," *New England Journal of Medicine* 351, no. 11 (September 2004): 1057–1067. See also "Who Is Most Affected by Outdoor Air Pollution," American Lung Association, lung.org/clean-air/outdoors/who-is-at-risk/children-and-air-pollution.

635 Dufresne et al., *Brut*, p. 13; "Canada: From Homeland to Oil Sands: The Impact of Oil and Gas Development on the Lubicon Cree of Canada," Amnesty International, June 16, 2010, https://www.amnesty.org/en/documents/amr20/002/2010/en/.

636 Doug Weir, "How Does War Damage the Environment?," Conflict and Environment Observatory, June 4, 2022, ceobs.org/how-does-war-damage-the-environment.

637 George Black, "The Victims of Agent Orange the US Has Never Acknowledged," *New York Times*, March 16, 2021, nytimes.com/2021/03/16/magazine/laos-agent-orange-vietnam-war.html.

638 Regarding the links between exposure to Agent Orange and respiratory cancers, see the U.S. Department of Veteran Affairs "Public Health" web page: "Respiratory Cancers and Agent Orange," USDVA, https://www.publichealth.va.gov/exposures/agentorange/conditi ons/respiratory_cancers.asp.

639 Jane Mager Stellman, Steven D. Stellman, Richard Christian, Tracy Weber, and Carrie Tomasallo, "The Extent and Patterns of Usage of Agent Orange and Other Herbicides in Vietnam," *Nature* 422, no. 17 (2003): 681–687.

The Politics of Refusal

640 "Saint-Paul raconte l'histoire des frères Adékalom," December 22, 2021, Saint Paul Town Hall, https://www.mairie-saintpaul.re/saint-paul-raconte-lhistoire-des-freres-adekalom/. See also "La Réunion des années Debré: répression coloniale et violences policières," *Révolte Décoloniale*, September 25, 2020, https://revoltedecoloniale.home.blog/2020/09/25/la-reunion-des-annees-debre-repression-coloniale-et-violences-policieres/.

641 Liboiron, *Pollution Is Colonialism*, p. 72.

642 Ibid.

643 "La Réunion n'est pas une colonie et ne l'a jamais été," December 19, 2019, https://www.zinfos974.com/la-reunion-nest-pas-une-colonie-et-ne-la-jamais-ete/.

644 Ibid.

645 Maynard and Simpson, *Rehearsals for Living*, p. 85.

646 Niiganii Zhaawshoko Giihigok, cited in ibid., p. 93.

647 Ibid., p. 95.

648 Ibid., p. 94.

649 Dhoruba Bin Wahad, "The Last of the Loud," Millennials Are Killing Capitalism, 2021, https://millennialsarekillingcapitalism.libsyn.com/the-last-of-the-loud-dhoruba-bin-wahad-philosopher-of-the-whirlwind; cited in Day and McBean, *Abolition Revolution*, p. 197.

650 Day and McBean, *Abolition Revolution*, p. 200.

Anti-Cleaning Politics

651 Marcus Rediker, "The Transatlantic Slave Trade Ships: Trajectories of Death and Violence across the Ocean," *The Funambulist*, December 14, 2014, https://thefunambulist.net/magazine/the-ocean/the-transatlantic-slave-trade-ships-trajectories-of-death-and-violence-across-the-ocean.

652 On punitive programs of rehabilitation among Indigenous youth, see Kevin Howells, Andrew Day, Stuart Byrne, and Mitchell K. Byrne, "Risk, Needs and Responsivity in Violence Rehabilitation: Implications for Programs with Indigenous Offenders," paper presented at the "Best Practice Interventions in Corrections for Indigenous People" conference, Adelaide, October 13–15, 1999, https://ro.uow.edu.au/cgi/viewcontent.cgi?article=3662&context=sspapers.

653 See Ruha Benjamin, *Race after Technology* (Polity, 2019).

654 M. E. O'Brien and Eman Abdelhadi, *Everything for Everyone: An Oral History of the New York Commune, 2052–2072* (Common Notions, 2022), pp. 200–201.

655 Miéville, "A Strategy for Ruination."

656 Ibid.

657 See Vergès, *Program of Absolute Disorder*.

658 Liboiron, *Pollution Is Colonialism*, p. 11.

659 Susie Cagle, "'Bees Not Refugees': The Environmentalist Roots of Anti-Immigrants Bigotry," *Guardian*, August 16, 2019, https://www.theguardian.com/environment/2019/aug/15/anti.

660 Cagle, "'Bees Not Refugees.'"

661 Miéville, "The Limits of Utopia."

662 See Françoise Vergès, *The Wombs of Women: Race, Capital, Feminism*, translated by Kaiama Glover (Duke University Press, 2020).

663 Cited in Cagle, "'Bees Not Refugees.'"

664 Miéville, "The Limits of Utopia."

665 John Berger, "Undefeated Despair," *Critical Inquiry*, 2006, https://criticalinquiry.uchicago.edu/undefeated_despair/.

666 Cited in ibid.

667 Miéville, "The Limits of Utopia."

668 Véronica Gago, *Feminist International: How to Change Everything*, translated from Spanish by Liz Mason-Deeze (Verso, 2020), p. 13.

669 Gago, *Feminist International*, p. 15, emphasis in original.

670 See "Herbier Résistant Rosa Luxembourg," a workshop that the artist Paula Valero organized with curator and filmmaker Pascale Obolo and the collective La Semeuse with a group of women of color at the Laboratoires d'Aubervilliers, April–October 2023, http://www.lesl aboratoires.org/date/herbier-resistant-rosa-luxemburg.

671 "Séverine et sa grande famille," France Inter, August 20, 2023, https://www.radiofrance. fr/franceinter/podcasts/des-vies-francaises/des-vies-francaises-du-dimanche-20-aout-2023-7183813.

672 Shulamith Firestone, *The Dialectics of Sex: The Case for a Feminist Revolution* (William Morrow, 1970).

673 Firestone, cited in Helen Hester, "Promethean Labors and Domestic Realism," *e-flux*, 2017, https://www.e-flux.com/architecture/artificial-labor/140680/promethean-labors-and-domestic-realism/.

674 Hester, "Promethean Labors."

675 Ibid.

676 Day and McBean, *Abolition Revolution*, p. 200.

677 Christine Vollaire and Philippe Bazin, *Un archipel des solidarités, Grèce 2017–2020* (Loco, 2020).

678 See the discussion in ibid, pp. 9–11.

679 Cited in Liboiron, *Pollution Is Colonialism*, p. 115.

680 Ruth Wilson Gilmore, cited in Angela Davis, Gina Dent, Erica R. Meiners, and Beth E. Richie, *Abolition Feminism Now* (Penguin Books, 2022), p. 52.

681 Interview with Avery Gordon in *Revolutionary Feminisms*, edited by Brenna Bhandar and Rafeef Ziadah (Verso, 2020), p. 188.

682 Goldoracle, QuedlaGold, and Goldebois, *Ni or ni maître*, p. 26.

Author Biography

Françoise Vergès (Reunion Island-France) is currently Senior Fellow Researcher at the Sarah Parker Remond Centre for the Study of Race and Racialization, University College London. A co-founder of the collective "Decolonize the Arts" (2015–2020), she is the curator of decolonial visits in museums and *L'Atelier*, a workshop and public performance with artists and activists. She is interested in the racial fabrication of "premature death," the multiple practices of resistance and South–South circulations of theories and cultural forms. She writes books and articles on the afterlives of slavery and colonization, climate catastrophe and racial capitalocene, the impossible decolonization of the western museum, decolonial feminism, psychiatry, and the "post-museum." Her publications include: *A Programme of Absolute Disorder: Decolonizing the Museum* (Pluto, 2024), *A Decolonial Feminism* (Pluto, 2021), *The Wombs of Women: Race, Capital, Feminism* (Duke University Press, 2020), *Resolutely Black: Conversations with Françoise Vergès,* with Aimé Césaire (Polity, 2020). She has written documentary films on Maryse Condé (2013) and Aimé Césaire (2011), and was a project advisor for documenta11 (2002) and the Triennale de Paris (2011).